York High
Yorktown

MW00862083

DATE DUE

Student Companion to
Arthur MILLER

Student Companion to

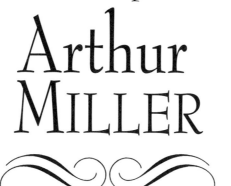

Arthur
MILLER

Susan C. W. Abbotson

Student Companions to Classic Writers

Greenwood Press
Westport, Connecticut • London

Library of Congress Cataloging-in-Publication Data

Abbotson, Susan C. W., 1961–
    Student companion to Arthur Miller / Susan C.W. Abbotson.
        p.   cm.—(Student companions to classic writers, ISSN 1522–7979)
    Includes bibliographical references and index.
    ISBN 0–313–30949–3 (alk. paper)
    1. Miller, Arthur, 1915—Criticism and interpretation.   I. Title.   II. Series.
    PS3525.I5156 Z5116   2000
    812′.52—dc21   99–089069

British Library Cataloguing in Publication Data is available.

Library of Congress Catalog Card Number: 99–089069
ISBN: 0–313–30949–3
ISSN: 1522–7979

First published in 2000

Greenwood Press, 88 Post Road West, Westport, CT 06881
An imprint of Greenwood Publishing Group, Inc.
www.greenwood.com

Printed in the United States of America

The paper used in this book complies with the
Permanent Paper Standard issued by the National
Information Standards Organization (Z39.48–1984).

10 9 8 7 6 5 4 3 2 1

Cover photo of Arthur Miller © Bettmann/CORBIS.

For my husband, Dave Wasser,
who makes me laugh, keeps me sane,
and fixes stuff

Contents

Series Foreword

This series has been designed to meet the needs of students and general readers for accessible literary criticism on the American and world writers most frequently studied and read in the secondary school, community college, and four-year college classrooms. Unlike other works of literary criticism that are written for the specialist and graduate student, or that feature a variety of reprinted scholarly essays on sometimes obscure aspects of the writer's work, the Student Companions to Classic Writers series is carefully crafted to examine each writer's major works fully and in a systematic way, at the level of the non-specialist and general reader. The objective is to enable the reader to gain a deeper understanding of the work and to apply critical thinking skills to the act of reading. The proven format for the volumes in this series was developed by an advisory board of teachers and librarians for a successful series published by Greenwood Press, Critical Companions to Popular Contemporary Writers. Responding to their request for easy-to-use and yet challenging literary criticism for students and adult library patrons, Greenwood Press developed a systematic format that is not intimidating but helps the reader to develop the ability to analyze literature.

How does this work? Each volume in the Student Companions to Classic Writers series is written by a subject specialist, an academic who understands students' needs for basic and yet challenging examination of the writer's canon. Each volume begins with a biographical chapter, drawn from published sources, biographies, and autobiographies, that relates the writer's life to his or her work. The next chapter examines the writer's literary heritage, tracing the literary influences of other writers on that writer and explaining and discussing the literary genres into which the writer's work falls. Each of the following chapters examines one or more major works by the writer, featuring those works most frequently read and studied by high school and college students. Depending on the writer's canon, generally between four and eight major works are examined, each in individual chapters. The discussion of each work is organized into separate sections on plot development, character development, and major themes. Literary devices and style, narrative point of view, and historical setting are also discussed in turn if pertinent to the work. Each chapter concludes with an alternate critical perspective from which to read the works, such as a psychological or feminist criticism. The critical theory is defined briefly in easy, comprehensible language for the student. Looking at the literature from the point of view of a particular critical approach will help the reader to understand and apply critical theory to the act of reading and analyzing literature.

Of particular value in each volume is the bibliography, which includes a complete bibliography of the writer's major works, a selected bibliography of biographical and critical works suitable for students, and lists of reviews of each work examined in the companion, all of which will be helpful to readers, teachers, and librarians who would like to consult additional sources.

As a source of literary criticism for the student or for the general reader, this series will help the reader to gain understanding of the writer's work and skill in critical reading.

Preface

The *Student Companion to Arthur Miller* provides a critical introduction to the plays of one of America's major playwrights. Beginning with a discussion of his life and career, Miller is placed within the context of his times, showing how he was influenced by and reacted to his culture and major events in his own life and the life of the American nation. The second chapter places Miller's work within its literary heritage, covering the various influences Miller has undergone, and the ways in which his work has and will continue to impact American theater. The remaining chapters deal with a selection of Miller's better-known plays, organizing them around some of the major themes of his work, and what Miller sees as the most influential occurrences of the twentieth century. In this way Miller's innovative ideas regarding tragedy are applied to the discussion of *Death of a Salesman*, and his treatment of the family informs the discussions of *All My Sons* and *A View from the Bridge*. *The American Clock* is a good representation of Miller's concerns regarding the depression, while *After the Fall* and *Broken Glass* are both tied to the Holocaust, and the House Un-American Activities Committee (HUAC) trials of the 1950s lie close behind *The Crucible*. We finish with *The Ride Down Mt. Morgan*, in which we can see echoes of Miller's early masterpiece, *Death of a Salesman*, and the threads of various concerns continuing through his work as he moves into his sixth decade as a leading American playwright.

Each chapter offers the student and general reader background that will assist in understanding and interpreting Miller's work. The biographical chapter begins with his childhood and takes us through the depression years, Miller's theatrical apprenticeship, eventual fame, and three marriages; also his association with the Holocaust, the HUAC, and the political organization called Poets, Essayists, and Novelists. This chapter introduces all of Miller's major plays, and a number of his other literary and motion picture projects. The chapter on his literary heritage begins with an outline of Miller's literary and dramatic precursors, then moves on to how he writes, the major aspects of his dramatic impact, other playwrights he has influenced, and the most common themes we see in Miller's work.

In examining the plays themselves, the remaining chapters feature close readings of the texts that include analyses of setting, plot development, character development, and thematic issues. In addition, there are discussions of Miller's use of various literary devices and craft in the plays selected, and an assessment of the social and/or historical context of each play. Each chapter also features an alternate reading on the play(s) being discussed. These readings introduce varied critical approaches to literature, among them feminist, psychoanalytical, and Marxist, along with reader-response, deconstructionist, and mythological approaches. These alternate readings demonstrate how varied readings may continue to highlight the sheer richness of Miller's work. Lastly, the bibliography provides information on Miller's published works, biographical material, selected general criticism, and both contemporary reviews and critical studies on each of the plays discussed.

The Life of Arthur Miller

With a worldwide reputation, Arthur Miller is one of America's best-known dramatists; after more than twenty plays, including the widely studied, read, and performed dramas *Death of a Salesman* and *The Crucible,* he is also, clearly, one of the most important. Throughout sixty years of playwriting, Miller has delighted, inspired, and shocked audiences all over the globe with plays that aspire to do more than entertain, but try to teach their audiences certain truths about their own lives. Miller's plays explore social and moral problems he sees being faced by the people who make up his audience. Raising issues which are central to the American consciousness, he writes about success and failure, guilt and betrayal, and most importantly, about love and responsibility. Not always popular with critics and audiences, partly due to his uncompromising insistence that we should accept unpleasant truths about our own lives, Miller's work has gone in and out of favor over the years, yet he continues to write into his eighties.

Miller remains committed to theater because he sincerely believes that it can change people for the better, and he feels that it is his responsibility as an artist to encourage such change. Miller views society as a complicated network of individuals who need to balance their needs and desires against those of the wider social group in order to live fulfilled and contented lives. His plays can be read as lessons suggesting ways by which people can improve their lives, largely by shaking off their adherence to false myths. He sees American society as having been misled by myths of success which advocate rampant materialism, social irresponsibility, and self-negating guilt. To this end, through all of his plays, Miller asks us to examine ourselves, and reassess our true responsibilities to both self and other.

CHILDHOOD

Arthur Asher Miller was born on 17 October 1915, in New York City; the second child of Augusta and Isidore Miller. Augusta was a first-generation American whose father had emigrated from Poland, and Isidore had himself emigrated from Poland at the age of six. An older brother, Kermit, and a younger sister, Joan, made up the Miller family, although there was also the extended family of aunts, uncles, and cousins from whom Miller developed many of his characters when he became a playwright. Miller felt that he was the opposite of his brother—a well-behaved, good boy, who took after their father—and saw himself, with his ambitions and darker side, as being more like their mother. Miller felt that he and his brother were in competition well into adulthood; two brothers at odds are frequently occurring characters in many of his plays, from *All My Sons* to *The Price*.

Despite internal family differences, Miller's social background gave him a secure sense of self. His upbringing was solidly Jewish, providing him with a strong moral and ethical center which is evident in his works and life. It has also given him a sense of reassurance and identity through troubled times. From an early age, Miller admired his mother's artistry and inquiring mind; filling their house with books and music, she displayed a fierce sense of life. Miller felt close to his mother, and saw her as having had a great influence on the way he views life. The portrait of Rose Baum in *The American Clock* is based on his mother, just as Moe Baum is ostensibly based on his father, and Lee Baum on the young Miller himself.

Miller's father was a quiet man; though unschooled, he had an innate authority and a strong sense of what he felt was right or wrong. Before being financially ruined by the Great Depression, he owned and ran a successful women's clothing business. Miller simultaneously hated and admired his father, annoyed at his incapacity to fully recuperate (both economically and emotionally) from the depression, yet able to recognize the man's inner goodness. This ambivalence toward his father lies at the core of many of the ambiguously presented father figures in his plays, such as Willy Loman (*Salesman*), Joe Keller (*All My Sons*), or Mr. Franz (*The Price*); seemingly strong men who love their children, yet make them suffer because of certain weaknesses. In hindsight, Miller realizes that it was the system that failed rather than his father, but at the time it was difficult to lay the blame elsewhere as he watched his father spend much of the day "napping," in between abortive attempts to get back into business.

At the age of eight, Miller attended his first play with his mother at the Shubert Theater in New York City—a melodrama in which a stereotyped cannibal tried to blow up a passenger ship—and was impressed by the "realness" of the experience, as opposed to the few films he had seen. But he did not consider writing his own plays at this time, being far more interested in sports. As Miller admits, "Until the age of seventeen I can safely say that I never read a book weightier than *Tom Swift*, and *Rover Boys*, and only verged on literature with some Dickens" (Kunitz 1955, 669). He attended a public school in Harlem until the age of fourteen, when his family was forced to move into a smaller home in Brooklyn after his father's business fell apart.

THE GREAT DEPRESSION

The Millers were a very contented family in the 1920s; wealthy enough to have their own chauffeur, and an attractive apartment on the edge of Harlem which overlooked Central Park. The Crash, and the depression which followed, did much to sour their formerly idyllic life, and we see such change depicted in detail with the Baum family in *The American Clock*. As the family finances tightened, they were forced to move to smaller premises. Augusta Miller sold or pawned all of her jewelry, lost her piano, and began to resent her husband's incapacity to win out over the general collapse of the country, just as happens to Rose Baum.

To Miller, the depression was a key event in American history, one which changed the nature of people's outlook on the world, and a time which personally taught him much about people and life. In his autobiography, *Timebends* (1987, 115), Miller describes the depression as a "moral catastrophe" and only "incidentally a matter of money," largely because it exposed many of the hypocrisies which had lain behind the prosperous facade of American society. The old order had been proven to be both incompetent and inherently hollow. Having the rug pulled from under their feet for no real reason that they could ascertain, people lost many of the old certainties, becoming obsessively terrified of failure, and yet feeling guilty when successful. Miller's father never fully recovered from the loss of a business he had worked so hard to build, and his mother was often depressed or embittered by the family's reduced circumstances. However, both refused to give up hope for the future; an optimistic attitude which Miller has carried with him throughout his career.

Miller recognizes the tendency of many Americans to idealize the 1930s as a humanitarian era filled with human solidarity, so when touching on this period in plays like *The American Clock*, he tries to show what he feels was the truer picture: the depression was a time in which there may have been isolated moments of compassion and thoughtfulness, but the majority of people were selfishly out to personally survive, and would tread on anyone who got in their way.

Attending Abraham Lincoln High School during this period, Miller had a better reputation for sports than for academics, and can be seen as something of a Biff Loman from *Death of a Salesman*. It was while playing football that Miller ripped a ligament which would later prevent him from joining the army in World War II. He graduated from high school in 1932, and trying to continue his education, unsuccessfully pursued a night school degree at City College. He soon realized that he should either work or attend school full-time. He began a series of short-term jobs—from singing on a local radio station to truck driving—to try and save up the $500 he would need to attend the University of Michigan as a full-time student.

Toward the end of 1932, a friend got Miller a job clerking in an auto parts warehouse in Manhattan which did not usually employ Jews—giving him his first real experience of American anti-Semitism. It was on the subway to and from this job that he began to read serious literature—most notably, the Russian novelist Fyodor Dostoyevsky's *The Brothers Karamazov*—and realize that writers have the amazing power to affect how people see the world around them. Miller views the two years which he spent in the auto parts warehouse as his "entry into the big world beyond home and school" (*Timebends* 1987, 213). It is his time working here which he later recalls in the short play *A Memory of Two Mondays*.

THE APPRENTICESHIP YEARS

It was partly Miller's growing interest in politics which had attracted him to the University of Michigan, with its notoriety as a radical enclave. Although his high school grades had been poor, Miller managed to get the university to accept him on probation for a year in order to prove himself, and by 1934 he had saved sufficient funds to attend. Enrolling as a student in journalism, during his first year he worked as a reporter and night editor on the student newspaper. Then, during his 1936 spring vacation, Miller spent six days writing his first play, *No Villain*, in order to enter the Avery Hopwood Writing Awards. The Hopwood Awards are competitive, financial awards given by the University of Michigan in a variety of literary genres, and Miller desperately needed the prize money in order to stay enrolled.

Miller chose to write a play because he felt it was closer to real life, and was more accessible than a poem or novel. To his surprise and delight, he won the first prize for drama. Winning the award made Miller feel confident as a playwright, as he explains, "It left me with the belief that the ability to write plays is born into one, and that it is a kind of sport of the mind" (Kunitz 1955, 669). At this point, he switched his major to English and enrolled in a playwriting class given by Professor Kenneth Rowe. Miller credits Rowe with teaching him about the dynamics of constructing a play. By the next year, his rewrite of *No Villain*, now called *They Too Arise*, won a major award from the Bureau of New Plays, and was produced in Ann Arbor and Detroit; Miller also won another Hopwood Award in Drama for *Honors at Dawn*.

On graduating from Michigan in 1938, Miller moved back to New York to join the Federal Theater Project. This Project was a government-run, national agency which had been formed to provide salaries for artists during the lean depression years. Having turned down an offer of $250 a week from Twentieth Century Fox to work as a scriptwriter for films, Miller took the weekly salary of $22.77 from the Federal Theater Project, because he felt that films were too controlled and the theater offered him a greater freedom. Unfortunately, soon after signing on, this project was shut down on the suspicion that it had been infiltrated by communists, and Miller had to find other avenues of work.

For the next few years, Miller earned his living by writing scripts and radio plays, mostly for the popular radio shows *Columbia Workshop* (CBS) and the *Cavalcade of America* (NBC), while working at the Brooklyn Navy Yard. Although few of his plays from this period were ever aired, it gave him a lucrative opportunity to develop and refine his writing skills, while still in contact with an artistic community—even affording him the opportunity to work with Orson Welles on one project. However, Miller was not content with writing for the commercial radio, feeling restricted and confined by the demands of the networks and their advertisers. During this time, he continued to write stage plays for himself, and search for a producer.

In 1940, Miller married his college sweetheart, Mary Slattery, despite the uncertainty of his future career, and the fact that she was a Catholic. They went out to Mary's family in Ohio to marry, even though her relatives had initial suspicions of this Jew marrying into their family. Miller won their respect by his forcefulness in clearing up a problem they faced with the dispensation they needed from the Catholic Church in order to carry out the ceremony. In 1944, the couple had a daughter, Jane, and Miller had his first Broadway play produced, *The Man Who Had All the Luck*.

In his search for a producer, Miller had attracted the attention of Joe Fields, a writer of musical comedies who wanted to be involved with something more serious. Fields had read Miller's latest play, *The Man Who Had All the Luck*, and liking it immensely, acquired the backing to direct it on Broadway. At this point, Miller's luck ran out; the play closed after only six performances, despite winning the Theater Guild National Award and being selected for publication in a collection of new American writing. It was through *The Man Who Had All the Luck*, with its depiction of Beeves's family relationships, that Miller first explored father-son and brother-brother conflicts, and the impact of materialism on American families. The play, about a prosperous businessman, David Beeves, who simply cannot accept his good life and eventually commits suicide, had been poorly produced (as Miller later recognized), and was summarily dismissed by critics. Discouraged by the way *The Man Who Had All the Luck* was received, Miller considered giving up playwriting for good. Turning his hand to fiction, he wrote *Focus* (1945), a controversial novel exploring issues of American anti-Semitism, which was a moderate success. However, the playwright within could not be silenced, and he began work on a new play about success, guilt, and responsibility, revolving around another controversial issue: war profiteering.

In 1947, he and Mary had their second child, Robert, and Miller found a producer for his new play, *All My Sons*, about a father who gets away with selling faulty aircraft parts to the air force, but ultimately pays the price, as his sons turn against him. Miller had spent two years developing *All My Sons*, and by the time the director, Elia Kazan, and the Group Theater began production, it was honed to perfection. This time there was no early closure. Championed by the *New York Times's* theater critic Brooks Atkinson, who welcomed such a serious work in a theater he saw as growing too socially trivial, *All My Sons* won solid reviews, some major awards, and professional recognition for Miller as a playwright. It also provided Miller with sufficient funds to purchase an old farm in Roxbury, Connecticut, to use as a vacation home for the family.

After *All My Sons*, Miller felt that the Red Hook shipping area of Brooklyn might offer him something new on which to write, but trying to gain the confidence of the longshoremen who worked there was next to impossible. Miller became intrigued by the story of Pete Panto, who had tried to lead a rank-and-file revolt against bosses who were possibly Mafia, and certainly corrupt. Panto had vanished, presumed dead, and seemed a heroic figure to Miller—someone defying evil and getting destroyed in the attempt—the very stuff of tragedy. He would later try to tell Panto's story in *The Hook*, a film he never had the chance to make, but his inquiries also gave him the material which he would later turn into *A View from the Bridge* in 1955. However, Miller would follow *All My Sons* with the play that really made his mark in American theater, *Death of a Salesman*.

PLAYWRIGHT OF THE YEAR

After the success of *All My Sons*, Miller felt free to create something more adventurous—hopefully, something never before seen on stage. He wanted to convey to his audience a sense of the simultaneity he felt existed in people's lives. He wanted to give audiences a sense of what went on in a person's head as his life played out around him. Seeing tension as the very stuff of drama, Miller tried to re-create in a play what he saw as the contradictory forces which operate on people—past against present, society against individual, greed against ethics. Though as yet unsure of his topic, he had the idea of a form which would help to convey these contradictions by being "both infinitely compressed and expansive and leisurely, the story itself both strange and homely" (*Timebends* 1987, 144). Finding himself unable to get the play started in his Brooklyn house, he went out to the Connecticut countryside, and on the property he had bought there, he built himself a small studio in which to work. He wrote the first act in two days, then took a more leisurely six weeks to complete it.

Death of a Salesman, a play about the life and death of salesman Willy Loman, premiered on 10 February 1949 at the Morosco Theater in New York City. The enthusiastic reviews of such eminent critics as *New York Times's* Brooks Atkinson swiftly made *Death of a Salesman* the "must see" play of the season. The response was tremendous; Miller won a string of major awards, including the Pulitzer Prize, the New York Drama Critics' Circle Award, the Theater Club Award, and the Antoinette Perry (Toni) Award. The play was soon performed throughout America and Europe, the published script became a best-seller, and it is the only play ever to be a Book-of-the Month Club selection. Drama scholar, Brenda Murphy talks about "the ease with which audiences all over the world have understood and sympathized with the plight of Willy Loman, and have grasped the issues of the play" (*Death of a Salesman* 1995, 126). At times comic, yet also poetic, tragic, and with a realistic veneer which made it easy to involve any audience, *Death of a Salesman* was a new type of serious play which merged the forms of realism and expressionism to suggest new directions and possibilities for all of American drama.

In terms of realism, much of the play seems very true to life: *Death of a Salesman's* characters act and sound like natural, everyday people, facing common social and domestic concerns, and the original stage set of the Loman family house was designed to look as real as possible, even giving Linda, Loman's wife, a working stove over which to cook. However, Willy's flashback dream sequences, the increasingly evident symbolism of various stage effects (lighting and sound), and the play's subtle protest against accepted social expectations, also satisfy the requirements of an expressionistic work, which does not present real life so much as subjective representation of life. On top of this, the play's clever use of time, which allows the audience to view both past and present occuring at the same moment on the same stage set, fully captured the concept of simultaneity after which Miller had been striving.

Death of a Salesman's portrait of Willy Loman managed to strike an emotional chord which continues to reverberate. A man of his time and yet also, somehow, timeless, Loman has attracted audiences all over the world and continues to interest audiences even to the present day. The 1983 production of *Death of a Salesman* in Beijing, The People's Republic of China, at the People's Art Theater, which Miller himself directed, was a landmark in foreign diplomacy. Aside from the Chinese production and numerous American and European productions, the play has been successfully produced in countries as diverse as South Africa, Korea, Japan, Mexico, the Soviet Union, and Australia. There have also been at least seven film and television versions. The play's tremendous success put Miller on a firm financial basis for life.

After *Death of a Salesman*, Miller got to work on his filmscript for *The Hook*, his story about waterfront corruption, which he wanted Elia Kazan to direct, having built up a strong relationship with him during Kazan's direction of both *All My Sons* and *Death of a Salesman*. Knowing from the start that it would be difficult to get backing for such a controversial film, especially given the growing paranoia of the times, Miller did what he saw as the socially responsible thing, and tried to expose the corruption he had discovered in his time on the waterfront two years earlier. Unfortunately, he was entering an era when social responsibility was being conflated with communism, and studios felt it too dangerous to back such projects. Miller would not be working with Kazan again until the sixties.

THE HOUSE UN-AMERICAN ACTIVITIES COMMITTEE AND MARILYN

The House Un-American Activities Committee (HUAC), had been set up in 1938, and had been behind the closing of the Federal Theater Project which Miller had briefly joined. However, the political and cultural climate in America did not allow HUAC to become really powerful until the 1950s. Led by Senator Joseph McCarthy of Wisconsin, the committee sought to expose and restrict anyone in government positions, the military, or the arts whom they suspected of harboring communist sympathies or beliefs, which the committee saw threatening the American way of life. Artists, actors, and writers were subpoenaed to prove that they were not or had not been active in the Communist Party. If they confessed to any communist activity, they were expected to name anyone else involved, or they would be sent to jail for contempt of court. One group of actors, writers, and directors who had been called up before the committee tried to resist the committee's coercion by taking the Fifth Amendment (refusing to testify on the grounds that they might incriminate themselves). Even though they had not confessed to any communist sympathies, they were all sent to jail, and became known as "the Hollywood Ten." The example of their harsh treatment scared many into going along with whatever the committee asked, rather than face such punishment themselves.

In order to further restrict potential subversives among the artistic and intellectual community, a blacklisting system, by which anyone even rumored to have "Red" sympathies would be refused work or prevented from displaying their art, came into creation. Unfortunately, by the time that fears of communist expansion were assuaged, and the committee's bullying tactics and McCarthy's own self-aggrandizing agenda were finally exposed, many people had lost careers, reputations, and even their sanity or life. The disconcerting experience of Miller and his friends during the years of HUAC's power lies behind much of the action in his play *After the Fall*, and forms the background to Eddie Carbone informing on Marco and Rodolpho in *A View from the Bridge*.

A number of people in the theater—such as Miller's friend, Elia Kazan, and fellow playwright, Clifford Odets—admitted having had socialist sympathies to HUAC in an act of public contrition, and named others of similar sympathies, thus putting those others under intense scrutiny. This was seen as an act of betrayal by those to whom the finger was now pointed, especially when it led to those people becoming blacklisted. Kazan's and Miller's friendship fell apart for a number of years following Kazan's testimony. When Miller was finally subpoenaed, like the Hollywood Ten, he refused to cooperate, seeing the whole thing as an unnecessary and cruel exercise, and was cited for contempt.

In 1950, actors Fredric March and his wife, Florence Eldridge, had been blacklisted from movie roles because they were unjustly suspected of being communists. In response, they decided to stage Henrik Ibsen's play *An Enemy of the People*, in which they saw the lead character's situation resembling their own: all are falsely accused by a kind of "mob hysteria" of threatening the well-being of the larger society. They asked Miller if he would write them a new adaptation, which he willingly did, working from a literal translation of the Norwegian. Given the climate of the times, the production was not a great success, and Miller was accused by the press of creating anti-American propaganda.

Miller was never actually blacklisted, and he was able to work in the theater during this time, but he did lose two potential film contracts. There was also some active campaigning against his plays by patriotic groups, such as the American Legion and Catholic War Veterans. Miller responded by publically speaking out *against* HUAC's influence, and *for* artistic freedom, although he found it impossible to get newspapers to print anything written directly against McCarthy. Meanwhile, he was strongly suspected of holding communist sympathies, and was being daily observed by the FBI. Although never at the center of the situation, Miller was affected, and more importantly, he realized just how far America as a nation was being affected by this growing atmosphere of distrust. HUAC changed the lives of many Americans, robbing them of their livelihoods and security as a result of the committee's investigations. This experience revealed to them the sheer tenuousness of human connection in which best friends were seen to turn on one another to save their own careers or reputations. It was during this period when Miller decided to write *The Crucible*, which draws a clear parallel between the American anticommunist paranoia of the 1950s and the 1692 witch trials of Salem, exposing both to be maliciously motivated with ritualistic, public denunciations of innocent people.

Nineteen fifty was also the year in which Miller had been initially introduced to Marilyn Monroe, while in Hollywood for the production of the first film of *Death of a Salesman*, and to promote his screenplay, *The Hook*. His first impression was pretty much what the world saw—the "quintessential dumb blonde" who was "ludicrously provocative" (*Timebends* 1987, 302). However, after a few brief, casual meetings, he began to see her differently. Drawn not only by what he saw as her great physical beauty, but also by her surprising freshness and idealism, and although still married to Mary and a father of two, he could not get Marilyn out of his mind. His mounting celebrity and the pressures of a writing career had been putting an immense strain on his marriage for some time, and meeting Marilyn was the final straw. Miller was attracted to both Marilyn's intense sexuality and her vulnerability, and she to his strength and sense of certainty; Marilyn seemed to hope that Miller would be able to protect her from the hostile world she saw around her. This was, ultimately, a task at which he failed, and about which he writes compassionately in his autobiography.

Meanwhile, under the influence of HUAC, Hollywood did not welcome Miller's disturbing depictions of America. Plans to produce *The Hook* were shelved, and the American Legion threatened to picket the film of *Death of a Salesman*. To soothe opposition, the production company, Columbia, offered to show *Death of a Salesman* accompanied by a film short supporting American businessmen and explaining how Loman was not a typical salesman. Miller objected, and threatened to sue Columbia if they did this. The film was released on its own, but was not a great success, as people were wary at this time of accepting anything critical of American values. Setting these problems aside, Miller turned his attention to an idea which had been forming in his mind for his next play, *The Crucible*.

Miller spent much of 1952 researching witch trials at the Historical Society in Salem, Massachusetts. Thus he ensured that the play would have an accurate historical basis, which could also guard him against accusations of creating a flimsy social satire. The play premiered in 1953 in New York City in a production by Jed Harris, which Miller saw as too cold and stylized, and it was greeted by a mixture of praise, suspicion, and contempt for its evident parallels to HUAC's "witch hunts." It was not until two years later, when a better production appeared, that critics proclaimed it a "great" play. *The Crucible*, with its clear message of resistance against tyranny, has grown to be Miller's most widely produced work.

In 1953, Miller was asked to attend the Belgian premier of *The Crucible*, but he was unable to attend because the U.S. government refused to renew his passport, seeing him as a dangerous dissident. In 1955, HUAC pressured city officials to withdraw permission for Miller to make a film he had been putting together about juvenile delinquency in New York. In 1956, shortly after Miller divorced his first wife and married Marilyn, he was finally subpoenaed to appear before the committee. Prior to the hearing, he went to England with Marilyn, who was making a film with the British actor, Laurence Olivier. While there, Miller revised *A View from the Bridge* into two acts for Peter Brook to produce in London; the play had appeared a year earlier in New York in a one-act format, on a double bill with Miller's nostalgic drama about life in an auto parts warehouse, *Memory of Two Mondays*. On his return to America, Miller was scheduled to speak before the committee.

In his autobiography, Miller relates how Francis E. Walter, chairman of the HUAC before which he had been summoned, reportedly offered to waive Miller's appearance if he would allow Walter to be photographed shaking hands with Marilyn; Miller could not accept such an undignified way out. Refusing to name any writers suspected of communist sympathies to the committee, Miller was convicted of contempt of Congress, and given a fine and a suspended jail sentence. If he had been subpoenaed in HUAC's earlier years, the sentence might have been harsher, but the public was now beginning to grow bored with the repetition of the committee's proceedings. Rather than accept this conviction, Miller decided to appeal. The conviction was overturned by the United States Court of Appeals the following year on the grounds that the questions which he had been asked to answer served no legislative purpose.

The late fifties into the sixties were difficult times, professionally, politically, and personally. Apart from the troubles with HUAC which had made producers a little wary of him, his second marriage was not going well, and there would be a series of deaths of those closest to him. Distracted by personal problems, Miller lost touch with his audience and faced a creative slump. Unable to understand the growing nihilistic and self-indulgent mood of the country, he felt uninspired and unwilling to write anything. The only main work which emerged from this period was the result of an attempt to help his wife, and cheer her up after she had miscarried a much wanted child. Marilyn was growing frustrated by the insipid roles she was being given, so Miller adapted an earlier short story he had written, "The Misfits," into a screenplay for her. This took Miller three years to write, but he created a serious role for his wife to play. However, due to her growing insecurities, the filming was close to a disaster, and the finished movie opened to mediocre reviews.

In 1961, Miller divorced Monroe. Their marriage had been going downhill for some time, with Miller growing increasingly aware, and weary, of his wife's insecurity, mood swings, and growing dependency on drugs and alcohol. Feeling shut out by her personal assistant, Paula Strasberg, Miller saw that Monroe was in trouble, but felt powerless to help her, and could no longer watch her destroy herself. That same year, his mother died. The next year, 1962, six months before Monroe died, Miller married his third wife, Inge Morath, a professional photographer, whose stable nature was far preferable to the roller coaster relationship he had had with Marilyn. He and Marilyn had both met Inge when she took rehearsal photographs during the filming of *The Misfits*. Marilyn had liked her for her sensitivity and kindness, but Miller also recognized her evident strength and independence; meeting again months later, Miller and Inge became friends.

Born in Austria, to independent-minded Protestant parents, Inge had been sent into forced labor by the Nazis for refusing to join a Nazi student organization. Surviving this ordeal, she moved to Paris, and worked with writer and photographer Henri Cartier-Bresson, before coming to America in 1951, assigned to Hollywood as a photographer. In Inge, Miller found his ideal wife, and he has described their years together as "the best of my life" (*Timebends* 1987, 493). The pair have had a close, contented marriage for nearly forty years, as well as a daughter, Rebecca. Living between their estate in Roxbury, Connecticut, where Miller has his own woodwork shop, a writing studio, and close ties to the local community, and their apartment in New York City, close to both the theaters and the photography studios, Miller and his wife have successfully pursued their independent careers. They have also collaborated on a number of books of reportage, such as *In Russia* (1969) and *Chinese Encounters* (1979), for which Inge has taken the photographs and Miller has written the text.

THE HOLOCAUST AND PRESIDENCY OF POETS, ESSAYISTS, AND NOVELISTS (P.E.N.)

Although many critics see *Death of a Salesman* and *The Crucible* as the high point of Miller's career, his output of excellent plays has, if anything, increased in the subsequent years. In 1964, Miller visited the Mauthausen concentration camp with Inge, and later covered the war crimes trial of a group of former Auschwitz guards in Frankfurt, Germany, for the *New York Herald Tribune*. His trip to the death camp partly inspired him to write *After the Fall*, along with a suggestion by film producer Walter Wanger that he write a screenplay based on Albert Camus's novel, *The Fall*. The play conveys the psychological drama which is taking place in the head of Quentin, as he tries to place his life, loves, and fears into perspective; many critics chose to read Quentin as a surrogate for Miller himself, especially given the presentation of Quentin's three wives who seemed remarkably close to those of Miller. It was the similarity between Maggie and Marilyn Monroe that raised the most response; although Maggie is a singer rather than an actress, she has many of Marilyn's well-known mannerisms and traits, and the same personal background. She is also portrayed as promiscuous, temperamental, and self-deceiving.

Miller was asked to offer a play for the opening of the new Lincoln Center Theater in New York City in 1964, and he chose *After the Fall*. The play drew fierce disapproval from many critics for what they felt was a vindictive portrayal of Marilyn (who had died while he was completing the play). On hearing of Marilyn's actual death, Miller was stunned; she still seemed so vivid to him that he could not, at first, believe she was dead. He did not attend her funeral, not wanting to become part of the publicity circus that would surround such an event, but privately mourned the premature death of a woman he still partly loved. Miller has, throughout, refused to accept that Maggie's character in *After the Fall* was strictly based on Marilyn, and would rather critics judge the play by its artistic merits than as a piece of autobiography. Both *After the Fall* and the other play he had produced that same year, *Incident at Vichy*, have closer ties to his preoccupation with the Holocaust. Miller revisited the Holocaust as a central theme in the television play adaptation of Fania Fenelon's concentration camp memoirs, *Playing for Time*, in 1980, and again in 1994 with *Broken Glass*, which considers the effect of the Nazi oppression of German Jews on Jews in America.

For Miller, the concentration camp is a powerful symbol for contemporary life, with its accustomed violence, lack of communication and social responsibility, and dehumanization of feelings. As Miller explains, the camp becomes the "final expression of human separateness and its ultimate consequence. It is organized abandonment" (*Theater Essays* 1995, 289). Miller cites the Holocaust as the period when the world learned to turn away, and feels that this is a problem which persists in society, whenever atrocities occur, from Bosnia to Africa to South America. He insists that we combat this tendency to ignore what is unpleasant in life and involve ourselves before another Holocaust can occur. Willing to practice what he preaches, Miller has been involved throughout his life with numerous social and political organizations.

In 1965, Miller was elected president of P.E.N., an international organization of playwrights, poets, essayists, and novelists, formed after World War II to combat censorship and nationalistic pressures on writers. He had been chosen, partly, as a writer who had admirers and followers in both the East and the West, who could act as a potential connecting force. Miller attended his first P.E.N. conference in Blad, Yugoslavia, in 1965. In 1967, he visited Moscow to persuade Soviet writers to join the organization and make it truly international. In 1969, he visited Czechoslovakia to show support for writers there, and briefly met Václav Havel, then a famous dissident writer, but who later became the democratic president of Czechoslovakia. Havel became the inspiration for Sigmund in Miller's 1977 play, *The Archbishop's Ceiling*, which depicts a group of writers trying to survive against various threats of suppression. Although he retired as president of P.E.N. in 1969, he continued to work with the organization to assist writers in trouble across the globe.

Miller sees P.E.N. as having given him a new lease on life, in giving him the hope that there are enough concerned citizens out there, willing to do something to make a difference. This in turn gives him hope that there is still an audience for his plays who are willing to accept his prompting that they should confront their own responsibilities for the unpleasant way society is turning out, and strive to do something to change this.

OTHER MAJOR PLAYS

In 1968, *The Price* premiered in New York City, and saw a return to more familiar Miller territory: the division and connection between family members. We watch as two brothers attempt to sell off their deceased father's furniture, and come to terms with each other. The production was a troubled one, with Miller having to take over the direction after the actors had fallen out with the original director. Also, the actor playing the role of the furniture dealer, Gregory Solomon, was rushed to the hospital with a serious illness, and had to be replaced by his understudy during the previews. But *The Price* had the longest run of a Miller play for some time.

Despite this renewed popularity, Miller continued to experiment with new forms. He tried his hand at a full-blown musical in 1974, called *Up from Paradise*, which was a revised version of his 1972 rewrite of the Cain and Abel story as a comic folktale with serious undertones, *The Creation of the World and Other Business*. Neither met much success. In 1980, *The American Clock* was produced in the United States. With its twenty-one songs and tunes, and more than fifty-character cast, it was envisaged as a kind of moving collage of American life in the 1930s. The first production failed to catch the spirit of the play, and it was not until Peter Wood's 1986 production in England that the play really came together and caught the audience's imagination and approval.

Miller has also produced a number of intriguing one-act plays, which are firm evidence of his constant exploration of theatrical limits. In 1982, *Elegy for a Lady* and *Some Kind of Love Story* were performed under the collective title of *2 by A.M.*—later changed to *Two-Way Mirror.* In *Elegy for a Lady,* a man gets advice and enlightenment from the proprietress of a boutique. In *Some Kind of Love Story,* a private detective interviews a possible witness in a criminal case. Nineteen eighty-seven saw the production of *Danger: Memory!,* made up of the one-acts, *Clara* and *I Can't Remember Anything.* While *Clara* shows a man's re-actions to the vicious murder of his daughter, *I Can't Remember Anything* de-picts the squabbling relationship of two elderly friends. All four one-acts center on two main characters who, through conflicts over their differing views of re-ality, either grow or fail to grow toward a deeper appreciation of their own shortcomings, strengths, and responsibilities. The plays use minimalistic or highly representational sets, and make great use of lighting, sound, and image to get their points across.

Despite a lack of critical acclaim for his newer works, into the 1990s Miller's dedication to his craft has not slackened. In 1991, a one-act version of *The Last Yankee* was produced, with the expanded two-act version coming two years later. *The Last Yankee,* set in a mental hospital, depicts the pressures facing mar-ried couples in a postmodern age of chaos and insecurity. Also in 1991, *The Ride Down Mt. Morgan* about one man's ego and the troubles he causes in his desire for complete autonomy, premiered in London, England. The choice of England was a reflection of Miller's growing despair over getting fair press in America. *The Ride Down Mt. Morgan* was revised in 1996, and presented to full houses at the Williamstown Theater Festival, Massachusetts. Its planned transfer to a New York theater, however, did not take place until 1998, and with a different cast.

Nineteen ninety-four saw a return to Miller's interest in both the Holocaust and the 1930s with a new play, *Broken Glass,* which had successful runs on both Broadway and London stages. Many saw this realistically rendered tale of a woman's paralysis and her husband's inability to face his complicity in this as a return to the earlier style of Miller, albeit somewhat stripped. However, 1998 produced the ethereal *Mr. Peter's Connections,* a play, firmly experimental, with its multiple timelines and blurring of reality.

FILM VERSIONS OF MILLER'S PLAYS

There have been numerous film and television productions of Miller's work; in some instances, he has written directly for these media. Screenplays which he has written for the movies include *The Misfits* (1961) and *Everybody Wins* (1990); and for television, *Fame* (1978) and *Playing for Time* (1980). A number of his plays have also been produced directly for television, including

The Price (1971), *Incident at Vichy* (1973), *After the Fall* (1974), *All My Sons* (1987), *Clara* (1991), *The American Clock* (1993), and *Broken Glass* (1996).

Film versions of other plays by Miller include an atmospheric version of *A View from the Bridge*, directed in 1961 by Sidney Lumet and starring Raf Vallone and Maureen Stapleton. Also, there are numerous versions of *Death of a Salesman*, but the film which Miller himself most likes is the 1985 television version for CBS, with Dustin Hoffman as Willy Loman. He strongly disliked the first film version in which Fredric March played Willy, feeling that March had been directed to play the character as a lunatic, which vastly oversimplified the play, and led to a mediocre production.

The Crucible has also been filmed more than once. Miller enjoyed the 1950s version, retitled *The Witches of Salem*, for which French playwright and philosopher Jean-Paul Sartre wrote the screenplay, but felt that the Marxist references Sartre had included were a little too heavy-handed. The version of *The Crucible* with which Miller has been most closely involved, and for which he has rewritten some scenes, is the 1996 movie starring Daniel Day-Lewis, filmed in Essex, Massachusetts, and produced by Miller's son, Robert. Only the more recent of these films are available on video.

OTHER DIRECTIONS

Although Miller is known first and foremost as a playwright, he has, over his career, turned his hand to numerous forms of writing. Aside from his plays for radio, television, and stage, he has published a successful novel, numerous short stories, a children's book, an autobiography, books of reportage, and many important articles and essays.

He published his first book, *Situation Normal*, in 1944. This told of Miller's experiences traveling around army camps researching for the film about war correspondent Eddie Pyle, to be called *The Story of G. I. Joe*. Miller had originally been contracted to write the screenplay, and had the idea of creating a new kind of democratic war movie which would treat the whole platoon as equals and not privilege one man as a solitary hero, but it soon became apparent that the studio would not accept such a leap away from their tried-and-tested formula, so he withdrew from the project. The following year, Miller tried his hand at fiction with a novel, *Focus*, which attacked American anti-Semitism, something of which he had firsthand knowledge.

Most of his short stories and a novella, many of which have been printed individually in magazines such as *Esquire*, *Harper's*, *Collier's*, and *The Noble Savage*, are now collected into two volumes: *I Don't Need You Anymore* (1967) and *Homely Girl, A Life and Other Stories* (1995). Some of these stories, such as "The Misfits" and "Fame," acted as the nucleus for other, longer works. Reflecting Miller's interest in foreign cultures, four of his books of reportage, which have been published with photographs by his third wife, Inge Morath, are about places they have visited together, such as Russia and China. He has even published a children's book, *Jane's Blanket* (1963), written for his first daughter. His 1987 autobiography, *Timebends: A Life*, is both highly readable and informative. It ebbs and flows through the years of Miller's life, refusing to conform to any strictly ordered chronology, making connections across great swathes of time—it is a testament to his belief in the process of time and the importance of the past.

Miller has penned a large number of articles and essays during his career, many of which have sparked off major controversies. A number offer his views on various political, social, and moral issues, including the Holocaust, anti-communism, Marilyn Monroe, and P.E.N. There are many more which comment on other artists, writing plays, and the nature and function of theater itself. In 1978 many of these were collected into a book entitled *The Theater Essays of Arthur Miller*, which was updated in 1995. In a number of these articles, Miller is very critical of the American theatrical scene's capacity for producing serious drama, seeing it as having been ruined by commercialism and a serious lack of subsidy. He has also granted numerous interviews over the years, in which he has further commented on art and life in general.

WHY MILLER WRITES

Throughout *Arthur Miller and Company* (1990), edited by Christopher Bigsby, various writers, actors, directors, and critics speak of Miller's political commitment to democracy, truth, morality, and humanity. Directors see his plays as complex and difficult to put on because of their many levels and fine balance. Actors find his work challenging and exhilarating. All realize that his plays demand audience involvement to be fully effective. For Miller, playwriting has always been an act of self-discovery and an effective means of communicating with other people. As a kind of prophet, a role in which he has been described by a number of critics, Miller uncovers America's flaws and tries to enlighten the people as to the harsh realities of their existence, in the hope that they might strive to improve their behavior and lives. With Miller's agreement, in *Conversations with Arthur Miller*, Steve Centola sums up Miller's work as deriving from a "vision that emphasizes self-determinism and social responsibility and that is optimistic and affirms life by acknowledging man's possibilities in the face of his limitations and even sometimes in the dramatization of his failures" (Roudané 1987, 343).

Literary Heritage

LITERARY AND DRAMATIC PRECURSORS

Critics have considered a great variety of possible influences on Miller's work, from Shakespeare to Russian writer Anton Chekhov, to American novelist Sinclair Lewis. The clearest influences, however, are those whom Miller himself has acknowledged: classical Greek playwrights, nineteenth-century Norwegian playwright Henrik Ibsen, nineteenth-century Russian novelists Leo Tolstoy and Fyodor Dostoyevsky, and contemporary American playwrights Tennessee Williams and Clifford Odets.

While studying at the University of Michigan, Miller was attracted to the sense of form and symmetry of events in classical Greek plays. Although he did not always understand what the plays were about, they made him feel aware of the nature and function of drama itself. Using the Greeks as his model, Miller has long insisted that the best drama is social drama. By that he does not mean socialist drama, but plays which are concerned with more than the life of the individual; plays which consider the whole society, and the ties between individuals and society. Miller sees a disturbing tendency in American drama to separate the individual and society, and to write about the separation rather than the connection, which he sees as ultimately dehumanizing. A fierce desire to help their fellowmen evolve into something better, and the belief that such an evolution is possible, made the Greeks humanists. Miller, too, is a humanist—concerned in his plays with examining human nature, with an end toward improving it. Miller's 1955 essay, "On Social Plays," contains an extended treatment of his views on Greek drama, and makes clear his interest in the way Greek plays manage to seamlessly integrate psychological and social concerns.

Miller's indebtedness to the Greeks is reflected in many of his plays, even up to his recent drama, *Broken Glass*; its evident concern with people's identities and place in society are issues which lie at the heart of most Greek plays. But *Broken Glass* also takes on a very classical structure, with its short length and sense of predictability. A Greek play's impact largely depends upon the audience knowing what will happen next. *Broken Glass* uses the same type of classical structure which Miller used for *All My Sons* and *A View from the Bridge*, where the predictability of the outcome is an important part of the play's message. Coincidence lies at the heart of Greek dramas, such as Sophocles' *Oedipus Rex*, and should be seen not as impossible or incredible, but as positive proof that we do connect and live in a world capable of order. It was through theater that the Greeks discovered hope for their whole society; Miller believes that there is a need to rekindle such hope in America today.

Miller is also captivated by the Greek sense of the past, encapsulated in their myths and concept of fate, and how this contributed to the structure of their plays. In Greek plays, the past continually resurfaces in the present, and causes problems for characters whose past connections are made public. The purpose behind this is to show the way in which every action has a consequence, and even if people follow the legal laws of the land, if they have broken a moral law, they will eventually be punished. In *All My Sons,* Joe Keller knowingly endangered people's lives, and sent his partner to jail; in *A View from the Bridge*, Eddie Carbone betrays his wife's relatives, motivated by an unacknowledged, incestuous desire for his niece; in *Death of a Salesman*, Willy Loman commits adultery: when the truth comes out, as it must, each character pays for past mistakes with his life. As Miller tells Christopher Bigsby, "I've come out of the playwrighting tradition which is Greek and Ibsen where the past is the burden of man and it's got to be placed on the stage so that he can grapple with it. That's the way these plays are built. It's *now* grappling with *then*, it's the story of how the birds came home to roost" (Bigsby 1990, 201).

While he was at university, Miller also discovered the work of Henrik Ibsen, whom he saw as the Greek playwrights' successor. One of Miller's early productions was an adaptation he had written of Ibsen's *An Enemy of the People* (1950). It was hardly surprising that Miller would have chosen to work with such a text. Until he began *All My Sons*, Miller admits that he had only once been "truly engrossed in a production—when Ruth Gordon played Jed Harris's production of *A Doll's House*" (*Collected Plays* 1957, 16)—and he is quick to acknowledge Ibsen as a chief dramatic influence, especially on his early work. Miller's sense of realism comes directly from Ibsen, as does the idea of creating characters with whom an audience can identify, so that they might recognize the relevance of the play's message to their own lives. *All My Sons* is the play which has been most heavily influenced by Ibsen, and critics have noticed parallels between *All My Sons* and a number of Ibsen's works, such as *The Wild Duck*, *The Pillars of Society* and *The Master Builder*, in terms of character and plot. In addition, Miller took from Ibsen an idea which remains central to much of his writing: the difficulty of finding true happiness in an essentially unpleasant and hostile world.

What Miller initially recognized in Ibsen's work was the playwright's craft; he saw Ibsen's plays as being works in which everything fit and nothing was extraneous. It was this precision which inspired him to spend two years perfecting *All My Sons*. The concept of the delayed revelation, in which the audience is given discreet clues and symbols of something not apparent at the time, but which later comes to light, is also something Ibsen promoted. In *All My Sons*, we see this in subtle comments which gradually clue the audience in to Joe Keller's initial crime and his son's subsequent suicide, as well as in the symbolism of the tree in their yard (which comes to stand for Larry, the son who committed suicide), and the repeated imagery of imprisonment (which surrounds Keller). As Miller developed new techniques of his own, he left many of those he had learned from Ibsen behind, but he has never dropped the belief he shares with Ibsen that while plays should tell interesting stories, they must always be moral and socially responsible.

Miller also speaks of an allegiance to writers like Tolstoy and Dostoyevsky, who felt obligated to acknowledge and reinforce certain religious and social responsibilities through their writing, rather than simply entertain or offer escape. Needing something to read on the trip to his work at the auto parts warehouse, and during times when business was slack, Miller discovered these great Russian novelists and felt instantly drawn to their world view. Uneasy with the sudden fame and fortune during the run of *All My Sons*, for a short time Miller went to work in a box factory for minimum wage, in an effort to maintain contact with the people for whom he wanted to write. Tolstoy had this same impulse, working in a Moscow shoe shop making shoes at the height of his fame. Miller is not as secure in his religious convictions as writers such as Tolstoy and Dostoyevsky, but he is as deeply concerned with morality and the consequences of its absence. Like Tolstoy, Miller feels that a writer should commit himself and be unafraid to bare his soul in his work. Miller has done this on frequent occasions, which is why so many of his male protagonists, such as *Death of a Salesman*'s Biff Loman, *The Crucible*'s John Proctor, *American Clock*'s Lee Baum, and *After the Fall*'s Quentin, are so closely autobiographical.

Miller has been influenced not only by foreign writers from the past, but also recognizes his debt to contemporary American playwrights Tennessee Williams and Clifford Odets. Miller feels an affinity to Williams because he sees himself as suffering from the same "sense of alienation" (*Timebends* 1987, 180) which Williams had felt. While Williams felt alienated by his homosexuality, Miller felt alienated by a sense of morality which was clearly at odds with a commodified and materialistic society. Like Williams, Miller also believed in the possibility that theater could make a measurable difference in the wider society. Attracted to Williams's concept of the "plastic theater," which Williams saw as incorporating experimental use of lights, sets, music, and other nonverbal additions, Miller agreed that such experimentation could offer greater flexibility on the American stage, and could be highly instrumental in a play's effectiveness. He has continued to experiment with these elements in his plays throughout his career.

In his autobiography, Miller acknowledges that he owes the greatest debt to Williams's *A Streetcar Named Desire* (1947), which was produced on Broadway two years before *Death of a Salesman*. He was amazed by the play's sheer vitality, with its liberated and liberating use of words, and felt that it paved the way for the acceptance of a new form of drama which America could proudly call her own (*Timebends* 1987, 182). Miller saw Williams's use of language, which had a lyrical quality, as a kind of poeticized realism that produced an everyday speech for his characters. This allowed audiences to see, more clearly, the meaning of a play and its relevance to their own lives. Miller recognizes that this was something Clifford Odets also had tried to achieve, even before Williams.

Miller admires a number of American playwrights who preceded him, such as Maxwell Anderson, S. N. Behrman, and Sidney Howard; but none of them worked on the same sort of plays he wished to write, except for Clifford Odets, and, occasionally, Maxwell Anderson. To the young Miller, the generally accepted first great American playwright, Eugene O'Neill, was admirable, but by the late-thirties (when Miller started writing) he had become dated, boring, escapist, and too erudite. Miller admits that he views O'Neill's works of the late 1940s as very different and worthy of praise, but these had not been produced or published when he was looking for a role model. In hindsight, he sees both O'Neill and Odets as important "prophetic spirits" of the American stage, and "playwrights of political consequence, not merely theatrical talents" (*Timebends* 1987, 232). However, in the 1930s, with plays like *Waiting for Lefty* (1935) and *Awake and Sing* (1935) stunning Broadway audiences, Clifford Odets seemed the playwright to emulate, with his lyricism of hopeful despair, revolutionary fervor, and commitment to socialism.

Miller was attracted to both Odets's attempts at social protest in a theater which is often hostile to such attempts, and the poetic rhythms of the playwright's work. *Waiting for Lefty* was a classic example of agitprop theater: plays which blatantly attempt to engage their audience with a call to arms. Although he has developed a far more subtle and sophisticated form of agitprop, many of Miller's plays retain something of this influence, as they call for some kind of responsive action from the audience to correct in themselves the type of destructive behavior displayed by the plays' characters. Odets also inspired Miller to create a dialogue which would sound like realistic speech, yet contain many of the elements of poetry: rhythm, symbolism, and those resounding phrases which make much poetry so memorable. Critics have commented, especially, on the poetic language Miller has created for *Death of a Salesman* and *The Crucible*, but this is something which is evident in all of his work.

HOW MILLER WRITES

A number of the plot ideas for Miller's plays have come from stories he has heard. For example, the protagonist of his first major play (*The Man Who Had All the Luck*), David Beeves, came partly from Miller's first wife's aunt, Helen, who told him about how her husband had hung himself. A cheerful, well-liked and successful man, his whole personality had suddenly changed as he turned introverted, paranoid, and finally psychotic. Miller's own family had had a similar case study, Moe, the husband of his cousin, Jean. *All My Sons* was inspired by a tale told to him by his mother-in-law about a young girl in Ohio who had turned in her father for selling defective parts to the armed forces during the war. *A View from the Bridge* is based on a story Miller heard from his old friend, Vinny Longhi, about a longshoreman who informed on two brothers to the Bureau of Immigration to prevent one of them from marrying his niece.

Other plots are based on Miller's personal experiences, such as *American Clock* and *After the Fall*; both of which can be seen as highly autobiographical. Leonard Moss points out how many of Chris Keller's speeches about life in the army in *All My Sons* echo Miller's own reporting on returning veterans in his earlier book, *Situation Normal* (*Arthur Miller* 1980, 21). *The Archbishop's Ceiling* comes out of Miller's experiences meeting writers from Eastern Bloc countries. In many ways, even a play like *The Crucible*, with its evocation of the HUAC trials in which Miller was forced to take part, falls into this category. John Proctor's affair with young Abigail behind his wife's back could be seen as an indication of Miller's own guilt at carrying on with Marilyn Monroe while he was married to Mary.

Many of Miller's characters are actually composites of people he has known—he pieces together various traits he recalls to create believable characters. The Loman men in *Death of a Salesman* were partly based on his uncle, Manny Newman, and Manny's two sons, Buddy and Abby. Gregory Solomon, in *The Price*, is a mix of Miller's own great-grandfather, with his dark sense of humor, and Boris Aronson, the set designer on a number of Miller's plays, who spoke with a Russian-Yiddish accent and tended to mangle the English language. Miller's mother is reflected not only in Rose Baum in *American Clock*, but also in Sylvia Gellburg in *Broken Glass*, with her sense of a wasted life at a time when women faced too many social restrictions. It is not that Miller is obsessed with his own life, family, and friends, but that he utilizes his personal experience and knowledge of people to create credible, realistic characters for his plays.

All of Miller's plays have been written with a strong personal agenda to inform his audiences about their own natures and lives so that they may strive to make those lives more meaningful. Meaningful, for Miller, means a life which takes on both individual and social responsibilities, and actively participates in trying to make the world a better place. Miller wants to write plays which the average man in the street could follow and enjoy. Such a man, Miller knows, would be impatient with long speeches, literary allusions, or anything that smacks too much of "culture." Thus, he chooses to write what he sees as fundamental plays in which the characters and plots are dramatized by action as much as speech. That speech might be poetic, but it savors of realism; and it is always a part of the action, being a result of what has happened rather than the cause.

MILLER'S DRAMATIC IMPACT

Miller has won numerous major awards acknowledging his lifetime achievement in American theater: in 1959, he received the Gold Medal for Drama from the National Institute of Arts and Letters; in 1984, the Kennedy Center Honors; in 1995, the William Inge Festival Award; in 1996, the Edward Albee Last Frontier Playwright Award; in 2000, he was inducted into the Jewish American Hall of Fame. For his eightieth birthday in 1995, tributes to the playwright were held at the National Theatre in London, and at the Town Hall in New York City. But what, exactly, has Miller contributed to the development of American theater, beyond more than two dozen plays?

There is a temptation to describe Miller as a realist, because his plays often seem to present speech and situation as they appear in everyday life. However, Miller dislikes definitions of his writing as realistic, because he sees himself as one who is not attempting to create reality, but rather interpret it. Constantly trying out new techniques, Miller has created works whose artistic form is part of their message. His influence on American theater has been a profoundly moral one, through which he has reintroduced humanistic concerns which place mankind's improvement as uppermost, and popularized a social theater which promotes social reform. Miller's recognition, depiction, and insistence of tragedy as it exists in everyday people's lives has been one of his most controversial contributions. He has also made stylistic innovations, such as the "subjective realism" mode of presentation devised for *Death of a Salesman,* or the poetic diction he has created for many of his characters, which have further influenced the development of American drama, and show his importance in American literary history.

MILLER AND TRAGEDY

In 1949, soon after *Death of a Salesman* opened on Broadway, Miller wrote an article for the *New York Times,* entitled "Tragedy and the Common Man," in which he insisted that "the common man is as apt a subject for tragedy in its highest sense as kings were" (*Theater Essays* 1995, 3). This started off a heated debate regarding the nature of tragedy that has been going on ever since. Traditional views of tragedy assume a hero who is either upper-class or very intelligent, and who challenges, because of some personal flaw in his nature, the moral values of his society. For daring such a challenge, the hero suffers, to prove to audiences that their society and its values are inviolable.

Willy Loman is clearly not the usual tragic hero; he is lower middle-class and none too clever. The world he inhabits is that of amoral, capitalistic big business, rather than one with any clear moral value. However, Miller insists that Willy Loman is a tragic hero, and *Death of a Salesman* a tragedy. He argues that tragic heroes are defined by their willingness to sacrifice everything in order to maintain their personal dignity—whatever their station in life. Loman has a faulty vision of what makes a person successful, which makes him flawed, but regardless of the opposition and the ultimate cost to himself, he refuses to give up that vision, which makes him, in Miller's eyes, a tragic hero.

SUBJECTIVE REALISM

As well as introducing America to a broader concept of tragedy, *Death of a Salesman* also introduced theatergoers to a new form, which carefully blends realistic and expressionistic devices to create the impression of what was actually going on inside the protagonist's head. While the play strives to create the actual reality of Willy Loman's house before the audience, it is also filled with symbols and effects which suggest something beyond the tangible world. As drama scholar Brenda Murphy explains, "Miller needed a dramatic form that would combine the subjectivity of expressionism with the illusion of objectivity afforded by realism" (*Death of a Salesman* 1995, 5). Miller was aided in the creation of this form by the play's original director, Elia Kazan, and its stage designer, Jo Meilziner. They had both recently worked with Tennessee Williams on the initial production of *A Streetcar Named Desire*, which had similarly tried to blend nonrealistic and realistic elements to symbolize death, madness, and a degenerated South.

In *Death of a Salesman*, Miller allows his audience to witness the present and the past as they simultaneously occur in Willy Loman's life. Through this, we learn not just what happens to Loman objectively, but we also gain a view of how Willy subjectively views events; the contrast between the two is what makes the play so fascinating. The subjective reality of *Death of a Salesman*, by which an audience can see both the truth and the truth as Loman sees it, is created through careful lighting, musical cues, and subtle writing.

POETIC LANGUAGE

Despite using the colloquialism of ordinary, everyday language, Miller raises his dialogue to the level of poetic language with the inclusion of sophisticated metaphors and a unique style. The words his characters speak often reveal an inner self which normal speech would leave hidden. Thus, we can see beyond Willy Loman's proud boasts, and a character like Joe Keller in *All My Sons* unwittingly (or seemingly so) betrays his past wrongdoing by the countless references to jail and punishment in his speech. Critics are growing increasingly aware of Miller's use of language, and see his plays as being filled with intricate imagery—although it is often hidden behind a façade of everyday speech. Miller actually created his own stylized language for the characters of *The Crucible*, based on the syntax and idiom in the transcripts he read of the original Salem witchcraft trials.

A close look at the vocabulary of any one of his plays reveals numerous clichés, colloquialisms, historical references, and symbols which all point toward a specific idea. Even his characters' names are often weighted in significance. Critics discuss the relevance of Willy Loman, by which the first name implies a babyish quality and the last a sense of inferiority, or the closeness of Keller to Killer, and the biblical network of characters' names in *The Ride Down Mt. Morgan*. Miller intends these countless references and allusions to assist his audiences in recognizing the universal dilemmas in his plays, and the possible solutions to these dilemmas which he explores and wants viewers to absorb.

MILLER'S INFLUENCE ON OTHER WRITERS

Miller's influence on American drama can be seen as both general and specific. He can be placed alongside Eugene O'Neill and Tennessee Williams as a major pioneer of the development of a distinctly American theater. Although many American dramatists have written plays which clearly echo or build on Miller's plots and concerns, his presence is most firmly evident in the rekindling of a serious attitude toward drama which has developed in his wake. Dan Sullivan, a reviewer for the *Los Angeles Times*, describes Miller as a "father figure" for American theater artists, who is most notable for his "integrity" and pursuit of truth (Bigsby 1990, 192). Writers have a profound respect for Miller, and feel inspired to assist in his lofty goal of trying to make the world a better place in which to live. Christopher Bigsby's book, *Arthur Miller and Company*, is a telling summary of what many contemporary writers feel about Miller: what they owe him, why they admire him, and what they have learned from him. Throughout the book, writers, along with directors and actors who have been involved with his work, offer their opinions and assessments of Miller. Men like Ralph Ellison, Joseph Heller, and William Styron speak of Miller's importance and contribution to American art; while playwrights David Rabe and Edward Albee praise his writing and social commitment. Kurt Vonnegut sums up their admiration when he describes how Miller's plays "speak movingly about America to almost all Americans, while telling the truth about America" (Bigsby 1990, 10).

Miller's commitment to serious drama and openness toward experimentation has influenced many younger American playwrights, such as Edward Albee. Albee's plays, including *Who's Afraid of Virginia Woolf* (1962) and *Three Tall Women* (1994), display Miller's social concern, and similarly play with theatrical convention. Many of Albee's plays assert the need for the individual to acknowledge the nature of reality and the necessity for genuine human relationships. There is also a concern with what Albee sees as the collapse of American idealism. As social criticism which refuses to pull any punches, his plays attempt to combat the artificial values he sees becoming too prominent in our society. The same can be said for any number of Miller's works.

Another contemporary playwright whose work displays values and aims identical to Miller is African American playwright August Wilson. Through their plays, Miller and Wilson both seek to provide what they see as a spiritually impoverished American society with propositions for survival and improvement. Wilson's *The Piano Lesson* (1986) teaches about the power of the past, and the pointlessness of blame similar to Miller's *After the Fall*, while Wilson's *Two Trains Running* (1991) depicts a community learning to band together in the same way as the characters in Miller's *The American Clock*. The balance between the individual and social interests and needs, which both Miller and Wilson promote, is shown to be achieved by asserting moral responsibility toward self and others. Thus, Troy Maxson in Wilson's *Fences* (1987) can be seen as a counterpart to John Proctor in Miller's *The Crucible*, as both characters must find a way to balance their responsibility to themselves with their responsibility toward others. Neither character finds such a balance easy, and both eventually die to maintain what they do achieve. Wilson's plays are clearly inspired by the same beliefs in democracy and human potential which Miller exhibits throughout his work.

There are also numerous well-known American plays that display more specific influences from Miller's work, most notably the influence of *Death of a Salesman*. For example, Lorraine Hansberry's *A Raisin in the Sun* (1959) portrays the Youngers, a family who, despite their ethnicity, are very similar to the Lomans. Both families struggle to survive and progress in a society which seems antagonistic to their dreams. Similar internal and external forces are shown to be operating on each family, and conspiring to hold everyone back. The aspirations, relationships, and desires of the Younger family are as universal as those of the Lomans, making both families recognizably human, and therefore highly sympathetic to their audiences.

The work of fellow Jewish playwright David Mamet exhibits many similarities to that of Miller, from Mamet's attempt to create a kind of poetic realism in the dialogue (albeit that Mamet achieves a very different tone), to the shared concern with the way capitalism and materialism operate on American society. It is easy to read *Glengarry Glen Ross* (1984) as an update of *Death of a Salesman*, with one of its central protagonists, Shelley Levene, being a modern-day version of Willy Loman. Both elderly, they are tired men, worn out by a world which has been antagonistic and hostile to their dreams. Both hide behind false descriptions of their own ability to sell, when in fact both have become outmoded and dismissed by the very people they desire to impress. Caught in a world which judges people by their earning potential, these two are essentially losers, and are forced to pay the price for that fact. Loman exits in a dramatic flash of selfless sacrifice in an effort to help his son, Biff, through which he transforms himself into a hero. Levene, however, can only disappear out of view, unable to offer any assistance to his daughter, after he is exposed as a liar and a thief. The business world, Mamet appears to be saying, has become an even harsher place in 1984 than it was back in 1949.

COMMON MILLER THEMES

A great variety of plots and characters appear in Miller's plays, yet there are certain thematic concerns which tend to reappear with frequency. On a general level, all of Miller's drama attempts to create a better society by exploring the demands of morality, and uncovering important individual and social needs. However, examples of some of his more specific concerns would be the importance of the past, issues regarding responsibility and connection, the nature of families, the damage caused by capitalism and materialism, and the law. There are elements of all of these throughout most of the plays studied in this book.

THE IMPORTANCE OF THE PAST

In Miller's view, the past informs the present, and to ignore it is to restrict the present. He asks us to learn from the past so we can recognize and place ourselves in the present. This is the problem which Quentin faces in *After the Fall*. He is trying to escape his past rather than embrace it, which is causing a lack of direction in his life. When, by the close of the play, he accepts the responsibility of all he has done, and all that has happened to him in the past, he and his new wife, Holga, can begin to live more fully in their present.

The way in which history impacts on the present lies behind all of Miller's dramas, from the Salem witch trials in *The Crucible* to the Holocaust references in *Broken Glass*. The 1692 witch trials are echoed in the unfairness of the HUAC hearings, and the anti-Semitism at home and abroad in 1938 highlights ethnic problems which continue to plague society. Written in the shadow of atrocities in Rwanda and Bosnia, *Broken Glass* conveys the necessity of a humanistic response to the contemporary world we inhabit, for without their humanity both Sylvia and Phillip Gellburg are in danger of becoming lost souls.

Miller insists that the past should not be ignored; events like the depression or the Holocaust will reverberate through all of our lives for all time, and it is dangerous to deny this. Miller believes that the job of any artist, "is to remind people of what they have chosen to forget because it's too hard to remember" (Bigsby 1990, 200). Thus Quentin, or Sylvia and Phillip Gellburg, are encouraged to remember everything they have been in the past, to help them define who they are in the present. Those who achieve the connection, such as Quentin and Sylvia Gellburg, are rewarded; those who do not, such as Phillip Gellburg, suffer the consequences.

LESSONS IN RESPONSIBILITY AND CONNECTION

Through many of his plays, Miller tries to demonstrate the connections he sees between individuals and society, to point out people's responsibilities, and to depict the disastrous results when these go unrecognized. Fascinated with the idea of guilt and blame, and how to continue living with these in the world, Miller sees the first step as accepting responsibility—for what one intended to do or even did by accident—because someone has to be responsible. It is only by accepting our responsibility for evil, as Quentin does in *After the Fall*, that we can break its hold over us and restore a moral order to society.

Miller's Jewishness is important when trying to follow the philosophical beliefs which lie behind his work. Jewish theology has distinct ideas about guilt and contains no real concept of sin. To do right is natural and sensible, for not to do right reduces the humanity of the individual. To passively accept guilt can only lead to complacency. Miller insists that we should actively transform guilt into responsibility, and that will allow us to transcend it ("Our Guilt" 1965, 11). People should be responsible for what they create, and the consequences of their actions are important as the actions themselves. This is something John Proctor comes to realize in *The Crucible.*

Miller asks us to choose to take responsibility for things we cannot control as well as for those we can, because a refusal of responsibility is ultimately a refusal of humanity. Ignoring responsibilities, either personal or social, will interfere with an individual's ability to connect. Through his plays, Miller tells us that he tries "to make human relations felt between individuals and the larger structure of the world" (Roudané 1987, 171). Recognizing the sense of connection they had in Elizabethan drama, Miller sees such a sense as lacking in our contemporary world, but tries to re-create it through his plays. True American democracy depends upon the successful completion of such connections. The grand finale of *The American Clock*, in which the entire cast unites in song, presents an excellent image of the power of true democracy to surmount any difficulty, even one so great as the depression.

THE FAMILY

Much of the conflict and tension created in Miller's plays comes from the relationships and interactions between family members. Miller's families tend to act as microcosms for the larger society; just as every family member struggles to find the right position in their family, so does every individual struggle to find their right position in society. Miller sees the typical "American family" as facing many difficulties: members frequently work against each other rather than in unity, they fail to take on sufficient responsibility, and they do not show sufficient trust in, or love for, one another. Just as the family appears to be failing, so is American society, and for the same reasons. This is clearly illustrated by *All My Sons*, in which we witness two families torn apart by the actions of their members, culminating in the destruction of both fathers. On the larger social scale, which Chris tries to get his father to see, Joe Keller's irresponsible actions may have killed countless airmen. This is brought home to Joe when he learns of his son Larry's suicide out of shame for his father, and is brought to the realization that "all" of those airmen were "his sons."

Fathers and their sons, especially, are central characters in many of Miller's plays, and their relationship directs much of the action. Director and theater critic Harold Clurman identifies in Miller a "strong family feeling," by which Miller assigns the father the role of "prime authority and guide" (Corrigan 1969, 145). Miller believes that fathers should stand for virtue and value, and offer their sons an example they can be proud to emulate. However, as Clurman explains, Miller's plays often depict a father whose "inability to enact the role of moral authority the son assigns to him and which the father willy-nilly assumes" becomes one of the central concerns (145). Fathers, such as Joe Keller in *All My Sons* or Willy Loman in *Death of a Salesman,* quite simply cannot live up to the perfection demanded of them by their sons. Neither the sons nor the fathers can forgive such failure, and all carry a guilty burden of responsibility for each other, which is impossible to shirk.

CAPITALISM AND ANTIMATERIALISM

Since his college days, Miller had felt that America was being run by men of business who were all after private profit, and who merely used those without wealth as pawns. Thus, it made sense to see money and finance as being behind many American conflicts. Howard Wagner, in *Death of a Salesman,* is the epitome of the cold-hearted businessman, who callously takes away Willy Loman's job when he starts to lose business, without a thought to the man's financial obligations and years of service. Stanton Case, in *Broken Glass*, is similarly dismissive of Phillip Gellburg when he fails to get him a piece of property he had wanted. Men like Wagner and Case are only concerned with the bottom line, and are more interested in things than people; thus, Wagner is shown to be more interested in his tape recorder than his employee, and Case with his yacht. What fuels the hard-heartedness of such men is their desire for acquisitions and wealth.

Miller sees the constant American quest to be successful, especially in terms of wealth, as a potentially destructive and harmful one. Competition itself often creates negative values which may lead to success, but at what Miller regards as too heavy a price. Successful people in Miller's plays are rarely happy in any relationship other than the one they have with their own success, which makes them lonely individuals. Lyman Felt, in *The Ride Down Mt. Morgan,* is such a man. While the best way to survive in a capitalist system is to become a better and more ruthless capitalist than your fellow workers, this system clearly privileges individuals over their society, and that is what Miller fears could lead to an eventual breakdown of that society.

Many see great wealth as a mark of a person's success, and this belief fuels many to try to gain such wealth, or at least to own the things it can provide. This is the impulse behind materialism, which can be defined as the desire for the best of everything, from services to goods, often leading people to place acquisition ahead of all other values. *Death of a Salesman*'s Loman family is a typical example of a family from the middle of the century who strive to acquire everything that society and advertisers tell them they need to be viewed as successful. Their resulting failure to gain all that they want, and the repercussions this has on their lives, illustrates the dangers of such materialistic beliefs. *The Ride Down Mt. Morgan* carries these concerns into the 1990s, with the protagonist Lyman Felt, a successful businessman who also happens to be a bigamist, and whose overwhelming appetite leads him to destroy not one, but two families.

THE LAW

The law and lawyers, in many guises, inhabit Miller's plays, and it is clear that the gap between legal and moral law fascinates the playwright. Many of his characters would be found innocent of wrongdoing by America's legal system, but there are certain moral laws they cannot escape. Actual lawyers abound in the plays: George Deever in *All My Sons*, Bernard in *Death of a Salesman*, Alfieri in *A View from the Bridge*, Quentin in *After the Fall*, Tom Wilson in *The Ride Down Mt. Morgan*. It is interesting to note how these real lawyers are largely ineffectual in either helping or judging those who have committed the crimes (moral or legal). It is an indication of the separateness of legal law from moral law, and in some cases the actual ineffectiveness of the former. In *A View from the Bridge*, Eddie Carbone brings on disaster by upholding a legal statute (against illegal immigration) rather than by violating one; it is a higher, moral order of law which he finds he cannot escape. The legal system, often seen as ineffectual and certainly limited, cannot help him to protect his niece. These are the main reasons why *After the Fall*'s Quentin gives up his law practice.

As Leonard Moss insists (1980, 111), many of Miller's plays incorporate the "accusation-defense rhythm of a trial" (111) in their structure, despite the variety of their narrative schemes. Hidden guilt is hinted at and gradually brought to light as such plays progress toward judgment, with the protagonists on some occasions atoning, but often paying a heavy price (sometimes their own lives). A play like *All My Sons*, in essence, is a courtroom drama, filled with trial metaphors. Although George is the only actual lawyer in the piece, all the characters seem to act as witnesses or offer personal opinions regarding Joe Keller's level of guilt. The audience could be seen as the jury, while Joe's son, Chris, acts as prosecutor and judge—demanding a death sentence. In *Death of a Salesman*, Willy is similarly tried by his son, Biff.

In a play like *The Crucible*, the main impetus is quite literally a trial, but we actually spend our time outside the courtroom, in order to better illustrate the unpleasant repercussions on a society which allows itself to be governed by

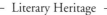

man-made laws which are unquestionably open to corruption in the pursuit of personal gain. This clearly indicates Miller's belief in the ascendancy of moral laws over the laws of the land. Man-made laws are too open to abuse, destructive loopholes, and personal agenda. Miller judges his characters by a higher moral standard.

3

Tragedy: *Death of a Salesman* (1949)

Miller wrote *Death of a Salesman* in the spring of 1948, in a small writing studio he built for himself on his property in Connecticut. Interested in carpentry since a teenager, when he bought a stack of lumber to build a porch onto the family house, he gave Willy Loman, the play's central protagonist, the same love of craftsmanship and working with wood. Miller's uncle, Manny Newman, also liked working with his hands, and he was a salesman with a wild imagination and tendency to brag. Providing the prototype for Willy, Manny was a small man, in love with fame and fortune, a man who would manipulate the truth to his own advantage and saw everything as some kind of competition which he, and his family, had to win. He was also prone to black moods and bouts of despair; it is quite possible that he committed suicide in the end, although Miller, a child at the time, was sheltered from this knowledge. Manny's eldest child, Buddy, like Willy's son, Biff, was athletic and popular, and the younger son, Abby, like Willy's younger son, Hap, was one for the ladies.

On meeting his Uncle Manny at a matinee performance of *All My Sons*, Miller asked how he was doing. Instead of replying, Manny went straight into saying how well his sons were doing, as if he felt he had to build them up in competition against their successful playwright cousin. The fact that Manny did not even pause before taking their conversation in an unexpected direction gave Miller the idea to write a play without transitions, where the dialogue would flow from one scene to the next without any apparent breaks. Instead of using a chronological order, in which single events followed on from one another, he wanted to create a form which displayed the past and the present as if they were both occurring at the same time. In this way, he would be able to transmit to the audience exactly what was going on inside the mind of his protagonist; indeed, an early title for the play was *The Inside of His Head*. He wrote the first act in one day, and six weeks later had completed the play.

Death of a Salesman covers the last twenty-four hours of Willy Loman's life. A victim of both a heartless capitalist society and his own misguided dreams, Willy's eventual suicide is presented with tragic dimensions. His beliefs may be misguided, but he stays true to them to the end. Although he has neither social nor intellectual stature, Willy has dignity, and he strives to maintain this as his life falls apart around him. We learn of past events leading up to the moment of his death by seeing Willy's memories acted out on the stage. Writing in a style which has become known as "subjective realism," Miller carefully blends a realistic picture of a salesman's home and life in the post-depression years with the subjective thoughts that are going through its central protagonist's head. Willy doesn't have flashbacks so much as immediate experiences in which time has been dislocated. The transitions between current action and memory are fluid, and occasionally the two occur simultaneously; the confusion this may cause for an onlooker is indicative of the greater confusion that is happening to Willy, who is trying to find some meaning in his life.

Miller's strong sense of moral and social commitment runs throughout the play. The aims of *Death of a Salesman* are twofold. First, Miller wanted to write a social drama confronting the problems of an ordinary man in a conscienceless, capitalistic social system. Second, he wanted that same play to be a modern tragedy which adapted older, tragic theories to allow for a common man as ill-fated protagonist. Willy's apparent ordinariness should not blind us to his tragic stature. Miller insists that a common family man's situation can be as tragic as the dilemmas of royalty, because he ties his definition of heroism to a notion of personal dignity which transcends social stature. Willy is heroic because he strives to be free and to make his mark in society despite the odds against him. Though he is destroyed in the process, he is motivated by love and his destruction allows learning to take place. Through Willy's sacrifice, Biff is able to accept his father's love, while recognizing the emptiness of the dream Willy espoused. Because of Willy's character, motive, and outcome, the action of the play is tragic. Willy Loman had accepted at face value overpublicized ideas of material success, and therein lies his tragedy. His downfall and final defeat illustrate not only the failure of a man, but also the failure of a way of life.

SETTING AND PLOT DEVELOPMENT

The opening setting is important, as it provides the background for Willy Loman's life and some of the rationale behind his death. Before we see anything, the script informs us that we hear a faint pastoral melody played on a flute, recalling both Willy's father (who played such an instrument) and the pastoral dream, which may have suited Willy's nature better than the harsh world of business he chose. As the curtain rises, Miller asks that the central focus be on a cross section of the Loman's small household, showing the kitchen and two bedrooms. Although the inside of the house is to be depicted realistically, Miller suggests only key furnishings should be included—a refrigerator dominating the kitchen, and a silver athletic trophy above Willy's bed. These moderate items represent the only achievements in Willy's life—a few basic luxuries for the house and a fleeting, winning moment from his family's past. The refrigerator we later learn is on the verge of breaking down, and the trophy was won by Willy's oldest son, Biff, just before he dropped out of high school and became a vagrant. The house is surrounded by apartments which dwarf and seem about to crush it, showing the intense social pressure under which the Loman family lives.

When the play begins it is nighttime, yet Willy is just coming home. He is exhausted, and his arrival at this hour has his wife, Linda, instantly worried. She is right to be worried, as it is clear that Willy is in trouble—he is a traveling salesman who is becoming totally alienated from the job against which he has defined his whole life. He cannot concentrate to drive his car to appointments, and when he manages to get out, he can no longer sell anything. Willy tells Linda how he could not drive and therefore returned home, and she tries to soothe him. Biff has arrived for a visit after a long absence, and their younger son, Hap, is also staying with them so that the whole family might be together. Relations are obviously strained between Biff and his father, partly because of Biff's evident lack of ambition in life—especially considering the promise his father still believes him to have. Willy starts to reminisce, trying to recall better days to cheer himself up, but his memories are confused and a little suspect. While he is remembering, his sons wake up and overhear their father.

Willy goes to the kitchen to get himself a snack, and the scene switches to the boys' room, where they discuss their father's condition. Despite being brothers, Biff and Hap have developed different outlooks on life. Of the two, Biff seems more grounded in reality, and is more worried about his father. He is as unhappy as Willy regarding his own lack of professional advancement, but cannot admit this to a father against whom he holds an unspoken grudge. Hap just wants to avoid anything unpleasant, preferring that his brother deal with their father rather than get involved himself. Although he momentarily confesses that he is not entirely content with his life as a deceitful womanizer, Hap is more concerned with his own image than his father's deterioration. The brothers talk about going into business together, but it is unlikely to ever happen, an idle dream from which they are soon distracted by their father, who has begun to loudly relive events from his past.

The apartment houses in the background are faded out, and the lighting suggests that the stage is covered with leaves, as the opening pastoral music re-asserts itself. With this change in atmosphere, Willy's dreamworld of the past is re-created for the audience as it occurs in Willy's memory. Willy remembers his sons as young boys, a time in the Loman family when they were all happily to-gether. The strength of Willy's memory brings the "young" boys onto stage, and all three become more vibrant than their current-day versions. Willy re-calls the fatherly advice he gave about how being liked is all a man needs to get on in this world—advice which has badly influenced his sons' lives, making them too self-assured and lazy. Willy boasts of his exploits to his sons, lying to make himself look better, and they are of an age where they still believe and idolize their father.

Bernard, the son of Willy's friendly neighbor, Charley, comes to warn Biff that he is failing his math class. The Lomans do not hide their contempt for Bernard, considering him beneath them because of his studiousness and lack of athleticism. They believe that they have more potential in life; however, it is a potential built on dreams and wishes rather than hard work or dedication, and as such is the flimsiest of constructions. Bernard's more serious attitude will be the one that achieves the only success among this group. While remembering, Willy cannot help but recall something of the truth rather than whitewash his whole past, and when Linda joins him (appearing in his dream as she would have been all those years ago), we discover they are barely making ends meet. Willy is not a very good salesman, and they are struggling to pay off all the modern appliances they have been buying to "keep up with the Joneses."

Willy has gone back to the time in his past when he realized he would not make the "big time" he desired. We learn that he has taken on a mistress in Bos-ton to boost his spirits when he gets lonely on the road. His guilt over this is ex-acerbated by his wife being so loving and supportive, even when his sales are down. Willy's memories, which started so contentedly, turn unpleasant as he recalls a darker past: his guilt over his adultery; Biff's laziness, thievery, and im-pending failure to graduate. Willy is plunged back into the present, partly to protect himself from such hurtful memories, and finds Hap in the kitchen try-ing to calm him down.

Willy has been making enough noise to wake the neighbors, and Charley comes over in evident concern for his friend. He stays to play cards, and tries to get Willy to accept a job with his company. Willy refuses, as his pride cannot al-low him to work for a man he sees as his inferior. This turns Willy's thoughts to a man he does respect, his older brother, Ben, and another memory plays itself out, even as he and Charley play cards. Willy recalls a rare visit he had from Ben in the past, and as he converses with the brother his memory has created, Charley becomes confused because he can only hear Willy's side of the conversation. Impatient with Charley's lack of understanding, Willy argues with him and Charley walks out, leaving the dream to take over. Linda joins the brothers, as she had all those years ago, and we learn of the influence Ben has had on Willy over the years.

Ben has not seen Willy for a long time, and even though he abandoned Willy at the age of three, Willy admires him because Ben became rich. Ben found success largely by luck, but Willy believes there is something more to it and that his brother can teach him. Ben is a hard man, without compassion, which has helped him become a successful businessman, running diamond mines in Africa and pursuing lucrative land deals in Alaska. Their father was a mix of his two sons; like Ben, he accepted no responsibility for his family, and, like Willy, he was full of great, unrealizable dreams. With Ben refusing to give Willy the answers he wants, the dream again turns sour, and Willy recalls Biff being caught stealing lumber at the time of this visit. Linda, of the present time, enters the kitchen to bring her husband back to the present, and he decides to go for a walk.

Biff joins his mother to find out what is wrong with Willy. Linda first, instinctively tries to calm Biff's fears, but then decides to let him know that his estrangement from his father is the root of the problem. She tries to get some answers from Biff as to why he is antagonistic to Willy, but Biff is as evasive as all the Lomans are when asked for direct answers. Biff is angry at his father for something he does not yet disclose, but which involves his mother. Linda just feels sorry for her husband, and wants to help him in any way she can. Showing that she is capable of facing the truth, Linda describes how exhausted Willy has become. Although he has not told her, she knows that Willy has been taken off salary, has been unable to make any sales to earn a commission, and has been borrowing money from Charley to hide the fact. Linda criticizes both her sons for their wasteful and selfish lives, and for not caring enough about their father. Biff reluctantly promises to stay around to help, but Linda demands more, telling him that Willy has been trying to kill himself, and that she has found evidence of him planning to gas himself using the water heater.

Willy comes back from his walk and he and Biff begin to argue. Considering what he has just learned, Biff backs down and tries to cheer up his father, suggesting that he might go and see an old employer, Bill Oliver, with whom he was once supposedly a favorite, to get a loan to start up his own business. Hap encourages this idea by suggesting that he and Biff are planning a sporting goods partnership, and they get Willy enthused by this dream. For a moment the whole family is buoyed up and together, until Willy and Biff fall back into arguing. Even though it was over Biff defending his mother when Willy treats her dismissively, Linda insists that Biff be the one to make up, which he does in order to keep the peace. Willy finally goes to sleep, dreaming of Biff's greatest moment, when he won the high school football championship. Meanwhile, Biff goes to remove the rubber tube Linda has discovered, which Willy has hidden to assist in his suicide.

In contrast to the somber note on which the first act closes, the second act begins brightly, as the spirits of the family have risen by imagining Biff's future success. The boys have already left, but Linda and Willy breakfast together and speak hopefully of the future. The boys plan to meet their father later in the day for a celebratory dinner. Willy has regained his energy and sense of hope, a change Linda encourages. He decides that now is the time to demand a desk job at the company, but it is clear on his arrival there that his boss, Howard Wagner, has little time for him and the outcome will not be good.

Fascinated by his latest acquisition, a wire recorder, Howard hardly listens to what Willy says to him. Willy makes his request, citing his thirty-four years of loyal service to the company, and Howard unsympathetically refuses. Willy tells him about Dave Singleman, an old-time salesman who had inspired him as a younger man to go into sales, and about what a great asset he has been to the company in the past. Willy probably exaggerates his sales figures, but Howard is not interested, he is just embarrassed; as soon as he is able, he fires Willy and suggests that he ask Biff and Hap for help. Reluctant to admit how useless his sons are, Willy pleads for his old job back, but Howard stays firm, leaving the office to let Willy pull himself together. The shock sends Willy back into his past to seek advice from his brother, Ben.

Willy recalls a job opportunity Ben had once offered him in Alaska, and how Linda had encouraged him to turn it down. In this way, he can justify his current failure as the fault of his wife rather than himself. To further boost his spirits, he again recalls Biff's championship game, but the mood gets broken by the memory of Charley mocking the importance of Biff's victory. Willy comes back to the present outside of Charley's office, where he has come to borrow more money. The adult Bernard is waiting to see his father, and feeling sorry for Willy, talks to him, despite Willy's erratic behavior.

With his tennis date, Bernard is now, ironically, the athlete, as well as being a successful lawyer about to take a case before the Supreme Court, and a happy family man with a second child on the way. Modestly, he does not gloat, or even tell Willy all of this, but kindly asks after Willy's family. Willy cannot help but see the unflattering contrast between Bernard and his own sons. Envious of Bernard's success, Willy lies about Biff's prospects, but cannot resist asking Bernard how he managed to do so well, while Biff turned out so poorly. Bernard cannot advise him, knowing that success cannot be guaranteed, but he asks him why Biff ruined his chances by refusing to retake the math class which would have allowed him to graduate and go to college. Something major happened between Biff and Willy around this time which influenced his decision, but it remains a secret, as Willy defensively begins to argue with Bernard. Charley arrives to break it up.

Charley again tries to get his friend to accept a job from him, but Willy gets angry, feeling his dignity is being threatened. Charley just gives him the money he needs, and Willy goes to meet his sons for dinner. Hap is already at the restaurant planning an elaborate meal, but he gets distracted when a girl arrives, and they make plans—he even persuades her to go and call a friend so that Biff will have a date. Biff arrives, and has come to his senses, realizing that the dream the family had constructed of him borrowing money from Bill Oliver and becoming a successful businessman was entirely unrealistic. Oliver did not remember who he was, not giving him a moment's attention, and in revenge Biff stole a fountain pen from his desk. Biff is determined that Willy also face the truth, though Hap wants him to maintain the lie and pretend that Oliver is interested, allowing their father his hope, even if it can never be fulfilled. When Willy arrives, Biff insists on the truth; he has been telling lies for too long. He tries to tell his father that he was only a shipping clerk, and that Oliver owes him nothing. Willy refuses to listen, and practically forces Biff to create a happier version of his meeting. Biff gets frustrated at his father, and causes Willy to return to that part in their past when his relationship with Biff had been torn apart.

We learn that Biff had gone to Boston to ask his father for advice after flunking his math, and found him with another woman. As Willy fitfully relives this awful moment, Biff of the present tries to tell him what really happened with Oliver, but Willy blocks it out. It is clear that Willy is distracted, and his behavior gets Biff so worried that he falls back on the lie to calm his father down, telling him that Oliver will loan the money after all. It nearly works, as Willy begins to come back to the present, but Biff cannot keep up the pretense, and as it slips, Willy retreats further into his past. He goes to the washroom as part of his dream, and Biff appeals to Hap for help. But Hap is too wrapped up in himself, and, like Howard, just wants to avoid any embarrassment. Distraught, Biff leaves, and Hap follows on with the women, callously leaving his father alone in the washroom.

Willy relives the whole experience of Biff losing faith in his father that time in Boston. It was the discovery of Willy's adultery, and in his young eyes, the betrayal of his mother which it signified, that originally shattered Biff's capacity to dream, turned him against his father, and caused him to lose all direction in life. If a father whom he had trusted could be deceiving his mother, then why should he believe anything his father had told him in the past? Biff is left without beliefs, and Willy returns to the present with the full realization of his own guilt in this outcome. Finding himself abandoned by his sons, Willy goes off to buy some seeds, having the urge to plant something, no doubt caused by his need to become a creator rather than destroyer.

The boys arrive home late to find their mother fuming at the way they have treated their father, and determined to throw them both out for good. Hap tries to smooth things over, but Biff, to Linda's horror, wants to confront his father again. Willy is outside planting seeds, and Biff and Linda go to join him. Willy is chatting to Ben, discussing his plan to kill himself so that Biff will get the insurance money to start his own business, and Willy will not have failed him as a father. Ben casts doubt on whether or not the insurance company will pay out, but does not discourage Willy from killing himself. Biff interrupts, telling his father that he has decided to leave for good, but Willy curses Biff if he dares to leave. Willy seems mostly concerned that Biff will blame his father for his failure, although Biff keeps assuring him that he does not. Biff tries one final time to get his father to face the truth, confronting him with the rubber tube he has taken, and declaring the whole family to be fakes.

Biff speaks the truth as he sees it: Hap has a lowly job without prospects and is wasting his life away; he himself is a thief and a bum who has never been able to hold down any kind of job; and he declares that his father is a "dime a dozen," just like the rest of them. His father refuses to accept any of it, accusing Biff of spite, but when Biff finally breaks down into tears before him, he realizes that his son loves him. Ignoring everything else Biff has said, Willy concentrates on this one uplifting truth, and thus decides to go through with his suicide plans so that his loving son will have enough money to make a success of his life. The family goes to bed, and, seemingly appeased, Willy promises to follow, but encouraged by the ghost of his brother, he drives off to crash his car one last time.

At the close of the play, there is a short scene titled, "Requiem," which takes place with Willy's family and good friend, Charley, standing before his grave as they discuss what his death means. Against Willy's optimistic expectation, no one else has shown up for his funeral. Hap seems determined to follow in his father's footsteps, forever the dreamer, while Biff refuses to fall back into that world of deceit. Charley is sympathetic, suggesting that dreams are all that some men have, while Linda is shown to be utterly lost without her husband. None of them really understand why Willy died, and all feel saddened by his absence, as each loved him. They leave the stage to the threatening apartment building which has lurked throughout the play, which symbolizes the indifference of the surrounding world to the plight of the Loman family, and others like them.

CHARACTER DEVELOPMENT

Willy Loman's whole life seems to have been a sellout, his sons have turned out badly, and his relationship with Biff has soured. But although a braggart and adulterer, Willy Loman is not a bad man, and he is loved by all who are close to him. It is their love which allows us to see his better side and sympathize with his plight. Willy also loves his family, and tries to give them what he feels they are worth, even to sacrificing his own life. Unlike his father and brother, Willy stayed with his family and tried to be responsible. Willy's problem is that he wants to be successful, but has not been given the personality, ability, or luck to achieve this goal. Overweight, overtalkative, and now over-age, he has become redundant in a business world which only tolerated him in the first place. But Willy refuses to give up without a fight. He is a human being and demands the respect and dignity most human beings deserve; this determination makes him heroic.

Willy is the salesman of the title, but the first salesman whose death we hear of is Dave Singleman. Willy idealizes Singleman's death, but realistically, the man passed away on a train still trying to make that big deal, and despite the many who attended his funeral, died alone. Salesmen must always be on the move, and such a life inevitably wears people down. Singleman was a salesman of the past who could still manage to get by on being liked; Willy attempts to emulate Singleman's life in a less sentimental age. Working against greater odds, Willy runs out of steam, and it is his death which ends the play. His funeral is not nearly so well attended, indicating a society in which people hold less importance, which seems finally to invalidate Willy's insistence on personality being the key to success.

Although Willy has always exaggerated his earning potential, he has made a living in the past; enough to allow him to turn down his brother's lucrative offer to work for him in Alaska. Unfortunately, times have changed, and efficiency, productivity, and the hard sell have become more important in the business world. Willy cannot keep up with such demands, and does not have the character to be sufficiently ruthless. Already sixty-three, he is too old to begin anew, even when it becomes increasingly obvious that he would have been far happier working with his hands as a farmer or carpenter. All he can do is look back on his past decisions to assign blame for his failure as a salesman, provider, and father. Try as he might, he has no one to blame but himself.

Willy recalls his idealized past, both as an escape and an attempt to discover what went wrong. Convinced his current unhappiness is due to his failure to make his mark in the business world, he searches for the answer to the question he has asked all his life: How do you become successful? Willy has convinced himself that the answer is to be well liked, and he passed this belief onto his sons. However, Miller makes it clear that being well liked has little to do with success. He uses various characters in the play to exemplify how people get ahead through hard work (Charley and Bernard), inheritance (Howard), or sheer luck (Ben). Neither Howard nor Ben waste any time trying to be liked, and both are depicted as selfish, impolite, and rich.

Related by his recording device (an early version of a tape recorder) to cold technology, Howard foreshadows the hard-hearted businessmen who decimate their work forces as cheaper automation takes over. Howard has not worked for his success, he inherited it from his father. He has no time for his father's old salesman and does not listen to what Willy tries to tell him. Howard represents a new development in the business world, the uncaring and exploitative way of doing business, in which being well liked holds no relevance, and all that matters is the profit line. Howard's company has used Willy up, and now Howard can dismiss him without a qualm. Howard's only evidence of humanity is his uneasiness at having to witness Willy's reaction to this dismissal. The person who comes closest to Howard in coldness and sheer self-regard is Willy's brother, Ben.

Ben, as a self-made man, tells his tale of finding a fortune in the African jungle as if it were a solution, but it is merely a boast. Ben is a selfish man, and he survives the jungle by plundering it. His father had left a wife and two young sons to seek success in Alaska and was never heard from again. Ben similarly ignores family responsibility as he follows his father's footsteps. Ben's hardness helped him survive, and he has made a fortune by luck. Willy could never do what Ben has done, and so Ben's advice is useless. Willy blames Linda for holding him back from going with his brother, but would he have taken that risk if he had been free? He is too fearful of the risks one takes to achieve things in the way Ben did, and he is right to be scared—the chances of such success are small. Willy, also, cannot be as selfish as his brother, and though he is not the perfect father, he loves his family and accepts the responsibilities their existence creates.

Charley, on the other hand, is successful, content, and a nice guy. Charley is satisfied with moderate success without feeling compelled to be the best, and he does not take shortcuts but relies on steady, hard work. He knows that winning a high school football championship is no guarantee of success in life. He also does not judge people by their success or failure, or unnecessarily boast of his own success. Ever in the background, not forcing himself, but trying to help his unfortunate neighbor through a difficult time, Charley loves and respects Willy in a way that few others do. Indeed, even Willy admits that Charley is his "only friend." Charley passes on his values to his offspring, as Willy does, but his are clearly the better values by which to live, for his son Bernard is a caring, compassionate adult, as well as a highly successful lawyer.

As children, Biff and Happy idolized their father and looked down on Bernard for his more cautious lifestyle and belief in work. However, Bernard represents an ideal in the play. He works for his success and it is well earned, but it is not the be-all of his existence. This is the lesson Willy needs to learn, but refuses to accept. Willy's sons look to him for guidance, but he feeds them unrealistic dreams. His wife supports and loves him, but he has an affair. Willy fails socially, as a salesman, and personally, as a husband and father, because he has no strong value system. Bernard succeeds both socially and personally, because he was given a strong value system by his father.

As a youth, Biff was led to believe that since he was "well liked" he could get away with anything. He begins to steal—a football from school, lumber for the house, a crate of balls from Bill Oliver. Willy is desperate that Biff should succeed in life, so instead of punishing him, he condones the thefts and makes excuses. Willy neglects to instill in his son the moral values a parent should teach a child. Biff appears successful in high school as a football player, but he reaps no benefit from this, as he never goes to college. Initially, he had planned to retake the math course he needed to get into college, but he catches his father with a mistress. Biff's self-confidence dissipates as he loses respect for his father. As a result of this, his belief in the fantasies his father has fed him cannot be maintained.

Out in the real world, away from the destructive influence of his father, Biff begins to recognize his own true nature. He takes some time to learn, spending a stretch in jail, but he eventually replaces his father's dream with one of his own. Whether or not Biff can achieve his dream of working with the land is not as important as the fact that it is more suited to his nature than trying to be a hot-shot businessman. He gains self-knowledge, and in recognizing his own mediocrity and insignificance, Biff may be able to build himself a happier life. It would have been better for Willy to work at something he was happy doing, like carpentry, instead of trying to be the number one salesman.

Hap does not reach the same level of awareness as his brother. Since his childhood, Hap has admired his father and older brother, forever fighting for their attention and approval. Biff left home, but Willy remained as a role model, and Hap has become a pale imitation of his father. He is a dreamer, though his dreams are more selfish than his father's, and more limited. He has no depth, living a shallow life which he pretends is more glamorous than it really is. He tells his parents he is getting married, but shows no evidence of this intent, and he continues to date any woman he meets. It is little wonder his parents ignore his marriage declaration, his own mother knowing him well enough to call him a "philandering bum" to his face.

Bereft of even the few decencies Willy retains, such as a conscience and a sense of responsibility, Hap presents an entirely disreputable figure. Despite his supposed love and respect for his father, Hap has no compunction about leaving Willy behind in a bar when he is clearly distressed, and even denies that Willy is his father to escape responsibility and embarrassment. He would rather chase women, even though he has as little respect for them as he shows to Willy. He declares that he wants to find a woman like his mother, but this is unlikely when he treats women so dismissively. Happy has no dignity or honor. He takes bribes from manufacturers, and he sleeps with the fiancées and wives of men higher in the firm than he, possibly to get even with them for being more successful than he will ever be. What is worse, his faith in his father's dream, despite his loss of faith in his father, remains undiminished at the close.

Linda's central importance seems to be as a voice of protest and outrage against what is happening to her husband. She insists that "attention must be paid" to Willy and his suffering. As Linda recognizes, Willy is a human being and it *is* a terrible thing that happens to him. Dreams, illusions, and self-deceptions feed the action of this play. Linda, in contrast, seems very much planted in reality with her concerns over house payments, mending work, insurance premiums, and her husband's care. She knows exactly what her sons are and she does not hold back on telling them, especially when they hurt her husband. Yet despite Linda's clear sight, she allows her family's dreams to flourish, even encouraging them. It is only when they are dreaming of a brighter future that the family can operate together, and for Linda, the truth is a small sacrifice to pay for the happiness of her family.

THEMATIC ISSUES

A central thematic issue in this play is Miller's consideration of the problematic and elusive "American dream" of success, and how its tends to be interpreted by society. Miller sees many people's lives being poisoned by their desire to be successful. People like the Lomans are doomed to try for success but fail, with all the resulting guilt that such failure brings. Others, like Ben and Howard, display an ability to make money, which deems them successful, but at the cost of their own moral integrity. Charley and Bernard, on the other hand, are successful, but do not allow their desire for wealth to run their lives. This enables them to maintain their moral integrity, and offer us a potential solution to this social problem which, Miller believes, lies at the heart of American democracy.

The Declaration of Independence of 1776 promised American citizens the rights to life, liberty, and the pursuit of happiness. While the first two rights are relatively straightforward, the third creates numerous difficulties as people strive to determine exactly what might bring them happiness. Finding the answer to this question—through hard work, personal achievement, popular fame, or great wealth—is the dream of many Americans, who have great expectations of life, and any failure in achievement leads to keen disappointment. In his own search for happiness and the fulfillment of the "American dream," Willy can be viewed as an everyman figure whose personal dilemmas speak to all times and to all people, but to Americans in particular.

The Loman family survives intact for many years, largely through their capacity to dream. Such dreams are highly ambivalent, especially when they turn out to be so patently false. They may provide a momentary respite from a harsh reality, but are usually more destructive in the long run. When Biff is led to dream that he and Hap can start a business on a loan from Bill Oliver, we see the family revitalized and Willy gain the strength to go and ask for a better job. But to feed the dream, Biff has to reinvent not only his own abilities, but also his relationship with Mr. Oliver. Such dreams can never be fulfilled, as they are based on lies. While the dream is maintained it may grant strength, but as soon as reality intrudes, the dream is shattered and lays the dreamer open to harsh disillusionment.

But the question remains in the play: Is it possible to live in dreams? Charley tells us, "A salesman is got to dream" (138), and seems to suggest that Willy had no other option. But where do Willy's dreams originate? It is evident that Willy's family experience has been influential in his development. Both Willy's father and older brother, Ben, are portrayed as archetypal pioneers—men who have successfully tamed the West—whom Willy is tempted to emulate, despite their evident self-absorption and lack of compassion. However, their sense of freedom and adventure clashes with Willy's more humane sense of responsibility and his caution; for Willy is not only the product of his family upbringing, but of a far wider array of cultural myths and values. It is little wonder that Willy is unable to find happiness, for he is being continuously influenced by conflicting ideologies, which can never allow him to feel any satisfaction.

While America was founded on the Protestant work ethic, which insists contentment can only be won through hard, honest labor, thrift, and a pride of craftsmanship, the numerous "get-rich-quick" schemes that sprang up through the early decades of the twentieth century suggest that hard work is unnecessary to attain the success Willy craves. Not only is the *means* to success made confusing, but also the ideal *location*. While the concept of the American frontier suggests great opportunity and the freedom of a pastoral life, this is balanced against the potential and excitement of the city. Willy wants the best of both worlds, and ends up with neither. It is impossible for him to be both the carefree adventurer who discovers great wealth at the cost of those around him, and a hardworking, responsible provider for his family.

Americans have a tendency to idolize success, paying homage to artists who get rave reviews, businessmen who make the largest profits, or politicians who win by a landslide. In *Death of a Salesman*, Miller tries to show a clear moral distinction between the success of callous people like Ben and Howard Wagner, whose greed and selfishness wins them fortunes at the cost of others, and people like Charley and Bernard, whose success is tempered with a concern for others. Willy foolishly admires the Bens of his world more than the Charleys. However, in America, being successful brings prestige, respect, and the envy of others, virtually regardless of how that success was achieved; while being unsuccessful brings the reverse fortune as people lose prestige, respect, and all hope of support from their fellow citizens. In a culture which places so much emphasis on success, failure of any kind becomes disastrous. It is in such a climate that the Lomans fruitlessly struggle to make their dreams come true, with their own natures, ironically, working against them at every step.

The difference between Ben and Charley, or Howard and Bernard, relates to another thematic issue which Miller's play explores: the changing role of capitalism in society and its impact on people's lives. Willy Loman is living in a time when the nature of business itself is undergoing intrinsic changes, partly due to the capitalist pressure to make more money and become more efficient, regardless of the kinds of ethical and honor systems which had guided American "gentlemen" of business in the past. Systems designed to share wealth were shunned as containing the dangerous seeds of communism, and anyone "respectable" was expected to try to make as much money as possible for himself alone, regardless of whomever gets left behind or trampled upon. A number of the characters in *Death of a Salesman* underline a definite clash between capitalistic business and morality, and it is clear that Miller would prefer us to follow the example of Charley rather than Howard or Ben.

Since the nineteenth century, there have been concerns that business is in danger of taking over people's lives if it becomes too concerned with profit margins alone. The idea that people should work to live, rather than live to work has increasingly faded into the businessman's background. While some cultures shun the acquisition of wealth as greedy and unseemly, in American culture, the desire for wealth and status has become an almost virtuous pursuit. This can lead to cases where obtaining of wealth begins to outweigh all other moral considerations. We should consider just how far Willy's desire for wealth has led him into morally lax situations, such as his overlooking of Biff's thefts, or his dalliance with a secretary in order to ensure that he gets to see her boss.

The morality of other characters, especially Ben, Howard, and Hap, is also questionable. Ben abandons his family, Howard ruthlessly fires an old man, and Hap admits to taking bribes; none of them feel any remorse, and a capitalist system encourages such behavior. The best way to survive in such a system is to become a better and more ruthless capitalist than your fellow workers—the road to wealth is only realized by treading on the backs of others. However, a character such as Charley seems to have found a way to survive in business with his morality intact, largely by limiting his expectations, and refusing to ignore the plight of others.

The desire to be successful, and the fact that a capitalistic society encourages such a desire, leads to a third major theme in the play: Miller's consideration of the force of materialism in people's lives. Materialism is defined by the desire for the best of everything from services to goods, and the abundance of which a culture makes available to satisfy those desires. In the search for the "good life," people like the Lomans, surround themselves with many things above and beyond the mere necessities of life. However, these goods are only available at a price, and not everyone in society can afford all that the advertisers convince them they must have to be considered happy. The Lomans try to keep up—with a refrigerator, a vacuum, and a new car—but they find themselves in a constant state of worry that they may not be able to meet all their payments. However, they do not dare be satisfied with less.

The drive for success creates a very competitive society in which people's standing in the community becomes measured by how much more they have than others. This often leads to unhappy lives, as people spend all their time and efforts in pursuit of wealth and prestige. If Willy had spent less time on the road and more with his family, he may never have lost his sons' respect. Consider, for example, how far Willy is motivated by his desire to do better than his neighbor, Charley. Instead of appreciating this kindly neighbor, who freely gives him money so he does not have to be embarrassed in front of his family, Willy continually forces him into arguments and criticizes his generosity. While he has less than others, Willy will never be happy, but trying to keep up with everyone else causes unnecessary stress in his life, and results in the further burden of guilt he must carry at not being able to provide his family with more.

The issue of family, and the relationship which exists between members of a family, are also of great interest to Miller. Father figures abound in Miller's work, and like Willy Loman, they are often portrayed as highly ambivalent characters. In the 1940s, the father was still viewed as the provider of life, both biologically and economically. Fathers were also responsible for teaching their children proper morals and values, through instruction and by setting themselves up as good examples. Children should be able to view their father with the proper mix of awe, devotion, and love. A major problem occurs with fathers like Willy Loman, because they prove themselves to be so fallible. They fail to exhibit the right morals and values in their own lives, thus making it hard for children to respect and follow their lead.

The kind of relationships Willy and Charley have with their sons are very different. They teach their offspring different sets of values, and we can see by their sons' resulting success or failure who was in the right. While Willy teaches

Biff and Hap that all they need to be successful is to be well liked, Charley makes sure Bernard understands that he has a better chance to get ahead through hard work. In many ways, Charley is the better father, yet Willy also loves his sons. Willy's own father and brother were not ideal family role models; both left to pursue their own dreams, disregarding all family responsibilities, yet Willy stays put, despite his brother's tempting offer.

Sociological studies of American families speak of a common expectation parents have that their children will "do better" than they. Indeed, they are dedicated to the idea that if children do not live wealthier and more accomplished lives than their parents, then those parents have somehow failed. The Lomans appear to believe this, and they live in an era where it is still possible, as proven by Charley and Bernard. Such an idea puts increasing pressure on each generation as the ceiling of opportunity draws closer, and it is understandable that Hap and Biff feel daunted by Willy's need for them to do better than he.

LITERARY DEVICES AND CRAFT

Miller's lengthy setting and character descriptions offer valuable clues for interpretation. Willy is presented as living in a claustrophobic, urban setting indicative of the harsh life he has chosen. His home is surrounded by apartment houses which emanate a threatening orange glow. When memory takes over, this glow gives way to a more dreamlike background with shadowy leaves and music, evoking a happier, pastoral era. At the close of the play, however, we see the looming "hard towers" of the apartment building dominating the setting once more. Without Willy's memories—and he is now dead and buried—the dream of a happier, pastoral life cannot exist in this city.

Many of Willy's activities can be seen as highly symbolic. He plants seeds just as he plants false hopes: both will die and never come to fruition, largely because the house has become enclosed by the city. The front porch, constructed out of stolen lumber, is indicative of how their lives, as well as their house, have been built on something false. Willy does not fit into the modern world of machinery; likewise, the values he espouses, where deals are made with a smile and a handshake, are those of a bygone age. To illustrate this point, Miller frequently depicts Willy's uneasy relationship with machinery such as his car, his refrigerator, and Howard's recording machine.

The names of characters also provide insights. *Willy* is a childish version of the more adult William, indicating an intrinsic immaturity in his nature. The Loman men all need to grow up and find true direction in their lives, especially Willy with his unrealistic dream of wanting everyone to like him. *Loman* has been read as indicating Willy to be a "low man," common and insignificant, as opposed, perhaps, to Dave Singleman, the salesman who is "singled" out.

Miller, however, declares this was unintentional, for he picked the name of Loman subconsciously from a movie he had once seen: *The Testament of Dr. Mabuse.* For Miller, the name "Lohmann" evokes the voice of a "terror-stricken man calling into the void for help that will never come" (*Timebends* 1987, 178), and this certainly applies to Willy Loman.

In contrast, the names of Willy's sons seem highly ironic. *Biff* seems to indicate an abrasive nature and someone who will have to fight to get what he wants, whereas Biff's life so far has been marked by his inability to stick to anything and quit anytime things get to be too hard. Born Harold, but called Happy by his friends, Biff's brother Hap invokes a happy-go-lucky personality. However, we soon learn that this is a deluded happiness; Hap isn't happy at all, but pushes his inner discontent to one side.

HISTORICAL CONTEXT

Although Willy Loman's situation is often described as timeless, *Death of a Salesman* can be read as an illustration of the historical economic interests and forces operating on American society during the period of Willy Loman's life. Willy has lived through major changes in the economic structure of his country. He witnessed the sense of hope and possibility at the beginning of the new century, a time when his father and brother both left home to embrace these possibilities to the full. He lived through the wild prosperity of the 1920s, a period when he felt he could become successful in the big city, through to the 1929 Wall Street crash, which marked the start of the Great Depression. The depression lasted throughout the 1930s, and Willy would have found his products increasingly hard to sell, as nobody had money to buy anything but necessities. With the economy being jump-started for the 1940s by the increased market demands and industrial advances of World War II, Willy has seen the renewed sense of vigor in the American economy, and this creates much of the hope he places in the prospects of his two sons. The play was written and is set in 1948, at the time when forces of capitalism and materialism came to the fore, and technology made its greatest inroad into the lives of everyday people. *Death of a Salesman* depicts the impact of these forces on the lives of an ordinary family—the Lomans.

If we ask the question of how far the Lomans might be trying to live up to standards which they are incapable of attaining, we must also consider whether they are failing because of their own inadequacies, or whether their failure is due to the unrealistic nature of such standards. In Miller's opinion, the blame of failure should not be attached to insignificant cogs in the social machine like the Lomans, but attributed to the larger social forces which operate on people's lives. Economics play an important part in the creation of such forces. By the time the play was written, Miller saw business matters at odds with conventional morality, with humanity threatened by the onset of technology, and the growing pressures of ownership. All these issues are reflected in the dilemmas of the Loman family and the other characters to whom they are economically linked.

The business boom which followed World War II saw a growth in mass production due to the increased development and understanding of technology. In 1928, Henry Ford declared machinery to be the "New Messiah," which could lead all Americans to their land of promise, as long as they embraced it without compunction, but by the 1940s, many feared the idea of the subordination of man to the machine, and worried over the effect this technological revolution would have on society as a whole. Willy certainly has very uneasy relationships with machinery in the play. Some people, like Ford, freely embraced mechanization as a way of becoming more efficient and increasing profits. But efficiency exacts certain costs, as Willy discovers when he goes to see Howard Wagner, a man who is captivated by technology.

Miller wants his audiences to recognize that dangers lurk within technological advances, and society's regard for mechanical efficiency may leave behind a concern for humanity. Willy illustrates how men need a sense of themselves as unique to be content—they need both a sense of their place in society and a separate sense of themselves as important individuals—and technology can endanger both. Technological advances changed American society very swiftly, and by the time of the play, everyone was desiring technological items. We see this in Willy's desire for items such as a car or a refrigerator. However, Howard's obsession with his tape recorder becomes a potentially more dangerous pursuit in the way it seems to overtake all human considerations.

ALTERNATE PERSPECTIVE: A FEMINIST READING

Feminist criticism takes many forms and looks at men as much as women, but what all feminist critics have in common is the need to uncover ways in which an intrinsically patriarchal society has historically subjugated women, and how it can be made possible for women to be free of such subjugation. Some critics search texts to find how the gender of the writer has reflected and/or shaped gender attitudes in the surrounding society; others are more concerned with style and the difference between masculine and feminine modes of writing. Critics often take another look at female characters written in the past, and try to reassess their roles as either patriarchal tools who passively accept and encourage their subservient positions, or as subversive figures who covertly fight the system in a variety of ways. It is unsurprising that we often find the first type of female character in the works of male writers, while the second is more common in the writing of women. *Death of a Salesman*, however, appears to offer examples of both, and often within the same character, depending on how she is viewed.

It is easy to be disturbed by the apparently passive female stereotypes we find in *Death of a Salesman*—the good housewife, the call girl, the mousy secretary—but Miller wanted his play to be realistic, pointing out these stereotypes, in part, to allow us to question them. In American society of the late 1940s, this is how many women were viewed. Women only had the vote since 1920, and despite the opportunities afforded by World War II when the shortage of able men at home allowed women to take jobs previously considered unsuitable, many women found it hard to see their role in society as any different from being good wives and mothers. Women of Linda Loman's generation were taught to be dependent on their men, stay at home, and raise the children. In more recent productions of the play, largely because women have a far stronger presence in today's society, Linda tends to be played more aggressively. The play can accommodate such an interpretation partly because of what Miller does not allow Linda to say.

Death of a Salesman is a profoundly masculine play, told from a man's point of view (Willy Loman). The men take center stage in what is a male-dominated world, where men do business, play sports, go adventuring, and try carpentry. Although more than a third of its cast are women, the play centers on issues of male bonding and relationships between fathers and sons. Women either have been marginalized and appear as loyal wives (like Linda) or easy women (like The Woman, Miss Forsythe, and Letta), or they have been silenced and hardly feature at all, such as Willy's mother, Ben's wife, or Charley's wife (the first two get a brief mention, the latter no comment at all).

Although Willy calls Linda his "foundation and support," and indeed she is, he shows little respect or regard for her in the way we see him treat her. He cheats on her and constantly, rudely tells her to shut up. What seems worse is that Linda accepts such treatment. She subordinates her life to Willy, shares his dreams, and appears to have none of her own. But Linda is not stupid or weak; she displays great perception and can be tough when necessary. She is the main reason this family has managed to stay together; hence, her depiction as a mender who tries to mend everything from stockings to people. She also knows what these repairs cost, and this knowledge gives her the strength to break the family apart, sending her sons away if they threaten her husband. In this light, Linda can be seen as working against the stereotype of the weak, maternal figure.

Many women called to assist in the wartime effort performed jobs outside the home which gave them new authority and ambition. To the dismay of many, some were reluctant to pass this authority back to the men on their return from the army. The "working girl" was becoming a social reality which some welcomed, but by which many more felt threatened. There are a number of examples of "working women" in the play, such as The Woman, Jenny, and Miss Forsythe, and it is interesting to note the way in which they are presented. To diminish such a threat, these women were often discredited and belittled wherever and however possible, largely to affirm old-fashioned opinions of what was right and proper for men and women to do.

On the surface, women like The Woman (Miss Francis), Miss Forsythe, and Letta are portrayed as being close to whores, as they are very easy with their favors. Fleshy characters, but not fleshed out, they become the scapegoats for the men's bad behavior, unable to defend themselves or have any opportunity to tell us how they feel. However, we know that The Woman *chose* Willy—she is in control here. Though shown as a temptress (laughing as she appears in a black slip to a background of sensuous music), as the cause of Willy's alienation from his son, she is also shown to have power which is antagonistic to that of the men. Other single girls like Miss Forsythe and Letta have the same power to divide men, as they tempt Hap and Biff away from their father. They are dangerous because they threaten to disrupt the patriarchal dream of a cozy home life with the "little woman," and so they also represent the growing independence and strength among women of the time.

4

The Family: *All My Sons* (1947) and *A View from the Bridge* (1956)

A View from the Bridge, with its tale of Eddie Carbone and his unspoken feelings toward his niece, has the same classical lines of *All My Sons*, performing like a modern Greek tragedy. For this reason, the two plays are usefully studied together. Each of these plays tells a family story. In *All My Sons*, we witness the interplay between the Kellers and the Deevers; in *A View from the Bridge*, we meet the extended Carbone family. Many of Miller's plays center on families, and by concentrating on their pleasures, problems, and relationships, Miller explores in microcosm, society as a whole.

All My Sons and *A View from the Bridge* have at their center that typical Miller figure—the male patriarch who is an utter failure as a father, and whose shortcomings consequently affect his whole family. In *All My Sons*, Joe Keller's actions are so terrible that one of his sons kills himself, and the other completely rejects him. In *A View from the Bridge*, the central protagonist, Eddie Carbone, is not even able to produce children and has a barren marriage. To compensate for this, he looks after his wife's young niece, but has developed unconscious sexual feelings toward her which impact everyone around him. Both men are capable of great love and have the best of intentions, but due to flaws in their characters, they mess up their own lives and the lives of their families.

ALL MY SONS (1947)

Miller wrote *All My Sons* over a period of two years, wanting to perfect it prior to performance. The basic idea of a war profiteer who shipped faulty parts to the armed forces was given to him by his mother-in-law, but the characters and complex relationships he created are all his own. The play opened in New York City at the beginning of 1947, two years after World War II ended. Miller felt that most people, at the time the play was first produced, did not really understand the play. Many complained that it was overly plotted and contained implausible coincidences, but as Miller suggests, especially in the shadow of Greek masterpieces such as Sophocles' *Oedipus* plays, coincidence is the very stuff of drama, if not of life. Others complained about the amount of death in the play, and felt it was too dark. However, the play had a lengthy run, won a number of major awards, and put Miller on the map of American theater.

SETTING AND PLOT DEVELOPMENT

The Kellers' backyard is hedged in, offering no escape for its inhabitants. To one side is the stump of a broken apple tree, which becomes increasingly significant as the play progresses. It is a fairly opulent yard, and whoever owns it is a financial success—that man is Joe Keller. Keller is a businessman whose business has taken over his life—even on a Sunday morning he cannot separate himself from commerce as he reads the want ads in the paper while sitting in his yard. A neighbor, Dr. Jim Bayliss, sits with him, and another neighbor, Frank Lubey, joins the group. Frank comments on the tree, pointing out its connection to Keller's son, Larry, for whom it was planted as a memorial. Larry has been missing in action for three years, and Frank, at Keller's wife's request, is preparing a horoscope to see if the day Larry disappeared was a favorable day on which nothing truly bad could have happened to him. Kate Keller wants to believe their son is still alive.

Ann, the daughter of Keller's old neighbor and business partner, Steve Deever, arrived the previous evening for a visit. Ann was Larry's girlfriend, but she has come to see Chris, the Kellers' other son. Jim's wife, Sue, comes to tell him he is needed by a patient. It is clear that Jim is unhappy with his job as a doctor, and Sue is unhappy with her husband. Frank's wife, Lydia, calls to get him to come home and fix the toaster. These people happily come and go, showing how Keller is popular and accepted by his neighbors; even their children play with him. Chris Keller comes out, and although he looks like his father, it is clear that he is more educated—he reads the book section of the paper. Then, a neighbor's son, Bert, arrives to play. Keller plays an imaginary game with the local children, in which he makes them his deputy policemen and pretends to have a jail in his cellar—highly ironic for a man who we will learn has broken the law but avoided punishment.

Both Chris and Keller are worried how the broken tree will affect Kate, who sees its breaking as an omen. She is the only person who still believes Larry is alive, although they never contradict her belief. But now Chris needs her to accept Larry's death because he wants to marry Ann. Keller refuses to help Chris deal with Kate, preferring to stay on the sidelines, but Chris provokes his father into agreeing to help by threatening to move away and leave the family business. Unlike his father, Chris hates the business, which scares Keller who feels he has sacrificed much to keep the business going for his sons. Kate enters, seeming content, but we soon realize this is a cover. She insists that Larry is alive, and that Ann is keeping herself free because she is waiting for him. When Chris tries to make her face the truth, she refuses to listen and sends him away to get aspirin. But Kate knows the score; as soon as Chris leaves, she tells her husband they must stop Ann from marrying Chris. Keller refuses to take sides, despite Kate's mounting anger. In revenge, when Bert returns, Kate sends him packing, ordering Keller to stop playing the jail game, as it is tempting fate. These two share a guilty secret, despite Keller's assumed innocence.

Ann is shocked to see Kate acting as though Larry will return. Ann has evidently accepted Larry's death and moved on. We learn that her father is due for parole, and though his wife will take him in, Ann and her brother, George, cannot forgive what he has done. Kate keeps asking Ann about Larry, so Ann bluntly tells her she is no longer waiting. But Kate is not ready to give up. When Frank comes to say hello and ask after her family, it is clear that Ann is uncomfortable even talking about her father. They discuss the case which got him sent to jail, a case for which Keller was also indicted, but later exonerated. Keller bluffed it out, and the neighbors soon forgave him, but Steve Deever was found guilty and seen as a murderer for selling cracked cylinder heads to the air force which caused twenty-one planes to crash.

Ann cannot understand why Keller holds no grudge against Steve, as she, George, and even Chris hate and utterly reject him. Ann suggests that Larry could have flown a plane with one of those faulty parts, and while Kate tries to shut them all up, Keller insists on explaining that the parts had gone to a model of a plane that Larry never flew. Keller defends Steve (and we shall later realize, also himself) by explaining how the parts got shipped in the first place. They were under pressure to produce and couldn't afford to lose a day's production, so the hairline cracks got covered up. Keller's explanation of Steve's behavior seems so convincing, you can almost believe it to be true, partly because Keller himself seems to believe it. There was no evil intent, but that doesn't matter to Ann or Chris, who see the end effect as overriding intent.

Ann and Chris are left alone and discuss their relationship. Chris admits his love, and Ann is relieved to hear him finally say it, as she loves him too. Chris, however, feels awkward, largely because of his war experiences. He saw many men die while he survived, and now he feels guilty taking advantage of his survival. Ann tries to persuade him that he has earned what he has and should accept it. Their chat is broken up by an unexpected phone call from George, which gets everyone on edge when they realize he has visited Steve. Tension mounts when Kate and Keller learn George is coming, for they fear he has learned something from his father.

Act 2 begins later that evening, waiting for George to arrive. Ann chats with Sue Bayliss, and we learn more about the Baylisses' unhappy marriage. Inspired by Chris's idealism, Jim wants to do medical research, but Sue insists he remain as a higher-paid doctor, and because of his family responsibilities, he capitulates. Sue sees Chris as a hypocrite living off his father's business, and lets Ann know that although the community has forgiven Keller, they believe he was guilty. He is admired for being smart enough to beat the charges. This raises the issue of whether or not Chris knows the truth, or does he really believe his father is innocent? Ann asks, and Chris insists he could not accept his father if he suspected anything, which prepares us for his eventual rejection of his father when he uncovers the truth.

Keller plans to bribe George into complicity by offering to set him up in town as a lawyer. He even tells Ann he is prepared to offer Steve a job, which horrifies Ann and Chris. Keller is nervous about his future relationship with Chris, and wants the children to forgive Steve, so they'll go easier on him if they learn the truth. He exits, then Jim arrives with George and suggests that Ann and Chris take him somewhere else. Ann nearly accedes, but Chris refuses to avoid a confrontation as it implies guilt, insisting George join them.

George enters in a belligerent state, wearing his father's hat and acting as an avenger. He wants to take Ann away from Chris, having learned that Keller set their father up. His father insists that Keller told him to cover up the cracks and he would take responsibility, but later denied this and let Steve take full blame. George had believed in Keller's innocence because Chris had, and they all look up to Chris, but this is the first time he has talked to his father about it. Chris refuses to accept this new version of events. Kate joins them, and instantly begins to mother George, deflating his anger and breaking the tension, to the extent that George can civilly greet Keller.

Keller talks to George, speaking of previous times Steve has not accepted fault after a mistake and tried to blame others, to convince George not to trust Steve's story. George is convinced by his argument and the atmosphere lightens, until Kate lets it slip that Keller has not been sick for fifteen years. George picks up on this, as Keller's whole defense had been that he was not at work the day the parts were shipped because he was laid up with flu—it becomes clear that he had purposely stayed home to avoid blame. Tempers are held in check while Frank comes by to report on Larry's horoscope, but George insists on leaving at once and wants Ann to join him. She refuses unless Chris tells her to go; still avoiding the truth, Chris sees no need.

Becoming frantic, Kate wants Ann to go, and Larry to be alive. She turns on Keller, physically striking him in her frustration. Chris insists that Ann stay, and that Larry is dead. Kate suggests that this cannot be true, because if Larry is dead then he was killed by his own father. Chris sees the implication in this, and finally accepts the truth: his father knew about the faulty parts. Chris turns on his father, who breaks down and confesses, trying to justify what he did—but his excuses seem feeble next to the moral implications of the act. Trying to convince Chris that he did it for him, thinking that will make it alright, just angers Chris further, and he attacks his father calling him worse than an animal, before he stumbles away in distress with Keller calling after him.

The final act is brief, taking place in the early hours of the morning, as Kate sits up for Chris's return. Jim keeps her company, confessing he knew Keller was guilty, but is sure Chris had not known. Jim believes this discovery will change Chris, forcing him to lose his idealism, but wishes it wouldn't, as the belief that some ideals cannot be compromised is uplifting. But Jim cannot believe Chris will turn in his own father. Jim goes to look for Chris, and Keller enters. He and Kate do not know what to do. Kate suggests that Keller offer to turn himself in to gain Chris's forgiveness, but Keller still doesn't feel he has done anything wrong—he did what he did for his family, and believes that justifies it. Even Kate knows there are some things bigger than the family.

Ann enters and tells the Kellers she will not try to reopen the case, but they must admit that Larry is dead in front of Chris so he will stay with her. Kate refuses, despite Ann telling them she has firm proof. Protectively sending Keller into the house, Ann shows Kate a letter she received from Larry, which causes Kate to break down. Chris returns to declare that he has decided to leave and start a new life alone. Having lived off his father's money and blinded himself to the truth, he feels compromised. Ann will not accept this, insisting that he needs to sacrifice his father so they can be together. Chris refuses, excusing his father as having simply followed the "dog-eat-dog" law of the land and, therefore, not being responsible. At this point, Keller returns and he and Chris have their final confrontation.

Keller tries to persuade Chris to stay—offering to give their money away, and even to go to jail, despite his lack of guilt. Ann forces the situation by giving Chris Larry's letter before Kate can stop her. This rekindles Chris's idealistic fury against Keller, as he reads how Larry committed suicide out of shame for his father's actions. The letter also drives Keller to accept his guilt, and recognize the responsibility to others which he has up until now ignored: "Sure, [Larry] was my son. But I think to him they were all my sons. And I guess they were" (170). Chris is determined to take him to jail, and Keller seems ready to go, entering the house to get his jacket. But while Kate tries to dissuade Chris, they hear a gunshot. Keller has taken his own life, and Kate and Chris are left distraught, holding one another in their grief.

CHARACTER DEVELOPMENT

Keller is a "man among men," because he has "made it" in this society, and that, to many, is cause for respect and admiration. His desire to pass his business on to his sons is rooted in love. Keller's regard for his sons is undeniable, and his belief in the sanctity of fatherhood is clear as he cries, "A father is a father" (136), and in this cry affirms his belief that blood should always be put before outside concerns. He tells Chris: "What the hell did I work for? That's only for you, Chris, the whole shooting match is for you!" (102), and is eager to include Chris in his business. This desire to bond with his son is, in a sense, what frees him from moral responsibility, and allows him to ship those faulty parts with a clear conscience.

Keller also shows pride in the ability he has to pass on such a thriving business firm, and it worries him deeply that Chris may not accept his gift. Despite a lack of education, Keller has gained ascendancy over many others: "I got so many lieutenants, majors, and colonels that I'm ashamed to ask someone to sweep the floor" (134). He revels in his financial, and therefore social, superiority. Having faced the accusations against him boldly, his boldness won him the case. But he has been morally misled by the mores of an unsavory society; a society Chris comes to describe as "the land of the great big dogs" (167). Keller has been taught that it is the winner who continues to play the game, and society can turn a blind eye to moral concerns so long as the production line keeps rolling—this is the essence of capitalism. It is what he tries to teach his son, but it is something his son does not want to hear. It is not until the end of the play that Keller sees what his sons saw all along: We have social responsibilities beyond the immediate family.

Keller cannot survive the rejection of his sons, and he literally ceases to exist once this occurs, as he commits suicide. Steve Deever, on the other hand, has almost ceased to exist from the start of the play. A shadowy figure about whom we hear a lot but never see, Steve has been estranged from his children since his incarceration. He has not the "courage" for suicide, but has almost vanished in his jail cell through the total alienation his children have displayed. Steve has a weaker personality than Keller, and it is hard to feel sympathy; he committed the crime for which he was jailed, but simply hoped he could escape blame, as Keller did, by making someone else responsible.

Kate is the real kingpin of this family. It is Kate whom they must all serve to please, and it is Kate to whom everyone turns for advice and comfort. Yet she is a woman who ignores realities of which she disapproves, such as the likelihood of Larry's death, and Chris and Ann's relationship. She focuses instead on anything she can adapt toward her version of reality. Kate feels the guilt of what her husband has done, and throughout the play she threatens to burst with the pressure of keeping his dark secrets. Her insistence that Larry is alive is intrinsic to her ability to continue supporting Keller.

Chris has been set up as a moral idealist by his friends and neighbors, which is a hard role to fulfill. They look to him to determine how they should behave—he inspires Jim to want to become a medical researcher, and the Deever children to believe in Keller's innocence and their own father's guilt. But Chris is unsure what he wants to do for himself. He feels torn between keeping his father happy by staying in the family business, and refusing to get caught up in the morally suspect world of commerce. Chris's character is summed up in his military epithet "Mother McKeller." He is both "mother" and "killer;" he has a desire to protect and destroy almost simultaneously, and this conflict finally burns him out. Chris tries to take on a responsibility for his fellow man against his father, but, ironically, without the support of his father, he finally crumbles and returns to the safe inertia of his mother's arms. Larry Keller's rebellion was better sustained in that he died for something he believed.

Aside from the disparity between the types of men who lead these families, the Deevers are very similar to the Kellers. Ann and George, like Chris and Larry, both reject their father for his crimes, while their mother stands by him. George has also had his outlook on the world changed by his war experiences, and he seems to have that same rash streak which no doubt led Larry to commit suicide. But George has not the same ability to follow through with what he starts, possibly a weakness inherited from his father. Trying to gain Keller's admission of guilt, he frequently backs down and allows himself to be calmed by the motherly attentions of Kate. Even when his lawyer's sharpness finally catches Keller in the lie which determines his guilt, George does little with his discovery, weakly declaring an intention to leave, and trying to persuade his sister to accompany him.

Ann, like Chris, is more cautious than George or Larry, which may be why she and Chris seem so suited. Also like Chris in her firm rejection of her father (and her later request that Chris too reject his father), she seems a fierce idealist. Because of Larry's letter, however, she knew of Keller's guilt from the start, and yet kept quiet until she saw no alternative to getting what she wanted, which compromises her idealism. This is a compromise Chris also will have to make if he is ever to be happy. Even though Ann will be marrying into the family which destroyed her father, she has realized that the worst thing to be in life is alone, and she is desperate to hold onto Chris. It is uncertain by the end of the play if she will succeed in this or not, as Kate, who has been trying to keep them apart throughout the play, seems to have reclaimed her son and holds him tightly in her arms. Ann, however, we suspect will not give in without a fight.

The neighbors offer interesting contrasts to the Kellers and Deevers, just as their obvious regard for Keller, despite knowing what he did, gives us a taste of this society's sense of moral value. Dr. Jim Bayliss has none of the solidity of Keller or sense of satisfaction. Both he and his wife, Sue, feel they could have done better with their own lives, as well as with each other. The main problem is Jim's desire to become a medical researcher, which he has had to sacrifice for the needs of his family. Frank and Lydia Lubey are happier, partly because Frank has no idealistic desires, but is content to conform. Frank was just old enough to avoid being drafted, and unlike Chris, Larry, and George, whose lives were all deeply affected by their war experiences, was able to stay home and raise a family.

HISTORICAL CONTEXT

All My Sons, written and set in 1947, with its tale of a family torn apart by secrets and lies, portrays many discordances which arose within American families during the 1940s. The decade began amidst the throes of destructive international conflict, and saw the development of even more destructive, domestic conflicts within the family itself. The depression of the 1930s had seriously undermined the prestige of many fathers in taking away from them the role of provider. Following on the heels of the depression, World War II accentuated these familial difficulties. Fathers and sons were dislocated from their homes by the draft, some never returning. Those who returned either found the world had changed in their absence, or felt a need to change it in the light of their experiences. Their efforts met great resistance, but the mood of change was in the air, no matter how hard some chose to ignore it. Both change and resistance would serve to deepen the gulf between father and child, and this is tellingly portrayed in Miller's tale of the Kellers.

World War II helped drive a physical or psychological wedge between many fathers and their children. But, in the case of the Kellers, the wedge is an ideological one. The task was to redefine the role of the father in the light of the changes taking place; the inability to achieve this sped the complete breakdown of the family unit, just as happens in the Keller household. Men like Chris and Larry Keller who had gone to fight were changed by their experiences. Affected by the sacrifices they saw their comrades make, they developed a heightened sense of social responsibility. This leads Larry to kill himself for shame at what his father has done, and Chris to set himself impossibly idealistic standards by which to live. Shaken by the horrors of World War II, society recognized the need for change, but the soldiers who fought often held different views from those who stayed at home as to how to initiate that change.

For those at home, and the older generation of Kellers, a return to the prosperous twenties, with its emphasis on work and individual family units, offered a greater security. But men like Chris, who by their service had experienced a new community-based society of mutual help where one's "family" was society itself, found themselves at odds with such an introverted concept. This socialist spirit, which had been growing in America since the depression, was at odds with the selfish capitalistic spirit which had captured the country in its postwar economic boom. But Chris, despite his new-found socialism, is still a product of the more traditional generation, and is reluctant to throw away his old values. While he dislikes his father's capitalism, he still loves his father, and he is confused as to what he should do.

Like so many young men of the 1940, Chris finds he needs a strong father figure to allow him to make sense of the changing worlds someone who would remain unchanging and inviolate, from whom he could derive stability for himself. Joe Keller, like many fathers of his time, cannot possibly live up to such an ideal, given that those same social pressures affecting Chris are also affecting him. Keller tries to offer Chris the only stability he knows in the form of his business, but Chris is looking for a moral stability rather than this material one. Keller's suicide at the close is symbolic in the sense that it shows the real transience and instability of the "father" in this era. Keller, for all his faults, tries to be the best father he can, given the constraints of the time, and his own nature and beliefs (themselves products of that time). But having successfully tapped into the ever-flowing stream of American materialism and competitiveness so prevalent in the 1940s, he is faced with offspring who have formed value systems totally alien to him. An inability on both sides to compromise leads to the destruction of all parties—a clear indication of the breakdown of the family, which was exacerbated during this period and continued to worsen as the century progressed.

A VIEW FROM THE BRIDGE (1956)

While exploring the corruption in the Brooklyn docklands in the late 1940s, Miller was befriended by two men who were trying to fight against the corruption and unionize the workers. One of these was a lawyer, Vinny Longhi, who offered to show Miller around. It was Longhi who told Miller the story of a longshoreman who informed on two brothers who were related to him and living illegally in his house. He had told the immigration authorities to try to break the engagement of one of these men to his niece. His actions had disgraced him in his neighborhood and he was forced to leave; there were rumors that one of the brothers later murdered him. Thus, the seed of *A View from the Bridge* was born, with Miller even keeping the figure of a lawyer as the person who tells the story.

Miller wrote *A View from the Bridge* in 1955 as one act, but was unhappy with the original New York production. He expanded it into the two-act version (which is more commonly known) the following year for the British director, Peter Brook. This longer, more polished version of the play opened to rave reviews in London. It would not be until the 1965 production starring Jon Voight and Robert Duvall that Miller would be satisfied with the play's performance in America.

SETTING AND PLOT DEVELOPMENT

What is important about this play's setting is the sense that Eddie Carbone is an ordinary man who lives in a community of ordinary men. He lives in a small apartment which is part of a tenement building, among other hardworking longshoremen. However, dominating the play's beginning is Mr. Alfieri, a local lawyer who commentates on the action of the play as events unfold. Alfieri seems pleasant enough, but his presence should allow us to realize that all is not as ordinary as it seems. He addresses the audience directly, introducing himself, the area in which he works, and the case of Eddie Carbone.

The play is set in the Red Hook section of Brooklyn, New York, and the inhabitants are largely Italian immigrants. Eddie is seen pitching coins with his fellow workers and neighbors, showing he is one of the group. As he moves into his apartment, he meets his niece, Catherine, to whom he is clearly attracted, and she shows off her new outfit in a naively flirtatious manner. Catherine has lived with the Carbones ever since her mother, Beatrice's sister, died. Eddie is worried that Catherine's dress and actions might be making her too attractive, and warns her about this and about men. She is upset by his disapproval, but is also nervous, as she tries to build the courage to tell him she has been offered a job even before finishing her secretarial training.

Meanwhile, Eddie tells his wife, Beatrice, that two of her Italian cousins have arrived. They are being smuggled past immigration that evening, and will start work on the docks the next day. Beatrice is overjoyed and scrambles to make the place look nice. Eddie is more cautious with his hospitality, feeling that his wife is overly generous, but also accepting it as the honorable thing to do. On learning that Catherine has a job, he shows reservations, wanting her to stay close to home and not be exposed to a lot of new men. Beatrice takes Catherine's side, and persuades Eddie to allow her to take the job. Beatrice does this largely because she wants Catherine out of the way, as she is unhappy with her husband's attachment to his niece. As Eddie accepts, the growing tension between them is deflated, and they make plans for the arriving cousins. Eddie is most concerned that they keep the cousins' presence a secret from the Immigration Bureau. To let Catherine know what a serious issue this is, they tell her the tale of a nephew who informed on his uncle and was thrown out of their community for such a betrayal.

The cousins, Marco and Rodolpho, arrive that night. The family welcomes them and learns of the terrible poverty from which they have come; Marco needs to make money to send to his wife and three children whom he left behind. Catherine and Rodolpho are attracted to each other, which gets Eddie upset and defensive; this makes Beatrice angry. Most of this pent-up emotion is conveyed in the stage directions rather than through what the characters say. Alfieri moves time along by commenting on Eddie's reaction to the growing relationship of Rodolpho and Catherine. Over the next two weeks, Eddie becomes obsessed by jealousy, using every opportunity to criticize, trying to imply that Rodolpho is a homosexual and therefore no real threat to Catherine. Beatrice makes it clear that Eddie's attraction to Catherine has been affecting their marital relationship; they have not slept together for three months, and she is coming to the end of her patience. Eddie feels guilty, but cannot stop himself.

Rodolpho is getting a reputation among the longshoremen as a joker, while Marco is known as a serious worker. Eddie tries to sour Catherine's relationship with Rodolpho by telling her he is only after an American passport. Catherine almost believes him because Rodolpho does behave irresponsibly, spending his money on trivial things. She wants to believe in Rodolpho's sincerity, but now she has doubts, and is angry at Eddie for causing them. Beatrice tries to encourage her to stick with Rodolpho, as she wants Catherine to become more independent, and realize the bad affect that her continual presence is having on Eddie. At this point, Eddie goes to Alfieri to see if he can legally prevent Rodolpho from marrying Catherine. The only way would be for him to inform on the brothers and have them deported. Alfieri warns Eddie that he has "too much love" for his niece and it would be best to let things take their course, but Eddie refuses to be consoled, just as he refuses to admit his real feelings for Catherine. Alfieri declares that he knew the outcome at this point, but could do nothing to stop it.

Back at the Carbone household, there is constant tension between Eddie and the cousins. Beatrice tries to keep the peace, but Eddie takes every opportunity to insult Rodolpho, and even tries to get Marco on his side. Marco stays neutral, and Catherine refuses to allow Rodolpho to be put down, so Eddie tricks Rodolpho into boxing with him to prove he is the better man. It breaks up before he can hurt him, but Marco recognizes what Eddie is doing and warns him off by showing his strength. He picks up a chair by a single leg—something Eddie cannot do.

By act 2, some time has passed and Catherine and Rodolpho are alone together in the house for the first time. Rodolpho has saved some money, and wants Catherine to marry him, but she is unsure because of the doubts Eddie put in her mind. To test Rodolpho, she suggests they go to Italy to live; he refuses and faces her suspicion without apology or explanation. It is hard to know if Eddie is right or not about Rodolpho, because his suggestions also arouse the audience's suspicions, but Rodolpho seems serious. Catherine is torn in her allegiance between Rodolpho and Eddie. However, Rodolpho offers her a freedom she will never have from Eddie, for he promises not to run her life the way Eddie does, and he wins her over. They move into the bedroom together.

Eddie arrives home drunk in time to see Catherine and Rodolpho coming out of the bedroom. He demands that Rodolpho leave the house, and Catherine says she will leave too. Having lost his inhibitions to alcohol, Eddie kisses Catherine on the mouth. Rodolpho defends his betrothed and the men fight, but Eddie easily holds Rodolpho, and to thoroughly embarrass him before Catherine, kisses him on the mouth. Catherine attacks Eddie to make him let go, and Eddie does, mocking Rodolpho's weakness, and warning Catherine not to go with him. With Beatrice's support, both stay. Eddie returns to Alfieri, who again insists there is no legal way for Eddie to bar the impending marriage. A phone booth which has been sitting to the side of the stage begins to glow to show the increasing temptation of Eddie's treacherous last resort—to call the immigration authorities. Alfieri warns Eddie against this course of action, but he cannot resist and makes the fatal phone call.

Meanwhile, Beatrice has moved Rodolpho and Marco to their neighbor's to keep them away from Eddie. Beatrice is angry at Eddie for causing so much upset, but he plays innocent and suggests it is Beatrice's fault. She knows he is wrong, and tells him that Catherine and Rodolpho plan to marry that week. She tries to persuade him to accept this, but Eddie, filled with guilt and shame at what he has done, asks Catherine to wait. The cousins will be rooming with two other illegal immigrants who are newly arrived, and Eddie uses this to suggest that they may have been tracked by the immigration authorities, and that Marco and Rodolpho should immediately leave the house to be safe. His warning comes too late, as the immigration officers arrive, and Beatrice and Catherine immediately realize who has called them.

The authorities take all four immigrants into detention. Marco knows Eddie's part in this, and before they take him, he breaks away to face Eddie in front of all their neighbors, spit in his face, and accuse him of betraying them. Despite Eddie's protestations to the contrary, the neighbors believe Marco and turn their backs on Eddie. Alfieri offers to bail out the cousins until the hearing on the condition that Marco agrees not to hurt Eddie. Rodolpho and Catherine plan to marry immediately so Rodolpho can stay, but Marco must return to Italy. Marco is outraged, but agrees to Alfieri's conditions so that he can work a few extra weeks and attend his brother's wedding.

Eddie tells Beatrice that if she goes to the wedding she cannot come home, and demands an apology from Marco before he will let his family attend. Catherine denounces Eddie, but Beatrice goes to his defense, taking partial responsibility for his actions, and agreeing to stay home. Rodolpho arrives to warn Eddie that Marco is coming, and the women try to keep them apart, but Eddie refuses to hide. Rodolpho tries to make amends, forgiving Eddie and apologizing for his treatment of Catherine, but Eddie does not listen—he is solely focused on Marco and regaining his lost reputation. As Eddie goes to meet Marco, Beatrice holds him, telling him she loves him, and trying to shock him into staying with the truth of his feelings for Catherine. But Eddie cannot face the truth, and goes instead to meet Marco and his death. Although Eddie pulls the knife, Marco turns it on Eddie and kills him with his own weapon. He dies in Beatrice's arms, acknowledging his love for her, while Alfieri concludes, stating his admiration for Eddie, despite his actions.

CHARACTER DEVELOPMENT

Whereas the forces acting on Willy Loman were largely external, those acting on Eddie Carbone are entirely internal. Eddie is totally inflexible; once he sets himself on his chosen course, his character cannot help but lead him to destruction. He dies still insisting that he has done nothing wrong, even though his desires for his niece and his betrayal of his wife's cousins to the immigration authorities are apparent to all. Blinkered like a horse, he refuses to see things from any other perspective than that of his own innocence. Such a refusal is not enough to save him, though it does make him more sympathetic. He intends good, but everything goes sadly wrong because he cannot handle his own emotions. When you betray all that you believe in, you betray yourself, which is what Eddie does. He knows informing is wrong, and he knows his love for Catherine is wrong, yet he cannot help himself. He tells Alfieri, when trying to imply that Rodolpho is not right, that even a mouse can break a hold if it really wants to, yet at the close, he does not break the hold Marco gets on his knife arm. This suggests that Eddie wanted to die rather than face the consequences of his betrayals.

From an early age, Eddie has been overprotective of Catherine. Because he can never have her, he wants to ensure that no one else gets a chance. He would like her to remain a beautiful, innocent Madonna who is pure and untouched, but her emergence into womanhood is something he cannot prevent. His shyness with Catherine turns into petulant resentment as his guilt grows, though he never consciously admits to his feelings for her. The only time the truth comes close to emerging is when he is drunk and kisses her. He casts doubts on Rodolpho's manhood to make himself feel more secure, and he tries to convince others so that he can convince himself, but all he has is very circumstantial evidence. He offers Catherine more freedom toward the end, but has left it too late. His guilt at his own betrayal of the cousins, and his failure to hold onto Catherine, lead him to face Marco in what is a virtual act of suicide.

Beatrice is a good woman, and she has been very patient with her husband, trying to keep the peace, even when it makes her look bad. A compassionate woman, she takes in anyone who needs help without a thought, from Catherine to her cousins. She wants Eddie back, yet won't throw Catherine out because she also wants to be fair to her niece. She even refuses to wholly blame Eddie for what happens, but accepts partial responsibility herself. Beatrice is generous, but no fool—she is not a doormat, and has limits. She loves Eddie and will fight for him, warning Catherine off and encouraging her to rebel, trying to smooth things between Eddie and the cousins, and even agreeing not to attend Catherine's wedding to stay with him. She demands her husband's attention, and finally gets it in his dying moment, as she holds him in her arms and takes full possession. Eddie sees his wife's love and acknowledges it before he dies, though he has bitterly complained along the way at her attempts to force him into being a better husband.

Catherine is naive, and initially responds to events very childishly. She tells Rodolpho that she knows more than they think, but if this is true, then Beatrice is right to hold her partially to blame for having led Eddie on—talking to him while one of them was only partly dressed, and acting the dependent baby when she was capable of being a grown woman. Catherine loves Eddie, and the extent of her love is left uncertain, but she listens to the warnings others give her and breaks away. By nature, she is more submissive than Beatrice and easily manipulated by others. However, she grows during the play, from being the eager child forever craving approval, to recognizing the forces at work on her and facing them—rejecting Eddie, and standing by Rodolpho in a show of mature courage. She and Rodolpho seem a good couple, and there is evidence that they are in love. Furthermore, both are able to give the other what they want—Rodolpho can stay in America and Catherine can have greater freedom, because Rodolpho does not wish to possess her as Eddie does, but to be her partner.

Marco is the older of the brothers and the more serious and cautious, while Rodolpho is younger and more eager and excitable. Marco is politely formal and carefully observes; he dislikes imposing on others. Marco is in America to raise money for his wife and three children, fully intending to return to them in a few years. He looks after his brother and quietly takes charge of situations; when he instructs, Rodolpho obeys. There is a palpable force to Marco, and he is not a man to cross. Though quiet, Marco is no fool. Seeing how Eddie tries to belittle his brother, Marco calmly defends Rodolpho, warning Eddie off with the minimum of fuss. His ability to lift the chair when Eddie cannot should prepare us for who will win their final conflict. Marco's dignity and sense of honor are clear, and because of these, his condemnation of Eddie is incontestable.

In contrast to his quiet, dark brother, Rodolpho is an exuberant blond who loves to have fun. A chatterbox full of jokes, dreams, and stories, he has come to America to experience everything he can. He wants to stay, as he has no responsibilities back in Italy and is excited by the possibilities in America. Catherine is instantly attracted to his lightness of spirit, which is emblematized in his hair color and friendly nature. Like Catherine, Rodolpho also grows during the course of the play, and we see a serious side to him that reminds us of his brother. He faces Catherine's suspicions with a quiet dignity, and maturely forgives Eddie, even accepting some blame for the way things turn out. Despite Eddie's accusations, we are given no proof from Rodolpho's behavior that any of them are true. Indeed, alone with Catherine he sounds most sincere.

Eddie's friends and neighbors act as a barometer of local opinion. They begin as close friends with Eddie, admiring him for helping his wife's relatives. They even side with him against Rodolpho, although they have a growing respect for Marco. However, they turn completely against Eddie as soon as they learn of his betrayal. In many Greek plays, the writer includes such a chorus—a group of minor characters who lead the audience by their reactions to events—and the leader of this particular chorus, though apparently separated from them, is Alfieri. Acting as observer and commentator on the play's action, Alfieri directly addresses the audience. He is only marginally involved in the events, and it is his "view" which we get as he stands on a metaphorical bridge between the characters and the audience. As a lawyer, he appears to represent the legal law in the play, which we realize has little influence on the events which unfold. In contrast to the neighbors, Alfieri shows sympathy for Eddie's downfall, and offers a more balanced view of the action.

HISTORICAL CONTEXT

The story which Miller was told by Vinny Longhi had lain dormant in his mind for some months. It reemerged during a trip to Europe with Longhi in which they visited Italy and got a sense of the background from which such people as the Carbones would have come. The working title for the script was

An Italian Tragedy. The Italian community in Red Hook was a close-knit body; the law of the land did not concern them as much as their own codes of honor and respectability. This was a society in which blood was thicker than water, and to betray a family member was the ultimate sin.

In 1950, Miller had tried to get the studios to take on a film script he had written about waterfront corruption called *The Hook*, but the film's dark picture was considered to be "anti-American," and out of fear of HUAC reprisals it had been shelved. Although set in Red Hook, *A View from the Bridge* does not say much about the racketeering that Miller had earlier sought to expose, although there are implications of something going on with the regular influx of illegal immigrants, and only certain people getting selected for work. But Miller's target was now the committee which had caused his earlier film to be dropped, and had pressured city officials to prevent him from making a film about juvenile delinquency in New York in 1955.

A View from the Bridge was written at the height of the HUAC trials when America was seized in an anti-communist fervor, and friends were being coerced to inform upon friends. Miller had already tried to expose the injustice of the HUAC procedures in 1953 with *The Crucible*, but now wanted to pass comment on those whom the committee has persuaded to inform, such as Miller's close friend, director Elia Kazan. When Miller was brought before the committee in 1956, he refused to give them any names. Using Eddie Carbone as his example, Miller shows that informing may have the law on its side, but it is morally indefensible and wrong.

ALL MY SONS AND *A VIEW FROM THE BRIDGE*

THEMATIC ISSUES

The issues of guilt and responsibility are concerns which Miller addresses in nearly every play he has written, but they are central to both *All My Sons* and *A View from the Bridge*. Miller often presents us with ambivalent characters who cannot be easily categorized as heroes or villains, such as Joe Keller and Eddie Carbone. They make mistakes, but they do not do so maliciously, and they often feel guilty for what they have done. But Miller wants us to realize that guilt is not the answer, because, as a passive reaction, it is destructive, as opposed to the active reaction of accepting responsibility. To passively accept guilt leads to complacency or even paralysis, but if we actively transform guilt into responsibility, Miller believes that we will be able to transcend it.

Like many of Miller's heroes, Eddie Carbone and Joe Keller have guilty secrets: Eddie wants to sleep with his niece, Keller knowingly shipped out faulty aircraft parts which may have caused numerous deaths. To get what they want, both have willingly put others at risk: Eddie tells the Immigration Bureau about his wife's relatives so they will be returned to Italy to prevent Rodolpho from taking Catherine away from him, and Keller ships faulty parts to ensure that his business continues to thrive. Because they refuse to accept responsibility for their actions, their guilt drives them toward destruction: Eddie pays with his own life, and Keller loses both his sons—one to suicide, the other to disgust.

A moral responsibility toward others and the self lies at the core of Miller's plays: To neglect either personal or social responsibility is self-destructive. But a moral responsibility can only be fully recognized by those who have an understanding of their own identities, as individuals *and* members of a society. Until the end of the play, Keller refuses to accept responsibility for anyone outside of his immediate family, and for that he loses his family. When he does, finally, accept responsibility, he takes his own life rather than live on in the knowledge of what he has done and what he has lost. Eddie, on the other hand, recognizes the responsibilities he has for others, but goes against them anyway, in a misguided belief of what his responsibilities are toward Catherine. By going against all he had previously believed, Eddie loses his sense of self, shown when he demands his name from Marco, causing his own death by refusing to accept responsibility for what he has done.

Miller utilizes a typical Greek tragic format in *All My Sons* and *A View from the Bridge*, which hinges upon issues of fate. Both Keller and Eddie are fated to die, partly because of who they are, and partly because of the world in which they live. There is a sense that both are inevitably rushing toward their doom, and that little can be done to save either one: given the same situation, each would make the same mistakes, and the result, therefore, is preordained. The Greeks believed in a world controlled by fates which were directed by the gods, but Miller prefers to believe that people's characters have the biggest influence in determining their fate.

Failure, in Miller's eyes, should not be blamed on an indefinable hostile fate or social system, but on individuals who refuse to accept their responsibilities and connection to fellow human beings. Miller sincerely believes that mankind has free will, and it is the choices people make in their lives which determine their direction. It is easier to blame others, but the fault often lies in ourselves. It is the flaws that exist in Keller's and Eddie's characters which ensure their defeat, rather than any divine authority. Individuals are responsible for their own fate in that they have affected this by the quality of the choices they have made throughout their lives.

Keller chose to ignore his responsibilities to anyone outside of his immediate family, including his friend and partner, Steve Deever, and the pilots flying the planes to which his faulty parts were supplied. Eddie chooses to act on his baser impulses, trying to keep Catherine away from other men, and informing on his wife's cousins. In Eddie's case, the deeper motivation is his lust for Catherine, an emotion he does not choose, but could better control. For Keller, his belief in family first, and the power of bluff, have been instilled in him by the approval of his society, but that does not make him right, and he stubbornly refuses to see the bigger picture.

Another important theme which runs through both plays is the issue of law. In *A View from the Bridge,* Alfieri represents the law, not justice, and Miller is careful not to mix these terms. When Alfieri tells us of many who were "justly shot by unjust men" (12), we come to see that the law is a complex notion, and has more than one side. On one hand, there is the legal law of the land which is often shown to be ineffective in Miller's plays, having no power to make the guilty pay for their crimes or protect the ordinary individual. But on the other hand, Miller insists that there is a moral law which does successfully operate, and judges both our individual and collective actions. Miller sees such a law as fundamental to the growth and development of American culture and democracy, for without this we are insufficiently protected against chaos and evil. Thus, while the institutionalized law can do nothing to seriously restrict or aid Joe Keller or Eddie Carbone, each pays a heavy price for breaking certain moral restrictions.

Keller is exonerated for a crime he committed, and allows his partner to take full blame. Deever was not wholly innocent, as he agreed to cover up the cracks, so we never perceive his punishment as unfair or feel any real sympathy for him, but Keller must pay for his actions. Even knowing Keller's guilt, his community accepts and forgives him—but his sons cannot. Keller's defense is that he did it for his sons, so he would have a thriving business to hand on to them, but when we consider the murderous indifference of his actions, we realize that he is morally lax and deserves punishment. George Deever, a lawyer, manages to uncover the truth, but seems unable to pursue this realization toward any legal action, leaving it instead to Keller's own son, Chris. The moral punishment which Chris forces home to Keller is the loss of his sons. Chris finds his father guilty of social irresponsibility, and demands that he be sent to jail to legally pay for his crime, but Keller chooses to punish himself even more severely, by committing suicide.

Eddie's case depicts even more clearly the chasm between legal and moral laws, because legally he does nothing wrong; indeed, legally you should inform on illegal immigrants, even when their need to make money is as great as Marco's. Worried about whether or not Rodolpho is taking advantage of his niece to get a passport, even though Eddie's motive may not be the purest, it is important to note that he finds no way to *legally* protect his niece. However, neither Eddie's lust for Catherine, nor his betrayal of Rodolpho and Marco can be morally defended, and for these he must pay—first with the loss of his name, and because he will not accept this punishment, finally with the loss of his life.

LITERARY DEVICES AND CRAFT

In *All My Sons,* many of the dominating symbols are physically present on the stage. Most important is Larry's tree. Planted at the news that he was missing in action, and broken down at the start of the play, the tree shows that the Kellers' false vision of Larry will be broken down during the play as they learn the truth about his death. The remainder of the play's setting is designed to emphasize the restrictions under which this family lives: "*The stage is hedged on right and left by tall, closely planted poplars which lend the yard a secluded atmosphere*" (89). The house "*looks tight,*" as it exudes an aura of restriction and privacy. We are in a time where as long as you keep your "dirty washing" private, the neighbors are unconcerned. This is shown by the neighbors' evident knowledge of Keller's guilt, yet continued friendship with the man.

Also, the names of Miller's characters are often significant, and this is true for the Keller men. It is not by chance that the name Keller sounds like "killer," or the "cellar," in which Keller metaphorically hides his guilt. Bert's belief that Keller's cellar is a jail helps to further underline the restrictions under which Keller exists. Meanwhile, Chris can be seen as a martyr, or even Christlike as his name suggests, but a Christ who has lost faith in his father, and so is unable to raise his Lazarus (Larry) from the dead. In contrast to the physical symbols and carefully named characters we find in *All My Sons,* many of the symbols in *A View from the Bridge* are conveyed by the dialogue and the character descriptions.

There is much irony in *A View from the Bridge.* For example, Eddie's cautionary tales of stool pigeons and their fates, with Beatrice declaring that he'll "get a blessing" for taking in Rodolpho and Marco, when it actually turns out to be Eddie who is the informer (he even describes himself as a "pigeon" later in the play, although he intends it in a different context), and his "good favor" becomes his downfall. Also, the song which Rodolpho sings, "Paper Doll," sets the scene for future events, as it sums up Eddie's attitude toward Catherine: "It's tough to love a doll that's not your own" (32). On other occasions, Eddie's eyes are described as being "like tunnels," to convey the sense of inevitability in his destructive behavior. The phone booth from which Eddie calls the authorities "begins to glow" as Eddie feels the temptation to make the call, and contributes to this sense of fate behind the play. As Eddie approaches the phone, Alfieri disappears into darkness and the phone lights up to place Eddie in the ill-fated spotlight which kills him, and it is a spotlight he freely chooses to enter. The sense that Eddie is the author of his own fate is further underlined by the irony of him dying by his own treachery, on his own knife.

ALTERNATE PERSPECTIVE: A PSYCHOANALYTICAL READING

Psychoanalysis, as practiced by pioneers like Sigmund Freud and his followers, provided a new key to the understanding of character. It showed how people's behavior is often dictated by hidden and unconscious motives, which can be uncovered by close scrutiny of a person's words and actions, and an assessment of their past. Freud's theory of repression, for example, suggests that much of what lies in the unconscious mind has been consciously put there as an act of self-censorship. Thoughts, instincts, or emotions which the person feels are unacceptable get hidden away into the unconscious mind, but they still exist and can surface when least expected, such as in dreams. Many are familiar with Freud's explanation of the "oedipal complex," which describes a commonly repressed childhood wish to displace the parent of the same sex and take that parent's place. He modeled this complex after the Greek tragic hero, Oedipus, who unwittingly killed his father and married his mother. It can involve a variety of wishes and fears, from desiring closer contact with the parent of the opposite gender to the fear of retaliation from the parent of the same gender. It is often manifested as a repressed sexual desire for someone socially forbidden as a partner.

In literary criticism, we use a psychoanalytical approach to try to understand certain fictional characters, or sometimes the writers themselves and the creative process. When psychoanalyzing characters, we look for both obvious and hidden motives behind what they do and say, and consider what these might tell us about them. Whether we are looking at a fictional character or the writer, we should learn as much as we can about social and personal background, and past experiences. What these characters repress into their unconsciousness can emerge in various disguised forms, such as in their dreams, the way they phrase certain comments, or even in neurotic behavior.

Kate Keller, in *All My Sons*, is a figure worthy of attention right from her ambiguous opening description: "*A woman of uncontrolled inspirations and an overwhelming capacity for love*" (102). "Uncontrolled" and "overwhelming" are the keys to her character—there is something about her that refuses to be dominated, and it will be she alone who stands firm against the cataclysmic events of the play. She insists on her son Larry's continued existence, because "if he's dead, your father killed him" (156). Even though the faulty plane parts Keller allowed to be shipped could not have been used in Larry's plane, Keller did kill his son, who committed suicide because of his father's actions. Kate represses the very idea of Larry's death, for to acknowledge it would be to reject her husband. Yet, she displays an underlying antagonism toward her husband throughout the play, which is unsurprising in light of her evident adoration of Larry.

Kate has a dream in which she sees her son falling and unsuccessfully tries to save him. This tells us that in her subconscious she really knows that Larry is dead, and because she envisions him falling through the sky, she blames her husband and his faulty aircraft parts for that death. Kate's anger with Keller shows most clearly when she actually smashes her husband across the face, but her behavior toward him is cold for much of the play, as she orders him about and tells him to be quiet. Kate finally acts on her contempt for her husband, though her disclosure may not be conscious, for it is she who betrays Keller to both George and Chris, and brings the truth into the open.

It is reasonable to ask why Kate has kept quiet so long and not acted sooner. Is it that, unconsciously, she wants control? We see this desire in her frequent attempts to dominate and insist on everyone doing what *she* wants. Her power is strong, and she has everyone on edge, wondering what her reactions will be and trying to please her: "What's Mother going to say?" Keller declares, worrying about her reaction to the broken tree (96). We should note the way in which she is "mother" even to him, especially as his control gradually slips. Keller has relinquished his power to Kate, for in the keeping of his secret, his wife has taken control over him. As Keller becomes more and more unable to control events, he turns to Kate for advice, and she suggests a course of action which will once more cover up the truth, a deceit to pacify their son: for Keller to pretend to offer to go to prison.

Kate keeps control by refusing to face the truth and forcing others to do the same. Her refusal to face Larry's death has the others running in circles. She also refuses to accept the rift between Chris and his father, and suggests that they use subterfuge to cover it up. The knowledge of Larry's suicide totally destroys Keller's ability to maintain any illusion, and he kills himself. But though she may have lost her husband, Kate regains control of her errant son as Chris turns to her, not Ann, for comfort. Chris had rebelled from his mother in his decision to marry Ann and in his desire to face the truth, but Kate now quiets him and suggests it would be better to forget. Chris turns himself over to her, and she takes charge, which does not bode well for the future.

Eddie Carbone, in *A View from the Bridge*, just like Kate Keller, tries to maintain control by refusing to face the truth. The relationship of Eddie and Catherine lends itself to a psychoanalytical interpretation, as it offers an interesting twist on the classic oedipal complex. Although there is much evidence in the play that Catherine has stronger feelings for her uncle than may be proper, the focus is on Eddie and his feelings for his niece. The usual oedipal complex has the child desiring the parent or parent figure, and that figure neither reciprocates their feelings, nor, often, even notices them. But in *A View from the*

Bridge, it becomes clear that Eddie fiercely desires Catherine, and it is the failure to fully repress this desire that forces him to go so strongly against his society's rules and betray the immigrant cousins. His unruly desire for his niece is the fatal flaw in his character that brings about his demise; just like the Greek hero Oedipus, he pays a heavy price for the disruption his actions bring to his community.

From Eddie's first entrance, we are aware that there is something out of the ordinary in his relationship with his niece. He is unusually shy, and at times awkward with her—especially when she shows affection and behaves in an unwittingly seductive way before him. He is also overly-possessive, not wanting her to draw the attention of other males. He rebukes her for the way she walks, the clothes she wears, even for a friendly wave to his friend, Louis. It is clear that he would like to keep her isolated from the rest of the world so he might have her all to himself. Miller's stage directions help us to understand that something is wrong with Eddie's reactions, such as when he becomes "strangely nervous" (18) and "somehow sickened" (20) on hearing of Catherine's intention to get a job, and "strangely and quickly resentful" (21) of his wife's efforts to make Catherine independent. Eddie does not want Catherine to grow up and escape his influence. Beatrice has noticed how Eddie treats her niece and is annoyed and jealous, but Eddie refuses to recognize any implications behind his treatment of Catherine, seeing it as paternal caution rather than sexual jealousy.

All through the play, Eddie refuses to acknowledge how he feels for Catherine, because he knows such feelings are wrong. He calls her "Madonna" (24), and through this designation keeps her pure and free from association with others, yet also unattainable even to him. But Eddie is so besotted with Catherine that he has not been able to sleep with his own wife for the past three months. When Beatrice and Alfieri imply that his feelings for Catherine are too strong, he responds with angry denial. However, on the night he comes in drunk, his guard is down, and in the passionate kiss he gives his niece we should recognize his true feelings. He endlessly tries to justify his distrust of Rodolpho by insisting that the boy is a homosexual and is only dating Catherine to get a passport, but his distrust is only created by Catherine's evident liking for Rodolpho. When Beatrice finally blurts out the truth, "You want somethin' else, Eddie, and you can never have her!" (83), Eddie is shocked and horrified. It is shortly after this that he confronts Marco in a virtual act of suicide, as if death were now his only escape from the truth he has tried so hard to avoid.

5

The Depression:
The American Clock
(1980)

Combining autobiographical memories of his own family in the form of the Baums, with various characters and situations he had read about in Studs Terkel's *Hard Times*, a series of sketches about people who had lived through the depression, Miller began writing *The American Clock* in 1972. The play premiered in 1980 at the Spoleto festival in Charleston, South Carolina, and later that same year on Broadway, but was not produced to Miller's satisfaction until the 1986 British production, which he felt best captured its spirit. This later rendition, though it contained the same plot line, was a rewritten rendition which emphasized different characters and made the play more cohesive by keeping the whole cast onstage throughout, and including more songs to link the scenes.

With forty-six named characters, plus extras, *The American Clock* is, in many ways, one of Miller's most ambitious plays. Miller considers *The American Clock* as a mural in which one sees individuals at close range, but when standing back, the larger society with its pattern of interconnections becomes visible. In the play, Miller tries to balance epic elements with intimate psychological portraits to give a picture of a society and the individuals who comprise it. The play's setting during the depression allows Miller to depict the complete collapse and regeneration of American society, and how this impacts on the people who lived through such times. What we learn from the play is that we should strive to overcome the dangers of depression and despair, accepting the responsibilities and potential connections offered to us by the society in which we live.

The American Clock shows a variety of false, misleading myths which must be set aside in order for society to progress and improve. What needs to be sought in their place is a better faith in the world we inhabit, and an awareness that there is always something beyond the self. The play's large cast depicts numerous examples of how we should see blame and guilt as destructive, and strive to love one another, accept connections, and set aside false, misleading dogma. A balance between individual and social concerns will allow us all to rekindle hope in the true possibilities of democracy, and in America itself.

SETTING AND PLOT DEVELOPMENT

Miller allows no scene breaks in *The American Clock*, presenting us with a fluid montage of constant action. The characters often address the audience directly, as if to include them as part of the throng to create the effect of a collage of people, past and present. The cast of the play represents the "whole country" (106), that is, the United States of America. To affirm this, Miller presents onstage two quintessential American pastimes—Jazz and baseball—with a guy pitching a ball, and the band playing "Million Dollar Baby" to emphasize the American obsession with wealth. Since the play begins in the 1920s, when wealth abounded, everyone willingly joins in the song as the whole cast comes on stage.

Miller creates an effect in which the speech of the individual people of America blends together to create one voice, the voice of America. Speech flows from one character to another, with Lee continuing the sentence Rose begins, then Moe taking over, then the rest of the cast, and returning to Moe for the conclusion. It suggests a community of one mind, connected by outlook, similar values and beliefs, and desire. Once all of the characters are present, they stay onstage for the remainder of the play. Scenes between various combinations of these characters play out, with occasional interjections and comments from those outside of the individual scenes, as well as numerous songs which bind the piece together. The young Lee and successful entrepreneur Arthur Robertson act as joint narrators.

Robertson's opening biblical image of the country kneeling to a golden calf evokes a prophecy of doom. We all know what happened to those original, misguided idolaters; they paid a harsh price for placing their faith in little but wealth. These people also will suffer, as the Wall Street crash is imminent, and it will spark off a sequence of events resulting in the Great Depression, the most widespread disaster faced by the American people since the Civil War. The red, white, and blue of America's flag, once an emblem of liberty and equality, is denigrated as a wrap for the golden calf, showing how Americans have come to obsess over notions of success and wealth above and beyond notions of democracy.

Robertson chats to a shoe black, Clarence, who has put all of his savings into the stock market. Clarence refuses to believe he could lose in this venture, despite Robertson's kindly and wise advice for him to sell out. By centering on Clarence as a typical investor, Miller shows us how the crash would have repercussions at every level of American society—it was not only the rich whose hopes were smashed. As Clarence leaves, relying on his investments for the future, Theodore Quinn is left to sing the final line of "Million Dollar Baby": "I found a million dollar baby in a five and ten cent store," to indicate the pervasive belief all Americans had in the 1920s, that they possessed an inviolable Midas touch.

The real antidote to the calamities of the depression, and Miller's suggestion of the only possible thing in this world which can be inviolable, is love. It is now introduced by the Baums, with Rose and Lee playing and singing "I Can't Give You Anything but Love." The song's sentiments contrast well with the opening scene of acquisitiveness, and it evokes the possibility of people who are not obsessed with things. And yet, this outlook has not yet occurred. The Baums, too, have lessons to learn in the course of the play. At this point, Lee becomes upset as his sense of his mother is shattered, because she has bobbed her hair. She is still the same loving mother, as her continued playing indicates, but for the time, he cannot see past the hair. Instead, he rallies himself with the fierce optimism of "On the Sunny Side of the Street," but optimism alone cannot prevent bad occurences. Meanwhile, the Baumses' wealth is displayed, with Moe's financial transactions, Rose's diamond bracelet, and the presence of their chauffeur. But all is not right with the family: Rose squabbles with her sister over who should take their father, is jealous of her husband's generosity to his mother, and her husband seems estranged from their son, Lee (not even sure of his age), and resentful of his sister-in-law.

As Moe and Rose leave for the theater, Robertson appears to explain his hunch about the impending market crash to his psychiatrist, Dr. Rosman, just prior to its occurrence. We then see the results of that crash, as we meet two financiers, Jesse Livermore and William Durant, discussing its impact. Randolph Morgan has thrown himself out of a window rather than face the investors whose money he has lost, and while Livermore sees this action as somewhat heroic (he will shortly commit suicide himself), Durant sees Morgan as a fool. Morgan's sister, Diana, unaware of his death, joins them in the bar. While Livermore tells her the market will soon recover, Durant advises her to forget such idle hopes and face the truth, that the country is in ruins. Robertson comes in, loaning Livermore some cash, and telling Diana the truth about her brother.

We return to the Baums, who are losing everything. Lee withdrew his savings just before the bank collapsed and bought a bike, but it gets stolen. Rose pawns her jewelry; Moe politely fires their chauffeur, who has been cheating on the garage bills; and Grandpa, clearly a selfish man, does not take their fall from wealth and move to smaller premises happily. He constantly complains, and Rose has to calm him down. Lee, meanwhile, naively considers which ivy league college to attend, not fully realizing the extent of his family's new poverty.

It is not just the city people who suffer. Due to weather conditions as punishing as the stock market, the farmers have lost as much as the city financiers, but there is no longer anywhere for them to run up credit. Miller shows Henry Taylor's farm being put up for compulsory auction by its creditors. The Taylors are shattered by this turn of events. The neighbors, threatened by similar treatment, rally around their fellow farmer. Disarming the police and taking the judge hostage, they scare off potential buyers and enforce a sale of Taylor's property for one dollar, returning it to him. It will be a momentary victory, for he has no money to run a farm whether he owns it or not, and he will soon be forced onto the road to find a living, and his unhappiness reflects this.

Judge Bradley, who initiated the sale, declares that the return of the farm to Taylor for a dollar is sheer theft and "a crime against every law of God and man" (135), but Miller wants us to recognize the unfairness of this. The judge insists that everyone must obey the legal system to ensure order, but Miller asks us to consider, Where is the order in having your livelihood sold off to the highest bidder, and your family home stripped away? Henry Taylor is a decent family man who has had an unavoidably fallow season. Judge Bradley may have man-made legal laws on his side, but every moral instinct says that Taylor should be allowed to keep his farm.

We then meet Banks, an African American vagrant, who tells of how a white fellow hobo helped him out. But Banks sees this as an unusual reaction, as most people seem out for themselves, and he leaves singing a blues song which asks "How Long?" as the stage is taken over by a sad and tiring group of marathon dancers, illustrating the ability of people to keep going despite utter weariness.

Lee realizes that college is not in the family budget, but before we can pity him we meet Taylor again, who has come to their house asking for work, and is quite literally starving to death. It is a level of poverty which can still shock the Baums, who survive in comparative comfort. They feed him and Moe gives him a dollar, but refuses to allow him to sleep in their basement. Moe feels sorry for Taylor, but cannot be fully responsible for him; Taylor must accept responsibility for his own condition. Lee, idealistically, is unhappy with what he sees as his father's refusal of responsibility. Grandpa's reaction, however, is worse; he insists that people are not connected, and you should only "worry about yourself," as he does (143). Moe's philosophy is a lot less selfish and may be a necessary balance; he helps a little, but not to a point where he damages his own prospects.

Robertson introduces us to the popular, carefree figure of Quinn, who enters singing and dancing. Quinn can still find enjoyment in these times. He has a faith to buoy him up, but in what does Quinn believe? Since the GE/Frigidaire price war, he has recognized the farce behind big business conglomerates, in which people have become so faceless that they can even end up cutting their own throats. He sees such large conglomerates as anti-business because they wipe out the "creative force of competition" in which he strongly believes (145). Unlike some businessmen, Quinn has a conscience, and can recognize that a company like GE only gets big on the sacrifice of smaller companies they destroy, and he disapproves. He views monopolies as un-American, because they are so undemocratic.

Quinn impresses a newspaper man (reporting on Quinn's election to president of GE), with his life story, and we learn that Quinn has worked his way up the corporate ladder by being aware of the individual elements that make up the company as a whole. But the reporter laughs at Quinn's proposal to try to help individuals by setting up a small business advisory service. Robertson suggests to Quinn that his view of rekindling small business in America is only a dream, and big business is the only possible future. He may be right, but Quinn realizes that it is worth engaging in a fight against such forces, even if victory seems impossible. Quinn decides to resign from the presidency of GE to register his disapproval of monopolies. Despite a lingering uncertainty as to whether it is wise to be renouncing the corporate world, he seems happier once the decision has been made, as evidenced by his continued song and dance.

Realizing his family's economic plight, Lee forgets about college and plans to get himself a job. His cousin, Sidney, in contrast, stays home and dreams of writing a hit song, while his mother encourages him to flirt with their landlady's daughter, Doris, to get them free accommodation. Luckily, Sidney and Doris actually hit it off, and later fall in love. Others, less fortunate, live in cardboard boxes beside the river. Moe walks Lee to his first job, and has to borrow a quarter from him to get downtown, which embarrasses Moe, but elates his son, who feels he is growing up.

The second act begins with Rose at her piano, desperately trying to cheer herself up. Robertson has been making money since investments have become so cheap, and Lee has finally gotten to college, where he discusses politics with fellow students, and learns that a university degree will be of little help in getting a better job. Wanting to be a writer, Lee aims to travel after he graduates, to gain experience, and heads down the Mississippi on a riverboat.

Down South, Lee becomes dismayed. Instead of helping each other, many have turned to violence and anger, and the poor are starving on the bottom of the heap. America has the food to feed them, only they cannot afford to buy it because there are no jobs for them to earn a living. This drove many close to madness as they saw hard-earned skills wasted due to the deflated economy, while a minority continued to get rich by taking irresponsible advantage, such as the tobacco bosses who continued to rake in profits while refusing to pay their workers a living wage. Lee's old friend, Joe, struggled to become a dentist but, now qualified, has no cash to begin his practice, and is reduced to selling flowers for a living, and visiting a prostitute for companionship. He explains to Lee his belief in Marxism; this is the same Joe who had, as a boy, written to Herbert Hoover, a staunch Republican president, to wish him success.

While Rose loses her piano, Lee meets Isaac, a successful African American café owner, who explains how African Americans were least hit by the depression, as they have been struggling to survive since abolition. The local sheriff offers his expensive radio to get Isaac to cook a chicken dinner with which he can impress his cousin, through whom he hopes to get a better job. When Lee returns home, he goes to sign on at the relief office, which he must do before signing on to the Works Progress Administration's Writer's Project. He can only get on relief by having his father pretend he hates him and has thrown him out of the house, a charade to which Moe agrees.

With his mix of characters at the relief office, Miller allows us to see just how disconnected these people have become in their times of trouble, as they squabble over the pettiest of things. Irene, an African American who espouses communism, tries to get them all to pull together and consider joining the Communist Party. She elicits their assistance for the starving Matthew Bush, but none of these people are interested in her political beliefs. As Lee is called up and asked to explain his position, the scene is initially amusing, but it brings out in Moe a feeling of disgust toward his son. Moe sees Lee as having compromised both their dignities, and he is also distraught at his son's evident lack of faith in everything.

Disgusted by a society he sees destroying its poor through selfish capitalism, Lee considers Marxism as an alternative, but soon becomes disillusioned with its evident dogmatism, and is unable to find anything else in which he can believe. His rejection of communism is shown to be wise, as Miller shows how communist beliefs were unable to sustain Lee's friend, Joe, who throws himself under a train in despair. Lee's girlfriend, Edie, tries to defend communism to him, but she is too idealistic to be entirely credible, and Lee's cynicism only provokes her into kicking him out.

Meanwhile, Rose is playing cards with the women in her family, while pretending to be out for the repossessors. She has adopted a vagrant, Stanislaus, who helps around the house in return for food and lodging. The women argue among themselves, and talk about their reduced circumstances, but each tries to put on a brave face. However, Rose tells the audience in an aside about her moments of panic when she has to lock herself in the bathroom so no one will see. She is approaching the end of her tether, and gets very impatient with everyone's lies and stupidity, finally bursting into tears. Moe arrives to calm her down, as the repossessors knock on the door and we move into the future.

Sidney, working as a security guard, meets Lee who is reporting on a prize fight, and beside them, the hobo, Banks, appears in soldier's uniform. World War II created many jobs, though it also killed many people, and a collage of songs takes us through to the Vietnam conflict, as the cast lists those they knew who died. Time has passed and life seems more hopeful, despite the wars and the deaths of people like Moe, Rose, and Fanny. Sidney has published some songs, and Lee has discovered something in which he can believe: America itself. It is a concept he finally understands through his vision of his own mother and the "headful of life" (203) he gains from thinking about all the contradictions for which she stood.

Lee's final identification of Rose with America as a whole rests in her ability to accept contradictory beliefs. Rose can simultaneously support concepts of capitalism and freedom, socialism and elitism, humanitarianism and racism—for at the heart of these beliefs lie her essential optimism and belief in life. These convictions allow Rose, and the rest of America, to survive and continue to function. Rose sings out at the close of the play, refusing to give in. Although a little wistful at first, everyone joins in her rendition of "Life's Just a Bowl of Cherries." The country has been saved, not just by the onset of war as Robertson suggests, but also, as Quinn adds, by a reaffirmation of belief in itself, partly engendered by President Roosevelt. Quinn leads the final chorus in a dance as everybody sings, including, hopefully, the audience, providing a prime picture of America the brave, prepared to sing and dance with life in the face of any disaster.

CHARACTER DEVELOPMENT

The American Clock depicts characters from every walk of life, to fully illustrate the far reaching effects of the depression. Some we only meet briefly, others recur throughout the play. The central characters are the Baum family: Rose and Moe with their son, Lee; Rose's sister, Fanny, with her son, Sidney; Rose's niece, Lucille; and Grandpa. They form the heart of the play. Miller uses the three main Baums to illustrate the major different reactions he perceived people had to the depression: Moe responds practically, Rose emotionally, and Lee ideologically. In combination, the three offer a comprehensive picture of the overwhelming impact of the depression on the American psyche and disposition. Apart, they allow us to explore personalized aspects of the larger social changes occurring during this period.

Wealthy enough at the start, though not necessarily happy, the Baums, like many, overinvest in stocks and suffer the consequences. We watch their descent into relative poverty, as they discover various strategies for survival. Moe is an ordinary man who displays extraordinary courage in the way he deals with his fall in fortune. He recognizes the importance of maintaining a strong sense of self in the face of all that befalls him and his family. He struggles to retain his dignity and honor. Despite bankruptcy, he tries to pay off his debts. Dismissing his chauffeur, whom he has been allowing to cheat him for years, is done firmly but without malice. He offers some aid to the suffering community he sees around him—feeding the homeless, giving small sums of money to people like Henry Taylor and Matthew Bush—without allowing it to grow out of proportion to the family's means.

Moe remains a strong figure to the end because he refuses to blame himself for what has happened, and avoids self-destructive guilt. What is most important about Moe is his continual refusal to buckle. He strives to provide for his family as practically as possible—moving to a smaller apartment, cutting back on all but necessities—and he does not hide behind feelings of guilt or shame when things grow tough. He acknowledges the real state society is in, and remains strong, even as he sees everything around him collapse and men like Joe kill themselves. "We are going to be alright. . . . It can't go on forever" (198–99), he assures his wife. His final words in the play display this refusal to give in: "I'm trying! God Almighty, I am trying!" (199).

In contrast to Moe's stoicism is Grandpa, who constantly complains and always suggests the most selfish and unrealistic of options. Miller makes it clear we should take no notice of Grandpa. We are shown how wrong his views are when he insists that Hitler can only stay in power for six months at most, and by his unrealistic response to Taylor's plight, suggesting he should borrow money to repurchase his farm. Grandpa lives in fierce denial of the changing times, and what he says is not credible. His daughter shares his ability to ignore reality, though in not quite so mean a spirit.

Throughout the calamities the Baums must face, Rose responds less practically than her husband, but far more imaginatively, and events take an emotional toll. Rose tries to look on the bright side, pointing out how the crash has brought families such as theirs closer together through sheer necessity. Her efforts to keep happy, however, are motivated by a refusal to admit their real poverty and position, holding onto dreams of a past gentility in order to survive. Through her books and songs she avoids truths and pretends that everything is fine and "S'Wonderful," pushing money troubles aside with a carefully chosen lyric.

But at times the truth is hard to ignore, especially as they are about to be evicted from their apartment. Despite their worsening condition, Rose continues to help other people, such as Stanislaus, who stays with them and works for his keep. Though she may lock herself in the bathroom to vent her despair and frustration, in front of others she preserves an attitude of control and optimism. She rests, however, on the brink of madness and despair. Rose is no fool; she sees what is happening to her and her family, but insists on viewing these events through the lens of her optimism. She survives by treading a fine line between hope and despair, and managing to keep her balance by her ability to live in contradictions—as Lee finally recognizes.

Lee is very young when the depression hits, and after losing previously thought unshakable beliefs, he must decide the values by which he will live. He displays, throughout, an awareness of his responsibility to others. He knows, instinctively, that the way Taylor gets treated is "all *wrong*" (140). Growing up in a nation which has had the rug pulled from under its feet, and will remain unsure of its footing for some time, Lee searches for an ideology which will satisfy his sense of community. For a long time, Lee finds it hard to have faith in anything; he considers various ideologies he sees vying for control, and seeks lasting ideals by which to live. What he uncovers is a network of contradictions, but he discovers a workable balance between them which offers him hope for the future.

Miller intends for Lee to assert the strongest "life force" in the play, and he seems to have more gumption than his cousin, Sidney, who sits around playing the piano, dreaming of writing a hit song. But appearances can be deceptive. Sidney may stay home, but he pursues his dreams no less forcefully. It is through Sidney that Miller shows us the redeeming possibilities of love among the younger generation. Sidney's mother suggests that he date their landlady's daughter in the hope of getting a free apartment. The relationship between Sidney and Doris begins out of necessity, but blossoms into true love, and the couple becomes one of the few who survive. The younger generation is also represented by Lee's friends, Joe, Ralph, Rudy, and Edie. Despite university degrees and high ideals, most find themselves unable to get the jobs for which they trained. While Ralph's belief in capitalism is finally rewarded by the influx of new business with the onset of World War II, Joe and Edie flounder in their inability to make communism work.

As joint narrators, Lee and Arthur Robertson offer different interpretations of past events, and help to link the play's episodes together. Lee, youthful and initially naive, attempts to make sense of events as they unfold. Robertson, older and wiser, is a man with an intuitive understanding of events even before they occur. Together, they analyze and offer interpretations of how America survived the depression and what lessons we can take from this survival for the future. Both are importantly involved in the action—not outside commentators, but involved participants—which gives their words a greater credibility. Although Robertson's foresight keeps him financially ahead, he is no greedy businessman, and is depicted as a model of good behavior; he is aware of the consequences of his actions on others and makes responsible business choices.

A key voice in both the opening and closing choruses is Theodore Quinn, a representation of American zeal and spirit. Quinn has lived the American dream, having risen to the top from lowly origins. However, he sees that the perceived pinnacle of the American dream is an empty goal. The massive conglomerate of GE is utterly soulless. Quinn decides to go back to basics in order to assist the "little people" to survive in a faceless corporate world. His desire to help others is rooted in his belief in the importance of American individualism. It is individuals he wants to assist, and his decision to leave the corporate world fills him with evident joy, shown by his upbeat song and dance routine.

There is an array of responses to the crash among the financiers of the time: some commit suicide, like Randolph Morgan; others comfort themselves for a time, like Jesse Livermore, with empty optimism over the possibility of men like John D. Rockefeller saving the day; and there are those who face up to the truth, like William Durant. Livermore's blindness is self-destructive and he ends up taking the suicide route, but Durant's honesty and realization that prosperity can never be assured allow him to survive. He loses General Motors, but ends his days running a bowling alley in Ohio.

We also meet regular workers, such as farmer Henry Taylor, ship's steward Stanislaus, and taxi driver Toland. All lose their livelihood due to the receding economy, and from no fault of their own. All must beg for a living or else starve, though their spirits survive in their insistence that they are prepared to work for what they get. A number of African Americans are also represented, from the unfortunate bootblack, Clarence, or the vagrant hobo, Banks, to the more organized communist enlister, Irene, or the successful café owner, Isaac. They are shown to be more resilient than their white neighbors, due to having suffered from hardship most of their lives as African Americans, and knowing beforehand the lessons of survival.

THEMATIC ISSUES

Miller wants us to learn something regarding the democratic spirit, based on responsibility and a sense of connection, by observing the way the group of characters in *The American Clock* come together by the close of the play. The idea of everything being connected has long fascinated Miller. He believes that a sense of connection is achieved by making people more aware of their responsibilities toward others and themselves. The goal toward which Miller strives is a truly democratic society, in which both individuals and the larger group may have a say and an importance, and recognize the rights of the other. To achieve such a society, it is imperative that people accept their connections.

In *The American Clock,* Miller depicts characters' attempts to restore a sense of community alongside asserting their necessity for individuality, for it is through community and individuality combined that they will find the strength to survive. Despite acknowledging the intrinsic imperfections and inadequacies of most people and their societies, Miller continues to place his faith in human potential, and allow his characters to show the audience how to reconstruct meaning and purpose in their lives. People like the Baums balance their personal needs against their social responsibilities, and survive as a truly democratic family.

The characters in *The American Clock* must not only learn to accept their individual and social identities, but they must recognize the undeniable connection between the two which serves to give each meaning. Miller believes that perspective allows us to be more tolerant and able to accept the possibility of individualism within the social group, which helps us avoid the ego trap that people like Grandpa Baum cannot escape. Perspective colors our view of ourselves and others, and to acknowledge that such a thing as perspective exists is the first step toward acknowledging the existence and viability of difference. It encourages empathy, tolerance, and our ability to look beyond the self—all necessary prerequisites for an effective democracy.

Another theme is evident in the play is the way in which Miller and his characters envisage the past. While Miller seeks to accept the role of the past and of history in his characters' lives, he wishes this to be based on an understanding that such a past may contain false myths which should be set aside. Myths of success, the possibility of an easy life, the perfectibility of life, and the attainment of complete happiness are all deceptive goals and can be destructive. A play like *The American Clock* seeks to explode the false myths by which many live, and direct them, instead, toward a clearer recognition of what they can expect from life, based on an honest assessment of the past rather than vague hopes for the future.

The power of the past lies in its ability to sustain, offer assurance, and point toward those values people need to rekindle to attain positive goals. *The American Clock* uses the horrors of the 1930s to illustrate how America survived in the past, in order to teach survival in the similarly threatening 1980s. The Baum family faced difficulties and survived by recognizing a balance between their own needs and those of others. Moe's dignified strength, Rose's vitality and ability to live with contradiction, and Lee's discovery of the importance of humanity as he sheds off limiting ideologies, all point toward a positive future and suggest values we should embrace.

For Miller, a major key toward survival is optimism, which is more than a refusal to give up on oneself or a close companion, but on society as a whole. *The American Clock* ends with a strong sense of optimism, even if some problems have not been fully resolved. We are left with a sense of hope, despite the evidence of continued difficulties, because we have been shown that however bad the world becomes, humanity's capacity for love, faith, and connection cannot ever be fully crushed.

Although the depression is often seen as an era of futility and slight hope, Miller points out that optimism continued, and is evidenced in the upbeat songs, musicals, and comedies of the period. America improvised her way through the depression, and survived largely because of the great American spirit. It is this spirit which Miller tries to depict, in a hope that it will strike a chord in his audience and they can rediscover such a spirit in themselves. *The American Clock* is a play about America. For Miller, the best part of America is its identity as a nation where hope is possible; indulging the people's optimism for the future, and encouraging them to continually strive for better lives.

Those who fall into despair and become pessimistic, like Jesse Livermore or Joe, quite literally destroy themselves. Those who refuse to give up on themselves or each other—whether it is the Baums, Sidney and Doris, or the vagrant, Banks—are rewarded by their ability to keep going and to keep hoping, which gives their lives meaning and direction. They realize that survival means never giving in to despair or to whatever bad befalls. The human spirit has bottomless resilience in its capacity to dream, providing the hope toward which they continue to strive.

HISTORICAL CONTEXT

The 1920s were years of great prosperity, which most believed could never end. But the 1929 Wall Street crash, in which stock prices plummeted, ruined the economy of the country, and plunged many into abject poverty. With businesses folding, jobs became scarce, and an additional devastating period of drought for the farmers sent America into an economic depression which was not alleviated until the onset of World War II. It is this period in American history which forms the backdrop to *The American Clock*. America survived the traumas of the depression, and Miller is interested in showing us how.

Miller sees the depression as a major landmark in the American sensibility, for it was the time when America was first made to face uncertainty. People had been so sure that the wealth of the 1920s would go on, and now their whole social system seemed to have failed. Miller designed *The American Clock* to celebrate the power of American democracy, which he sees as having been instrumental in the country's survival against uncertainty. He sees the wealthy, decadent 1980s, the period in which he wrote *The American Clock*, as a return of the selfish and heedless attitudes which were prevalent in the 1920s. To prevent a repeat of the devastation caused by the depression, he wrote *The American Clock* as a wake up call, to warn people to be less self-absorbed and dependent on wealth.

Miller saw people in the depression years surviving partly through an irrepressible belief in the future, and in their sense of community. He reminds us of those qualities in this play, in which people survive by random acts of kindness, often given by people who do not even know the recipient (Brewster helping Taylor, Callaghan helping Banks, Moe helping Taylor and Bush), and by an underlying spirit which refuses to accept defeat. The 1930s showed the people of America a world in which connection and responsibilities had to be acknowledged in order for everyone to survive; suffering became the great equalizer, as everyone suffered, and social and moral action was necessary at every level of society. These are lessons which Miller felt the American people needed to rediscover in the self-serving 1980s.

Miller has described the depression as a time when, "Life might be frustrating, but it was exciting, and people in general seemed not to be bored. It was partly that progress was always in the air but also that to do anything at all still required so much effort" (*Timebends* 1987, 64). It was a time when people were more in touch with the basics of life and death, down to choosing meat while it was still alive at the butcher's. People didn't expect perfection, it just wasn't seen as a necessity. At the end of the day, Miller says, "it was really quite simple: we had to hope, and we found hope where we could, in illusions too, provided they showed promise. Reality was intolerable, with its permanent armies of the unemployed, the stagnating and defeated spirit of America, the fearful racism everywhere, the waste of everything precious, especially the potential of the young" (71).

LITERARY DEVICES AND CRAFT

The whole structure and form of *The American Clock* is a fairly unusual one for Miller. Creating a mural of life in America in the 1930s, he allows no scene breaks in order to present us with a fluid montage of constant action. The characters often address the audience directly, as if to include them as part of the throng. The effect he achieves is a collage of the American people, past and present. With so many characters, the work needs a strong collaborative effort on the part of the cast, to form themselves into a cohesive community which is constantly shifting, changing, evolving, and ultimately surviving before our eyes. Importantly, it is a community we see concretely existing before us.

Despite its fluidity and constant shifts of mood, time, and place, there are also, importantly, aspects within *The American Clock* which remain fixed throughout. Such aspects allow us to perceive constants which offer a sense of continuity and comforting permanence. The band remains onstage from start to finish, the Baums offer a central focus, and a key voice in both opening and closing choruses is Theodore Quinn, a perfect representation of American zeal and spirit. The play is also unified by its joint narrators, Arthur Robertson and Lee Baum, and a catalogue of songs, mostly from the era, which act as an additional commentary on the action.

The central image of the play is that of its title: an "American clock." It is Robertson who introduces us to this image: "There's never been a society that hasn't had a clock running on it, and you can't help wondering—how long? How long will they stand for this?" (154). Robertson's image sees time ticking away for everyone, indicating that nothing lasts forever and all things must change. In this constant change, hope can always be found if sought, for despite the fact that change can be for the worse, it is just as possible that it may be for the better; indeed, change often holds both options simultaneously. Although we see the conditions for the play's characters continually worsen, as long as they maintain the idea of an American clock which will keep ticking, regardless, they can retain hope.

ALTERNATE PERSPECTIVE: A MARXIST READING

The Marxist literary critic examines ways in which economics, class structure, and political beliefs shape a culture, and how these are revealed in that culture's literature. Influenced by the writings of Karl Marx, the nineteenth-century philosopher who wrote the *Communist Manifesto* in 1848, Marxist critics believe that it is through the economics of any society that one can come to understand the whole society. They tend to look for evidence in a text of an economic system, and who controls both the means of production and produce of labor. Put more simply, they are interested in who is shown to have the power, and on whose side the author appears to stand; by this they deduce the political sympathies of the author.

Miller has been accused by many of being a communist, and as a young man he held leftist egalitarian convictions. While living in Brooklyn during the depression, like so many Americans, Miller first heard about Marx. He began to think about whether or not America truly had a classless system, and saw that it had not, which overturned the world as he knew it. Drawn to the idealism of a noncompetitive system whereby everyone was equal and could love each man as his comrade, he momentarily flirted with communism, but soon realized its inherent flaws and essential impossibility on the terms which Marx had dictated. Yet he still considered himself a socialist, and felt that the economic problems of the time could only be resolved by socialist solutions.

Miller has a strong conviction that art ought to help change society, which he admits came to him via communist propaganda. Stalin had insisted that art was a "weapon" of revolution and writers were "engineers of the soul," but Miller soon rejected the larger political agenda of communism, seeing it as too restrictive of the individual. Miller is a socialist, but one who strongly believes in an American democracy over communist dogma. He has always preferred to give his energy to art rather than propaganda, and such a desire has always put him at odds with the Communist Party.

Given the evidence that the character Lee in *The American Clock* witnesses of continued elitist thought and the human rapacity of the bosses which has run rampant throughout a capitalistic American society, he, like his childhood friend, Joe, and like his biographical counterpart, Miller himself, considers Marxism as offering potential answers. But unlike Joe and like Miller, Lee soon sees the flaws in the communist system, resting largely in its dogmatism and idealism. It is a system which ultimately fails to sustain Joe, who later throws himself under a train in despair. Lee's girlfriend, Edie, is right when she declares in communism's defense that "Everything's connected" (186), but she is shown to be essentially too idealistic to be entirely credible. She works as a cartoonist, drawing Superman; in the same way, her whole world is largely built upon well-meaning fantasy. Marxism describes a capitalistic world in which relationships have come to be ruled by money. When that money is taken away, as in the depression, the people must find something else to bind them together. But Miller does not see communism as offering any fruitful alternative.

At the relief office we hear from Irene, an African American woman who has been with us from the start, but significantly kept fairly quiet in the background. Irene espouses communism and sees it as a sane response to the times, as it encourages a much needed solidarity in an era marked by chaos and loss. She believes communism will allow for equality—promised by the Constitution and Bill of Rights, but denied in practice—to touch everyone, regardless of skin color. She is right that solidarity is the answer, but Miller wants us to know that people need not embrace communist dogma to find this. We are shown a wonderful image of this solidarity as Irene persuades Grace to give the remains of her baby's bottle to feed the starving Matthew Bush. Apart from Irene, none of these people are communists. Moe's dime, given to buy the man some more milk, is not given as the ten cents needed for dues to the Workers Alliance, but as a payment to be a member of a caring human community. Though she is a communist, it is really Irene's knowledge and experience as an

African American woman that will help these people. As someone who has faced hardship all of her life, Irene offers her experience in survival to her fellow white Americans. She informs them that the way to survival is to be part of a community in which everyone willingly helps each other.

Although evidently against conscienceless capitalism—not allowing us for a moment to sympathize with those fallen wealthy such as Randolph Morgan or Jesse Livermore, who had exploited others in their prosperity—Miller is not against the individual wealth of men like Arthur Robertson, Theodore Quinn, or Isaac, which has been fairly won. Miller does not condemn individuals who have power over others, so long as they use that power responsibly. Due to foresight, Robertson loses none of his wealth during the depression, but he is a man who acts responsibly with his wealth, ensuring that no one will suffer as a result of his financial dealings. Neither his prosperity nor our high opinion of him suffer during the play. Quinn, the bright entrepreneur, is led away from the big corporate businesses which are becoming too soulless, to offer aid to smaller businesses. Although capitalism remains his aim, it is of a sort which he feels promotes healthy competition and is, therefore, acceptable. Isaac operates on a smaller scale, but by enforcing the laws of supply and demand makes a tidy profit from his community, including the local sheriff who needs Isaac's fried chicken to impress his cousin to get him employment with the state police.

Although the play is set during the depression, a time when it seemed as though the balance of power might forever be changed, as the wealthy lost everything and the economic playing field of America was swept bare, Miller portrays the reality of the situation as being very different. The poor were as devastated as the wealthy, and had no strength to rise and take control—indeed, control remained firmly in the hands of the people who had previously held it. Despite their schemes to get wealthy, men like Clarence the bootblack and Frank the chauffeur end up with nothing. Workers like Banks, Henry Taylor, Stanislaus, or Matthew Bush survive largely on handouts they receive from those who maintained some of their wealth and all of their conscience. Those looking to *The American Clock* for any sign of Miller's reputed communist sympathy will be out of luck, for the action of the play supports the previously existing hierarchy of wealth rather than allow or encourage it to be replaced by any other system.

6

The Holocaust: *After the Fall* (1964) and *Broken Glass* (1994)

For Miller, the Holocaust is one of the most central events of the twentieth century, and one from which everyone can learn much about human nature. Miller sees the Holocaust as the period when the world learned to turn away from atrocities and pretend they were not happening, partly because people felt helpless to stop them. Miller insists that we should combat this tendency to ignore what is unpleasant in life, and involve ourselves before another Holocaust can occur. Humanity is "in a boiling soup," Miller tells us, "we change the flavor by what we add, and it changes all of us" (Martine 1979, 178). Therefore, it is not acceptable to refuse to act on the grounds that what a single person does cannot make a difference. A number of Miller's plays have a close connection to the Holocaust, some actually reliving events from that period, like *Broken Glass*, and others, like *After the Fall*, using the Holocaust as an important symbol.

AFTER THE FALL (1964)

Rather than the usual Broadway opening, Miller permitted his first play of the 1960s, *After the Fall*, to open the new repertory theater at the Lincoln Center. Unfortunately, the whole venture was a disaster. The backers had failed to understand the necessary finances a repertory company would need, and the group trying to put the company together squabbled among themselves. Early audiences responded well, and attendance had been so good that Miller wrote another play to add to the company's repertoire, *Incident at Vichy*. But the negative reviews by critics who were ironically playing out a type of denial similar to that which the play sought to expose, coupled with the Lincoln Center project clearly coming apart, brought early closure to *After the Fall*. Most critics refused to go beyond the figure of Maggie as representing Marilyn Monroe, whom they had already built up into some kind of media goddess who could do no wrong, and saw Miller's portrait as unflattering, and the whole play an insult. It was many years before the play would be acknowledged as one of Miller's best works.

After the Fall is not a realistic play which tries to emulate real life onstage, but an expressionistic piece which attempts to create the fluid memories of its central protagonist, Quentin, as he tries to evaluate his life for an unseen "Listener." Because of its very visual structure, *After the Fall* is easier to watch than to read, but if one considers it more as a poetic libretto than a chronological narrative, in which mood is a key factor, and various characters will interrupt to speak key phrases which resonate at various points in the action, it is easier to follow.

SETTING AND PLOT DEVELOPMENT

Throughout the play, the open stage is kept predominantly bare of furnishings, though Miller suggests that the setting include three rising levels made to look like sculptured lava with ledges and contours to accommodate the cast. These levels curve back and forth across the stage in no fixed pattern, with the dominating symbol of the "blasted stone tower, of a German concentration camp" at the top. By this threatening tower Miller wishes to convey the continuing, dark presence of the Holocaust in the minds of the cast and audience. Throughout the play, Quentin relates various events of his life to the beliefs and attitudes which allowed the Holocaust to happen.

The stage begins in darkness, but as the light rises, we see characters enter to take their places at various levels on the stage. All are connected to Quentin, the central protagonist whose memory creates them, and who enters last. His creations seem to be communicating to him in whispers ranging from anger to appeal, but as he begins to speak they fall still and silent. Quentin addresses an unknown "Listener" who appears to exist just beyond the front of the stage. The figure addressed remains unknown throughout the play, as Miller leaves it to his audience to decide who it might be: psychiatrist, priest, judge, old friend, God, or even the audience itself.

Quentin insists he just came by on a social visit, and tells the Listener how he quit his job as a lawyer the previous year (though we later learn he was fired), and that his mother has recently died. As he mentions various characters and events in his life, we see the relevant characters, some of whom are already present in the background, stir onstage, or come into view. On a recent trip to Germany, Quentin met Holga, who is about to arrive in America for a conference and will see him again. It is largely to assess the possibilities of his future relationship with Holga that Quentin now analyzes his past, reliving scenes and trying to come to terms with who he is. After two divorces, and a series of unsatisfactory relationships with other people, Quentin is unsure if he should be considering a third marriage, even though he feels close to Holga. He remains hopeful, but uncertain whether he should trust such a feeling when his life has been filled with the despairing events he proceeds to reenact.

The first of his creations we meet is Felice, a woman for whom he acted as divorce lawyer, and with whom he subsequently had a brief affair, even though he admits he did not return her love. His first two wives, Louise and Maggie, are presented briefly, as well as Holga, to emphasize his obsession with female relationships in his life. He begins to recall his mother's funeral, as a precursor to assessing her influence on him, and how shortly before this he and his older brother, Dan, had announced her death to their father. He uses these past experiences to analyze his own character, by trying to understand what lay behind the things he said and did, and how he responded to events.

While in Germany, prior to his mother's death, Holga showed Quentin a concentration camp. This has deeply affected him, largely because he was unsure how to react. Although not Jewish, Holga spent two years during World War II in a forced labor camp. While visiting the camp, she tries to discover Quentin's feelings toward her; he is reluctant to either commit himself or leave her. This leads to a consideration of the survivor guilt which affects them both—she from her wartime experiences, he from his life experiences. Quentin cannot understand why shortly after this he will be unable to mourn his mother, so he moves into recalling what she was like.

Quentin's mother, Rose, was a vibrant character who simultaneously admired and denigrated her husband, partly resenting her lost opportunities in life, while spoiling her youngest son, Quentin. Although initially fairly wealthy, Quentin's family lost their funds after the Wall Street crash, and although there was nothing he could have done, Rose bitterly blames her husband. Quentin feels affected by his mother's dismissive treatment of his father, and the way she tried to get him to side with her against his father. Caught between his parents, Quentin needs Holga to teach him how not to despair over such matters. She tells him her dream of having an idiot child from which she initially ran away, but whom she finally embraced, realizing that to get on with your life you must learn to take the bad with the good and just keep going.

Quentin recalls his first wife, Louise, and their close friends, Elsie, and her husband, Lou. Elsie was continually trying to seduce Quentin. Though he resisted her advances, he uses this as ammunition in his belief that women cannot be trusted. Lou, a college teacher, was subpoenaed to appear before the House Un-American Activities Committee (HUAC), an experience which threatened to destroy his life and career. Quentin had planned to act as his defense lawyer at the hearings. Wrapped up in his own worries about HUAC, his career, and other concerns, Quentin has been neglecting Louise, who is fed up with being ignored and plans to see a psychoanalyst to change her life. Quentin traces the gradual breakdown of their marriage against the background of his relationships with his friends and colleagues.

Another of Quentin's friends, Mickey, is also subpoenaed by HUAC, but unlike Lou, he gives them the names they demand, partly to keep his job secure, and partly because he feels he had been fooled by communism and should speak against it. Mickey asks Lou to join him, but Lou takes the high moral road and refuses, demanding that Mickey not name him because it would mean instant dismissal from his teaching post. Mickey accuses Lou of being a hypocrite, as he once published a book deliberately whitewashing Russians (at the insistence of his wife, Elsie) rather than tell the truth and make the communists look bad (an action over which Lou already feels ashamed). Just as he felt caught between his parent's arguments, Quentin now feels caught between his friends, and again opts out of getting deeply involved with either—protecting himself by staying apart.

Louise's psychoanalyst has improved her confidence and she is now more assertive, which Quentin finds very unsettling. He also carries the guilt of an earlier affair (possibly Felice), about which his wife discovered. Their marriage is falling apart, and they no longer have any real relationship. Louise sees Quentin as an idiot, just as his mother viewed his father. He finds refuge in the comparatively naive Maggie, an attractive receptionist at his law offices, seduced by her warm-hearted innocence. Maggie is an apparent magnet for men and abuse, and Quentin feels drawn to protect her. Quentin is being pressured by his law firm not to defend Lou, and is unsure what to do. Discussing this with his wife only reveals the deep rifts that have developed between them. He is saved from having to defend Lou, as his friend commits suicide. The first act ends with Quentin uncertain as to how far he betrayed his friend, Lou, and his wife, Louise. His future wife, Maggie, calls him and he lights a cigarette.

Act 2 continues from where act one ends, indicated by Quentin lighting a cigarette at the start. The women from his life all make brief appearances as Quentin decides what life episode he should next analyze. He begins by returning to his current, troubled relationship with Holga, then back to his growing estrangement from his father when he went off to college at his mother's insistence. His main concern is to locate his own identity, feeling it has become lost in the pressures placed on him by others. He relates how he got together with

Maggie, four years from their first meeting, after she has become a famous singer. One night she phoned him out of the blue and invited him over; although still married, he went.

Maggie is attracted to Quentin because he takes her seriously, something few men have done. He feels guilty because he does not think he was ever as noble as she believed, but he did try to save her from being taken advantage of by others, even as he felt himself taking advantage of her. They begin an exciting affair that culminates in marriage (after he and Louise have divorced), but tensions quickly build between them. Quentin is ashamed of Maggie's sexually free past, and she becomes possessive and demanding. Looking after her has become a full-time job he had not planned, and as her demands grow, he becomes more uncomfortable with their relationship, and they split further apart. Turning to excessive alcohol and drugs, Maggie is becoming an increasingly difficult performer, to a point that Quentin feels he can no longer stay with her. He sees leaving Maggie as a betrayal similar to when he backed down from supporting his friend, Lou, or when his mother tricked him as a child to go on vacation without him. He tried to get Maggie to take responsibility for her own life, but she refused and ended by killing herself, the ultimate act of irresponsibility. Quentin is still unsure how much blame he should shoulder for this, but accepts that he was partly at fault.

Quentin's final discovery is that no one can be totally innocent, as we are all willing to betray others to save ourselves when placed in such a position. In this way, Quentin sees that blame for an event like the Holocaust needs to be accepted by everyone, however distant the event, for we are all capable of acting as the Nazis did. In the face of such knowledge, the only remedy is not to give up hope, and it is this aspect of Holga's personality that draws Quentin. He decides to take a chance and allow himself to love again. The play ends as he leaves the stage with Holga and his demons in pursuit.

CHARACTER DEVELOPMENT

In some ways, Quentin is the only character we can assess, as the play is created by him, and each of the other characters only exist in the way they relate to him. Working up to his third marriage, Quentin's life appears to have been a series of betrayals and letdowns. His apparent honesty about his own role in these allows us to sympathize even when he is the betrayer; at least he attempts to face the truth and accept responsibility for past actions. Quentin tends to detach himself from people when things get too problematic, which has led to a series of failed relationships. For his relationship with Holga to work, he must now find strength to commit, and fight this tendency to hang back from responsibility. Miller allows Quentin to be very human, with the same kind of flaws, doubts, and uncertainties many of us face. In this way, if Quentin can find hope, as he finally does, then Miller is letting us know there is hope for us all.

Quentin is a lawyer, and treats his life as if it were a law case he is investigating. In many ways, he is his own "Listener" and the play could be seen as an interior monologue in which Quentin judges himself, acting as prosecution and defense. He sees his relationship with his mother as being at the heart of his trouble with other women, because he still resents her betrayals—going on vacation without him, and using him in her battle against his father—and, therefore, expects all women to ultimately act in the same hurtful way. But Quentin must learn to accept his own share of the blame, which he does by the close. Having found himself, ironically, guilty, he leaves the stage with the hope of a brighter future with Holga.

Felice, Elsie, Louise, Maggie, Holga, and Rose (his mother) are the main women in Quentin's life. Each one is different, in terms of herself, how she is viewed by Quentin, and how she treats him. Each represents a different type of relationship. Felice idolizes Quentin, having had a brief affair with him after he was her divorce lawyer. Though Quentin admits he never loved her, he did help her rebuild confidence in herself after a messy divorce and see herself again as a desirable woman. However, Quentin decides he took more than he gave, and feels guilt over their affair. Elsie, the sexual temptress, on the other hand, allows us to see that Quentin does not always respond to feminine wiles, and can say no.

Louise was Quentin's first wife, and the play depicts the lengthy breakdown of their relationship. Quentin first begins to take her for granted, and then, when she becomes more independent, he realizes how little they have left in common. All that remains to their marriage are suspicions, accusations, and guilt. Although Louise is depicted through Quentin's eyes as cold and self-centered, she is also shown to be an intelligent woman who comes to realize she no longer has any place in her husband's list of priorities. She reaches a stage when she sensibly decides to take charge of her life, no longer waiting for Quentin to fix everything. Since he believes in the sanctity of marriage and because they have a daughter together, he tries to resuscitate their marriage, but his efforts are neither consistent nor totally sincere. Their eventual divorce seems an inevitability to both sides. He finds excitement in the arms of Maggie, a former receptionist at his law firm who becomes a famous singer. Maggie offers him the chance to be needed, which Louise has long since refused, and an active sex life, in which Louise has no interest (even making him sleep on the sofa).

Maggie offers something of the "tyranny of innocence;" her dependency on others and their opinions is so extreme that she has no real concept of self, becoming whatever plaything men demand to make them happy. She is the ultimate victim, and places herself firmly in that role. Quentin tries to teach her self-respect, but it is a lesson she is incapable of learning. Utterly naive about her own attraction and the way men use her, she draws Quentin into an embrace which threatens to stifle. Promiscuous and self-destructive, her increasing use of alcohol and drugs alienates her even from those who want to help. She has made a number of suicide attempts to gain attention, but finally Quentin refuses to help her, insisting she take responsibility for her own life. She cannot, and kills herself, leaving Quentin with the burden of guilt that this is something he may have prevented had he been a stronger man, yet also with the understanding that his relief at being free is all too human a reaction. Although Maggie is a famous singer rather than a movie star, it is hard not to see Marilyn Monroe behind this portrait, even though some of the details are not exact.

Holga is the complete opposite of Maggie, which is a major part of her attraction for Quentin. Her greatest strength, and one which Quentin strives to emulate, is that of self-knowledge. She is undemanding and independent, even while she offers to make a serious commitment to their relationship if he accepts. It is her steadfastness that allows him to recognize the possibilities of future commitment, despite one's past betrayals. Under her tutelage he embraces his "idiot child," and accepts this negative side of his nature as a part of his human whole for which he will be responsible, even as he may strive to lessen its influence.

Quentin's mother, Rose, like Felice, idolized and blessed Quentin, though she was also not above manipulating him for her own ends. Rose is convinced that her younger son is destined for greatness, constantly holding him above his brother, Don, who generously bears no resentment. Feeling she has a special bond with Quentin, she "seduces" him to act as an accomplice in her battles against her husband, continuously forcing him to take her side and subtly denigrate his father. However, despite her deep love, Quentin sees her capability for betrayal, as when she goes away on vacation without him and makes him feel abandoned.

Quentin's friends, Lou and Mickey, are used to show the two extremes of response to HUAC. While Lou refuses to comply and offer any names, Mickey tells all to keep his job. Lou loses everything and is ultimately destroyed, while Mickey tries to justify what he has done to assuage his own guilt, but loses many friends in the process. Many believe Mickey to be based upon Miller's old friend, Elia Kazan. Each character is given a chance to explain his decisions, and Quentin refuses to take sides, for each has good reasons for following the course of action he does. Quentin himself eventually makes some concessions to HUAC in order to keep his job, something Miller never did.

HISTORICAL CONTEXT

Survivor guilt is central to *After the Fall*, and its direct connection to the Holocaust is inescapable. Only months prior to its writing, Miller and his wife, Inge Morath, visited Mauthausen concentration camp, after which they attended the Frankfurt war crimes trials on which Miller wrote an essay for the *New York Herald Tribune*. Miller felt he had witnessed firsthand people's dangerous and irresponsible drive to forget or pretend innocence in order to deny guilt, and he objected to such a reaction, believing instead that we should each accept some responsibility for evil in the world. For Miller, *After the Fall* "was about how we—nations and individuals—destroy ourselves by denying that this is precisely what we are doing" (*Timebends* 1987, 527).

In the late 1950s, Walter Wanger suggested to Miller that he write a screenplay for the French novel *The Fall* by Albert Camus. Miller felt drawn to Camus's story, in which the main character is forced to question his own ability to judge given the knowledge that he himself had erred, but Miller wanted to take this idea further and address questions Camus does not face. In Camus's novel, the hero fails to help a suicidal girl and feels guilty. Miller wondered what would happen if the hero actually tried to help, but then realized this could achieve no good, as such people can only help themselves; very similar, of course, to the dilemma he was facing with Marilyn Monroe in the dying year of their marriage. Miller also wished to explore the reasons for which the hero might offer help, to assess whether or not there could be selfish motives. Miller left Monroe, whom he felt he could no longer help, and a year later married Inge Morath, whom he saw as a far more balanced individual, very like Holga in *After the Fall*. Just as Holga helps Quentin, Inge helped Miller to discover his own sense of balance, and realize that although one should not give up on others, one's duty must always be to save the self first. It is not surprising that his marriage to Inge has lasted.

Miller insists that the play was "neither more nor less autobiographical than anything else I had written for the stage" (*Timebends* 1987, 521), but found that most critics refused to look beyond the autobiographical elements on its initial showing. It is easy to compare the details of a play like *After the Fall* with what we know of Miller's own biography (three wives from very similar backgrounds, similar dealings with HUAC, and almost identical family backgrounds), but it limits Quentin to only see him as Miller's alter ego, as well as doing some disservice to the playwright himself. There is undeniably something of Marilyn Monroe in Maggie, as a type, but it is certainly not a strictly biographical portrait. When he had written the part of Maggie, Monroe was still alive, but she died as the play was being finished. Miller is convinced that this timing is what ruined the play's reception—it didn't help that the director, Elia Kazan, had the actress playing Maggie wear a blonde wig.

BROKEN GLASS (1994)

Broken Glass premiered in 1994 at The Long Wharf Theater in New Haven, where it underwent a number of changes during its short run. It later opened in New York, but despite promising reviews soon foundered in a Broadway climate that Miller insists has become increasingly hostile to serious drama. The play had a successful run in the more heavily subsidized British theater, which still willingly patronizes serious drama, and was subsequently filmed by the British Broadcasting Corporation (BBC).

In *Broken Glass,* Miller tells the story of Sylvia and Phillip Gellburg, who after years of marriage realize that they hardly know each other at all. Obsessed with work and his own desire to assimilate, Phillip has little time for his wife until she demands his attention by falling prey to a mysterious paralysis after seeing the events of Kristallnacht—a night when citizens throughout Germany rioted against the country's Jewish population—in the newspaper. Up until now Sylvia has been a quiet housewife, but she needs to express her buried fears and longings. Dr. Harry Hyman is called in to help, and though he is not a specialist, decides the case is a psychiatric one, and proceeds to treat Sylvia. Hyman, however, has problems of his own, which become apparent during his interaction with the Gellburgs.

SETTING AND PLOT DEVELOPMENT

The play takes place in Brooklyn toward the end of 1938, and a beginning atmosphere, both melancholy and menacing, is created by the playing of a lone cellist. This same cellist opens most of the play's scenes, the first of which is at Dr. Harry Hyman's office, where Phillip Gellburg sits waiting for Hyman to arrive. Gellburg's black business suit is meant to emphasize his overseriousness, paucity of lifespirit, and the overemphasis of work in his life. Hyman's wife, Margaret, enters to explain her husband's tardiness, and she and Gellburg make polite conversation. He corrects her pronunciation of his name, pointing out his Finnish origins, as if such details set him apart from other Jews. She gets him talking about his wife's recent paralysis, filling the audience in on the background, then Margaret leaves, assuring Gellburg her husband will find a cure.

On his entry, Hyman tries to lighten the atmosphere with some jokes, but Gellburg is incapable of levity, so they turn to discussing his wife, Sylvia. Hyman has noted her interest in the unpleasant way the Nazis are treating the Jews in Berlin at this time, and feels this may have some relevance to her case, especially in light of Gellburg's dismissal of the significance of such events. But Hyman, too, finds it hard to sympathize with German Jews, as his past experience of Germans has been too pleasant to credit such barbaric behavior. Neither see the reports as cause for concern, as Sylvia does.

Hyman understands that the paralysis of Sylvia's legs is not physical, but a psychological problem, and diagnoses her as having hysterical paralysis; though he is unsure as to the cause. He questions Gellburg about his marriage, but Gellburg is reluctant to open up. They discuss the onset of the paralysis as the couple were going out one evening, and the memory causes Gellburg to break down. Hyman promises to cure Sylvia, calming Gellburg by changing the subject. He gets him talking about his job with the mortgage department of Brooklyn Guarantee and Trust, where Gellburg is the only Jewish employee. They return to Sylvia to consider if her paralysis is a pretense to get attention, or even a revenge on her husband for something. Gellburg wonders if she might be possessed, but Hyman rejects such superstition. Gellburg leaves, and Margaret reenters. She is jealous of Sylvia as her husband has an eye for pretty women, but Hyman placates her by flirting and beginning to make love as the scene ends.

We move to the Gellburgs' bedroom, where Sylvia, in a wheelchair, is reading the newspaper, as her sister, Harriet, tidies. Harriet asks Sylvia what is wrong, and although unsure herself, Sylvia tries to explain, but Harriet cannot follow, so they move onto more concrete topics: why Harriet's son will not go to college, and the pictures of Jews in the paper. Harriet does not see why her sister would care about events in Germany. As Harriet leaves, Gellburg enters to tell Sylvia about his day, and show her a letter from their son, Jerome. Sylvia is not as pleased as her husband over their son's choice of the army as a profession. There is evident tension between them, as Gellburg unsuccessfully tries not to upset his wife; he is obviously frustrated by her paralysis. He tries to follow the doctor's instructions and be nicer, but Sylvia is bemused at his attempts at kindness. He tells her that Hyman diagnoses her problem as psychological, and asks her of what she might be scared; she can think of nothing. Gellburg suggests it may be the Nazi business, but she sees that as ridiculous. As both get upset, Gellburg tells Sylvia he loves her, and pleads with her to get well.

The couple have a secret about their relationship which Gellburg wants to discuss, but Sylvia refuses; we shall later learn that it is the matter of his impotency. Their marriage has been troubled; they even considered separating, but have left their problems to fester rather than talk about them. Sylvia is resentful of the sacrifices she feels she has been forced to make. Trying to take charge, Gellburg insists that she stand up, but she collapses when he tries to force her. The scene closes as Gellburg once again breaks down—beneath his dour exterior, he is desperate.

We return to Hyman's office, where Harriet has come to discuss her sister's case. She reminisces over some of Hyman's sexual exploits as a young man, and although flattered, he turns the conversation to Sylvia, asking about Sylvia and Gellburg's background. He learns Gellburg is not too popular because he acts superior and is odd about his own Jewish status. The couple met quite young, when Sylvia worked as a bookkeeper. Harriet tells tales of how Gellburg's temper has led him to abuse his wife in the past, but these episodes have their roots in Gellburg's feelings of inadequacy. Even Harriet has to admit that Gellburg loves his wife, although he cannot always admit it.

The next scene takes place in the office of Gellburg's boss, Stanton Case. Case refers to Jews as "you people," and his patronizing treatment of Gellburg betrays his anti-Semitism. Gellburg has been scouting out a property for Case to buy for a new clubhouse (to which Gellburg, as a Jew, could never belong), but advises him against buying the one Case likes, because he suspects the neighborhood may be on a decline. Case offers Gellburg a drink, but leaves him alone to drink it.

Scene 5 returns to the bedroom as Hyman pays a visit. Sylvia brightens on seeing him, but the doctor castigates her for not doing her exercises. He flirts to try and get her to open up, for he is getting frustrated at his inability to solve her case. She asks him not to give up, and tries to change the topic to his sexual exploits, but he asks about her husband. Sylvia explains how after they married Gellburg wanted her to stop work, which she resentfully did. Sylvia has developed a deep affection for Hyman, and with his encouragement, she even tries, unsuccessfully, to stand. She questions him about his recollection of Germany, where he had studied medicine because of the Jewish quotas they had at American schools. Trying to win her deeper confidence, Hyman tells her to imagine they just made love, and then leaves. Sylvia is stirred and attracted by this idea, but still cannot move her legs.

We return to Hyman's office, where Gellburg waits to discuss his wife's case. Margaret keeps him company until her husband arrives, but annoys Gellburg with her prying for information, so leaves. Gellburg is edgy, upset by their lack of progress, and openly hostile. With embarrassment, he confesses his impotency to Hyman and asks if he can recommend a doctor. He also tells Hyman how he made love to his wife the night before, after a long period of abstinence, and that she seems to have slept right through it and does not recall. Miller leaves it unresolved for the moment as to whether it is Gellburg or Sylvia who speaks the truth, but it is clear that one of them is lying. The doctor is reluctant to take sides, which further angers Gellburg, who sees his masculinity at threat. He fires Hyman, and storms out. Margaret reenters, wanting to know what happened, highly suspicious that her husband may be having an affair with

Sylvia, and suggesting he pass the case on to another doctor. He refuses because he is too intrigued by the case to let go.

Act 2 begins back at Case's office. He is annoyed because Gellburg wrongly advised him over the property he had wanted, and he lost his chance to buy it. Unfairly, he suspects Gellburg's loyalty, which leaves Gellburg worried and speechless. The scene switches to Hyman visiting Sylvia—he is clearly ignoring Gellburg's dismissal. The two begin by reminiscing about the neighborhood, but then Sylvia offers to tell Hyman about her recurring dream, in which she thinks she is being chased by Germans and gets attacked by a man who looks like her husband. The man kisses her, then tries to cut off her breasts. The dream told, Sylvia kisses Hyman and bursts into tears. Hyman realizes Sylvia is genuinely scared of Gellburg, has fallen for her doctor, and is at the edge of desperation. He asks if she and Gellburg made love the night before, and she feels insulted that he would ask. She declares they have not made love in twenty years, since their son was born, and Hyman believes her. She pleads with him to stay, but begins to get agitated by his presence.

In Sylvia's mind, she has connected the German Jewish troubles, her husband's estrangement, and her suspicion of Hyman's diffidence toward her; confused, she switches from one to the other. As her hysteria rises, she also rises to her feet, but then collapses on Gellburg's entry. Hyman sends him for a cold towel, and they both administer to Sylvia, who calms down. Hyman leaves, insistent he will return. Sylvia tells Gellburg how she nearly walked, and insists they keep Hyman. She turns on her husband, telling him he gives her bad dreams and must sleep in another room. He admits he lied in telling Hyman they made love, and they begin to air grievances they have kept quiet for far too long. Sylvia feels she has wasted her life; Gellburg feels he became impotent because of his wife's resentment over being asked to give up work and her vengeful refusal to have more children. Gellburg pleads with Sylvia to give their marriage another try, but although she seems to pity him, she is reluctant to do so.

In the next scene, Gellburg has gone to see Case to apologize about the building they lost, but Case remains unforgiving and suspicious that Gellburg has colluded with a rival Jew. This rouses Gellburg's anger, and he rightfully accuses Case of anti-Semitism, which Case resents and denies. Gellburg has a heart attack, and Case calls for an ambulance, noticeably not offering his Jewish employee any personal assistance.

At this point, there is a scene in the play which was added for the London run at the suggestion of the director, David Thacker. Earlier American performances did not include this meeting in Jerome's bedroom between the play's three female characters, in which they sympathetically discuss Gellburg and his possible recovery. He has requested to come home from the hospital early, and

Hyman is with him in the next room. Sylvia shows herself to be feeling guilty that she pushed him so far and was not more accommodating. Both Harriet and Margaret accept the lack of communication the Gellburgs had as not only normal, but inevitable, given their characters. Sylvia gets them to wheel her in to her husband.

In the play's final scene, Gellburg is in bed rather than Sylvia, and Hyman is telling him he should not have come home so early. The two have become friendly, and Gellburg's attack has given him a moment of vision; he has decided to change his life—his job and his relationship with Sylvia—if he lives. Gellburg realizes that his wife has been afraid of him and hopes he can rectify this, as he truly loves her. He and Hyman discuss what Jewishness means to them, realizing being Jewish is not easy, and both of them have been guilty of trying to hide their Jewishness (although the doctor is not as ready as Gellburg to admit this). Hyman has married a gentile and no longer believes in any religion, but Gellburg's experiences have helped reaffirm his previously dwindling belief in Judaism. The men discuss their relationship with Sylvia, and Gellburg asks for Hyman's help. Hyman suggests that Gellburg try to be less self-hating and more forgiving. Hyman leaves before Margaret brings in Sylvia.

Gellburg apologizes to his wife for what has happened to their marriage, but she cuts him off, accepting the blame for herself, and explaining why. She felt they never really trusted each other, and that she has lost touch with herself. Gellburg admits he has not been as confident in their marriage as he pretended, and accepts his portion of blame. He speaks of his past self-hatred, and admits that he also has lost touch with himself. He gets agitated as he pleads with Sylvia to give their relationship a second chance, and drives himself into another heart attack. Horrified at her husband's plight, Sylvia offers forgiveness and finds herself, finally, able to stand. Miller leaves it purposefully unclear as to whether or not Gellburg survives, and what Sylvia will do next. What further complicates matters is the fact that in a short span of time, Miller published three different endings for the play, each subtly different.

Much has been made of the various endings of the play and Miller's difficulties in finalizing the piece, but there are sufficient similarities in all three endings to make Miller's intentions clear, despite the differences. It hardly matters if Gellburg dies or not, an issue which varies between the versions, as the focus is now on Sylvia; she rises to her feet in every version. Gellburg attracts our attention throughout the play, but Sylvia now insists we look at her, as she faces certain truths and allows herself to take center stage. A progression has been made, which may seem minor, but it is enough to suggest the possibility of hope. Miller has stated a final preference for the ending that the 1996 BBC production uses, on which this summary is based.

CHARACTER DEVELOPMENT

Gellburg's problem is far more complicated than Hyman's assessment of him as a self-hating Jew. Declaring himself and his son to be the first or only Jews to do things, he seems not embarrassed but proud of his Jewishness. But is he proud of his achievements *as* a Jew, or *despite* his Jewishness? This question remains deliberately ambiguous. Partly due to his recognition and fear of American anti-Semitism, Gellburg has severed his connection with other Jews, yet his own Jewishness is unavoidable: he has a Jewish wife, he speaks Yiddish, he is prone to Jewish folk beliefs, and his achievements mean more, either way, *because* he is Jewish. But Gellburg is so self-involved that he has no place for a community in his life. Even though he has striven to be accepted, he cannot feel comfortable in the anti-Semitic American community, nor is he happy in the Jewish community for which he feels such antipathy. What is worse, Gellburg has no place in the larger community of mankind; he has no sense of himself anymore, and has lost touch with his humanity. He does not know who he is or who he would like to become.

The blackness of Gellburg's dress and the paleness of his complexion emphasize the emptiness inside the man. He is, as Miller says, "in mourning for his own life," and it is a life he himself is largely responsible for stifling. Reservedly stiff and "proper" (until the more truthful realities of his life insist on recognition), Gellburg offers up glimpses of inner torment in his outbursts of anger and hesitancy. His pent-up anger conveys an increasing sense of threat. Even in silence, his dark, brooding presence onstage commands attention as we wait to see if he will explode. Internally, Gellburg is a mass of contradictions he finds hard to control. He has lost the ability to connect and communicate his true feelings to Sylvia. We are constantly told he loves and adores his wife, and the difficulty he has admitting this to Sylvia is related to his fear of such uncontrollable feelings.

Gellburg desires a sense of control in his life, acting like a "dictator" at his grandmother's funeral, or playing the tyrant at home in order to seem in control—but it has not helped. Only his work gives him a sense of power and control, but he loses that as he realizes how empty his work is; he can no longer find pride in a job which is based on dispossessing others, and quits. His heart attack pushes him to reevaluate his life, and he realizes that he needs to change if he is to fix his relationship with Sylvia and his community. He determines to be a better husband and a better Jew—if it is not too late.

Sylvia, in direct contrast to her husband, has been in touch with the community all along, but so much that she has lost her sense of self, as she exclaims: "I'm here for my mother's sake, and Jerome's sake, and everybody's sake except mine" (44). She has lived her life so long for others she has lost connection with her own selfhood, and she begins by blaming others for this. But Sylvia has let herself become as pale and drained of vitality as her husband. Having withdrawn from their marriage as much as Gellburg, she "punished" her husband when he would not let her work by restricting life in refusing to have another child. Despite her condition, she has shown no interest in healing the relationship with her husband, and is derisive toward him when he attempts to reconnect. She tells Hyman she pities Gellburg, but not once in the play does she speak of loving him. She has failed to consider his private nature when speaking to her father about their sex life, which instead of helping only exacerbated Gellburg's feelings of guilt and embarrassment. Caught up in her own confusions and feelings of betrayal, it is not until the end of the play that she realizes Gellburg, too, has suffered.

Sylvia had settled and accommodated herself to a point which ultimately became untenable even for her self-effacing spirit, and this manifested itself in her objections to the Nazis' treatment of Jews in Europe. When Sylvia rises for the first time in the play, she is driven to do so by her fear that no one will do anything about the suffering in Germany; it also marks an important turning point in her relationship with Gellburg. She may have allowed herself to be a victim, like so many of the Jews in Europe, but now she fights back, and it is increasingly Sylvia who gives the orders.

Sylvia is momentarily distracted by Hyman's vitality, and fooled into believing she has a stronger connection to the doctor than her husband. However, she eventually acknowledges the truer connection existing between her and her husband, which both have stifled. This acknowledgment, coupled with her decision to face her responsibility for the way she is, gives Sylvia the strength to rise. Her paralysis has been an emblem of her loss of control, related to a denial of responsibilities she had to herself as much as others. She realizes her own complicity in this, declaring: "What I did with my life! Out of ignorance . . . Gave it away like a couple of pennies—I took better care of my shoes" (112). She finally takes on responsibility for her condition, and ceases to hide behind blaming others. It is the acceptance of such responsibilities which offers a person real control in their life, and allows her to ultimately stand, quite literally, on her own two feet.

In contrast to the pinched, repressed Gellburg, Hyman *seems* full of life–a romantic hero, who even rides a horse. But Hyman informs us that doctors are often "defective," and we should look for his defect. Hyman is a selfish man, and though he has a capacity to enjoy life, he is dissatisfied with the quality of that life, which leads him to flirtation and adultery. As a doctor, Hyman may understand his insecurities as much as he fears them, but he is unable to do more than build a smoke screen with that knowledge, because he is unable to make any real connection. He admires Sylvia's sense of connection and is drawn to it, but how she achieves it is a mystery to him. Hyman is left hanging at the close as an illustration of those individuals for whom answers are ever out of sight, despite their ability to ask questions, because of a fundamental lack of commitment in their lives. Hyman acts at being a part of the community by taking on a neighborhood practice, but as his wife points out: "Why, I don't know—we never invite anybody, we never go out, all our friends are in Manhattan" (6). His capacity to create illusions makes him attractive, but it also leads him to hide from certain necessary truths, such as what was going on in Germany.

Hyman has a reductive level of response to everything by which he tries to recast every complex situation into overly simplistic terms. This precludes any necessity for deep commitment and leads to an easier (if somewhat shallow) life. When problems loom, be it his wife's displeasure or Nazi oppression, he creates an illusion to protect himself and prevent him from having to address the problem. His diagnoses tend toward inaccuracy, as he simplifies issues to suit his own narrow, personal view of the world. Telling Sylvia to focus her concentration on her legs to awaken their power, and Gellburg to show his wife a little more love are inadequate responses to the true difficulties this couple face, and show him up as a poor physician.

Margaret and Harriet are relatively minor characters, but each allows us to learn more about the background of the major figures in the play to whom they are related. It is through Margaret and her constant suspicions of her husband that we recognize Hyman's history of infidelity and true lack of social commitment. It is through Harriet's gossiping that we get closer to the truth of Sylvia and Gellburg's relationship. As a character, Stanton Case, Gellburg's ruthless boss, seems stereotyped as the WASP (White Anglo-Saxon Protestant) anti-Semite, a not-so-subtle inversion of the more usually stereotyped minority, such as the Jew. He passes his time at the yachting club while Gellburg does his dirty work, then discards the Jew swiftly after his usefulness is over. He illustrates the strong presence of American anti-Semitism in the 1930s.

HISTORICAL CONTEXT

Although he did not experience anti-Semitism directly as a child, Miller was aware of its presence. Asking for a library ticket at the age of six, Miller panicked over saying his father's obviously Jewish name, and recognized the difficulty of trying to guard against the randomness of such evils as anti-Semitism. At the age of ten, feeling overlooked after his brother's bar mitzvah, Miller decided to punish his family by running away from home in the style of the heroes he had read about in books. He took his bike north into Harlem, a heavily African American neighborhood, but never once felt intimidated. In his 1987 autobiography, *Timebends*, Miller cites this experience as lying at the heart of his belief in the intrinsic human bond and affinity between all people, regardless of their ethnicity.

Miller sees racism as having its roots in a fear we should strive to overcome, for to belittle the humanity of others can only restrict the life of the self. While people's ethnicity may make their surfaces appear different, they are all ultimately a part of the same race—the human race. In later years Miller would be horrified at America's refusal to offer the Jews more help during World War II. In this refusal, he recognized America's internal tendency toward racism, and felt that it was a betrayal of the country's own pretensions toward democracy. Miller wants his writing to be accessible to all people, mediating between different types to allow them to feel what he calls, "The universality of human beings, their common emotions and ideas" (*Timebends* 1987, 83). Miller believes this will strengthen American democracy as it makes people aware of their connections to others. A love of, and fierce belief in, democracy lies behind much of Miller's work.

Miller sees Nazism as defined by its strong conformist pressure, chilling technological power, and erosion of autonomy—all of which led to people being stripped of their humanity. Miller resists such forces, just as he insists the Nazi regime should have been resisted. Believing strongly that an event like the Holocaust involves everyone, Miller insists there can be no turning away without cost. The denial, resignation, or ignorance we observe in *Broken Glass* is tantamount to complicity. Nonaction, Miller informs us, whatever its rationale, becomes destructive when it allows certain other actions to occur. Thus the issue of potency versus impotency is central to the play. Though represented mainly by its sexual connotation, Miller wishes the implication to spill into every aspect of life. What use is Doctor Harry Hyman's evident potency when he himself is incapable of true commitment or fidelity to either his culture or his wife? What value is Phillip Gellburg's commercial success when he understands so little of who he is and what he does? What use is even Sylvia Gellburg's compassion when she has lost touch with her own selfhood so much that she no longer retains even the capacity to stand?

Though set in 1938 in the wake of Kristallnacht, *Broken Glass* responds to problems which have not evaporated for 1990s audiences, but become more urgent. The notion of difference, when pursued too stringently and unalloyed with the acceptance of universal humanity, can lead to unnecessary fragmentation, harmful restrictions of the individual, and the destruction of society as a whole. Written in the shadow of atrocities in Rwanda and Bosnia, *Broken Glass* conveys the necessity of a humanistic response to the contemporary world we inhabit.

THEMATIC ISSUES IN *AFTER THE FALL* AND *BROKEN GLASS*

One issue which concerns Miller in these plays is the way human beings, for all their power of speech, are often poor communicators. Quentin and Louise, in *After the Fall*, live on in a pointless marriage because neither has the courage to admit the truth. Indeed, Quentin has had difficulty honestly communicating with everyone in his life up until the hopeful exception of Holga. And though Sylvia, in *Broken Glass*, finally speaks openly and directly to her husband, we must remember that this is only after twenty years of self-imposed silence. Gellburg and Hyman are equally self-restricted in their attempts to communicate. At one point, Gellburg dismisses Hyman, mainly as a result of self-consciousness regarding his impotency. Hyman's passionate response, instead of calming Gellburg, serves to make him more uneasy. Failing to communicate, Hyman does not react to Gellburg's fears but his own; he feels guilty for having flirted with Sylvia and thinks Gellburg may suspect. Each isolates himself from the other by his own self-involvement, and confusion results as each fails to recognize the other's feelings of guilt and inadequacy. It is such failures of communication that lie at the heart of both plays' aura of ambiguity.

Quentin, Louise, and the Gellburgs avoid their personal needs and fears by immersing themselves in work or the home. Their problems fester and grow, nurtured by their mutual silence. Each secretly holds the other to blame: Quentin sees his wife Louise as unsupportive, and she sees him as condescending and neglectful; Gellburg sees Sylvia as emasculating, and she sees him as tyrannical. None of them are fully honest or supportive of their partners. Quentin does not allow Louise to understand his fears or listen to her complaints, and Gellburg is too involved in his own divisions to tell Sylvia how much he loves her or allow her the freedom she wants. Louise feels neglected and used, but instead of talking to her husband, turns to a psychiatrist. Sylvia, having married a provider for the sake of her family, is full of regret, but instead of speaking out, maintains a twenty-year silence during which she helps drive her husband to impotency.

Also central to both plays are the issues of guilt, blame, responsibility, and how these relate to a person's identity. The characters in *Broken Glass* either deny guilt or are crippled by it, and consequently, are all uncertain of who they are. The play is set in an alienating period to emphasize this problem of identity. But *After the Fall*, set in the 1960s, seems more optimistic in that it sets out to show how one can go on, as Quentin does, with guilt, having accepted blame and whatever responsibilities go with such an acceptance. After the Holocaust, Miller realized that everyone is capable of evil, and so demands that everyone be partly responsible for any evil that is performed in the world.

Miller sees the American tendency toward denial as self-destructive, and through *After the Fall* asks people to accept guilt for the world's evil. That evil is represented in the play by the continual presence in the background of a death camp watchtower. Miller wants us to know that while remaining connected can bring suffering, it is necessary to remain human. Quentin confesses his sins and conquers denial, reconnecting his life and forging a self-identity with which he can continue to live. He learns what Miller sees as the lesson of the Holocaust.

Miller believes that events such as the Holocaust involve everyone, and we need to be aware and potent to effectively combat such evil forces. This is done by enforcing a continual recognition of self and community, and the history of both. Those who balance self-awareness with connection to others will live with dignity and direction. Through this they may also discover the stability they desire to survive contentedly in an alienating, fragmented world. This is the goal of Quentin's search in *After the Fall*, and the exploration of identity in *Broken Glass*. Both plays explore the necessary balance between self-awareness (individual identity) and a sense of security through connection to others (social identity), which allow us to live better lives. Sylvia Gellburg, like Quentin, ultimately accepts her guilt and achieves this balance, quite literally being able to rise to her feet at the close of the play.

Broken Glass is centered on people's search for a positive, sustaining identity, because people must define themselves before they can become productive members of a community. Neither Gellburg nor Hyman fully achieve this feat, as each is too concerned with his own self-image. Although the people in *Broken Glass* are Jewish, Miller wants them to be considered universals; a man like Gellburg may have problems as a Jew, but they stem from his problems as a human being. The essential nature of Gellburg's dilemma, resting on uncertainties regarding his own nature and worth, is faced by Americans from all kinds of backgrounds. To discover who he would like to be, Gellburg must put his Jewish heritage into perspective; he must learn to balance his ethnicity with his self-identification as an American citizen. In this way, he can come to accept a positive self-image which combines individual and social needs. To strive for a kind of dual identity, which allows for both an individual and a social self, is the best road to contentment. The attainment of this kind of self-identification becomes a worthwhile lesson in self-acceptance, tolerance, and understanding.

LITERARY DEVICES AND CRAFT

After the Fall is a highly experimental piece, as its form, presentation, and setting display. During the play, characters move around an eerie-looking split-level setting, appearing and disappearing as one scene leads into another to keep the action fluid, and in an effort to create the fits and starts of a person's memory. The action jumps back and forth in time and is intentionally confusing, just as Quentin's recollections pour in on him and prevent him from following a strictly chronological timeline. Various scenes get interrupted by outside characters who could not have been present at that specific event, as Quentin makes connections between what people in his life have said and done from his early years up to the current moment. Ultimately one senses a kind of progression, as Quentin tries to cover what he sees as the most formative events of his life, in order to decide where next to go.

Among the play's central symbols are those of the death camp tower and the idiot child. While the death camp tower acts as a reminder of the constant presence of evil in the world, the idea of the idiot, initially a contemptuous accusation on the lips of Rose, Louise, and Maggie toward their respective husbands, becomes a more positive image. It is Holga's dream of the idiot child which puts it into perspective, for Holga manages to recognize that the child represents those parts of a person they wish to dismiss, but should embrace as part of the whole. Therefore, it becomes evident that despite constant attacks on their self-esteem by those around them, both Quentin and his father need to embrace themselves for the people they are if they wish to gain contentment.

While the title *After the Fall* conveys Miller's recognition that we live in a world after the fall from innocence, when evil has become patently manifest in both major events like the Holocaust, as well as the numerous personal betrayals of everyday people, the title *Broken Glass* can be interpreted in a variety of ways. It is certainly intended to bring to mind the shattered glass of Kristallnacht, when, as part of their riot against the Jews, Germans broke the windows in Jewish homes, businesses, and synagogues. It may even allude to the glass which the bridegroom breaks at a Jewish wedding ceremony, and so refer to the Gellburgs' marriage itself, which in this play is in dire trouble. The various rabbinical explanations for the breaking of the glass—from being a reminder of the destruction of the temple in Jerusalem, to a symbol of our imperfect world—all involve sadness. This symbol of sadness, so prominently displayed on a joyous occasion, serves as a reminder of the duality of human existence. We may celebrate, but others are mourning; we may enjoy peace, but others are suffering war. Our response to this should be to accept that the world is not perfect, without giving up on our efforts to make it perfect. This is a lesson both Gellburgs need to learn, having each been resentfully trapped for years in a stifling marriage which neither has attempted to improve. Indeed, they could almost be pictured as living in some kind of glass bell jar which becomes shattered by the close of the play, when they finally break out of their self-imposed silence and begin to honestly communicate with each other.

There are many other symbolic elements in *Broken Glass*, such as Sylvia's physical paralysis, which represents the moral paralysis of many Americans in the face of the Holocaust; horrified by the reality of what was happening, it became far easier to pretend that nothing was happening at all. Doctor Hyman, whose numerous associations with sexuality (through his name, sexual history, and predilection for horse riding), cuts an ironic image in that his apparent potency is discovered to be a farce—he has a barren marriage, a chronically suspicious wife, and is unable to accurately diagnose or cure either of the Gellburgs. There is also Gellburg's whole appearance, with his pale face and black dress, which depicts the sheer lack (and fear) of life with which his character is afflicted.

ALTERNATE PERSPECTIVE: A READER-RESPONSE APPROACH

Reader-response criticism emerged in the 1970s as a reaction against the entirely textually based "new criticism" then popular, which refused to consider anything outside the text as relevant to an analysis—neither the author's intention nor the reader's response—and would only look at relationships between elements they could find within the text that they felt gave it its own distinctive character or form, such as repeated words or symbols. Reader-response critics go beyond the text, focusing on what texts do to the mind of the reader; concentration is fixed on what a text does, rather than what it is. By asking that we view literature subjectively rather than objectively, we become active rather than passive readers. Any text is seen as incomplete without a reader, although effective readings are expected to conform to certain elements in the text, and should not stray too far into new territory. Despite the flexibility of the reader-response approach, it is possible to arrive at an inappropriate or incorrect reading if it cannot be supported by the text. Reader-response critics have taken varying stances regarding how meaning is controlled: some believing it to be done by the text itself (which directs the reader toward certain reactions); some seeing each individual reading as unique; and others seeing the existence of a community of readers whose similar reactions define a common cultural ground—all three approaches can be rewarding.

Drama in particular lends itself to reader-response, as many playwrights, including Miller, see theater as an art form in which the audience completes the text through their presence and response. Furthermore, if texts, as the reader-response approach implies, only have importance while they are being read, then *when* they are read is a major determinant in their meaning, and they will read differently from one time to another (so a 1960s play may contain different meanings for a 1990s audience). This constantly changing aspect of the text again lends itself to drama, since every performance is necessarily unique. A typical reader-response strategy is to first consider your own response, then look to see if there is anything in the work which has shaped that response, and finally assess how others might respond.

It seems obvious to read *After the Fall* and *Broken Glass* as confessions in which various characters ask for our judgment, but on closer inspection we should realize that these characters have already come to terms with their guilt; indeed, that is the thrust of both plays' action. What Miller wants is to draw audiences in to recognize their own guilt and complicity in terms of the denials and betrayals with which we continually live; this we may only do by analyzing our own responses to these plays. Miller's strategy is not immediately apparent, as he teaches these lessons by presenting us with our past, and leaving us to make the connection to our present.

Rather than responding directly to social issues contemporary to their production, *After the Fall* and *Broken Glass* appear to be anachronistic, or at least nostalgic plays, and therefore "safe" to watch as they will not make high moral demands of their audiences. *After the Fall*, written during the Vietnam conflict and at the height of civil rights activity, seems to ignore these events and turn its attention to the previous three decades which witnessed the Great Depression, the Holocaust, and the machinations of HUAC. Similarly, *Broken Glass*, coming out of the troubled 1990s, looks back to the late 1930s as World War II gains impetus and the Nazis prepare to take over Europe while America looks on in disbelief. But Miller is not escaping to the past so much as using it to offer commentary and a useful lesson with how we can deal with contemporary difficulties. By following how Quentin and the Gellburgs face up to disturbing elements in their lives, we may learn how to apply the same strategies to our own.

Despite their historical appearance and close involvement with the past, both plays deal with contemporary issues on a universal rather than particularistic level. Issues of denial, guilt, betrayal, and the casual brutality of the human race firmly connect Vietnam, civil rights, and more recent atrocities in Rwanda and Afghanistan to the events of *After the Fall* and *Broken Glass*. Our response to the difficulties we see in these plays reflects our response to our contemporary social problems, and all too often, Miller tells us, our complete denial and refusal of responsibility. It is all too human a reaction to accept, promote, and believe in comfortable illusions rather than harsher truths, but Miller insists it is an abdication of moral duty to do so.

The response of many to *After the Fall* is to dismiss it as painfully autobiographical, and given the nature of Quentin's confessions, too exhibitionist to be seriously considered. People have objected especially to Miller's portrayal of Maggie, whom they take to be an unflattering and tasteless portrait of Marilyn

Monroe. But such hostile reactions to *After the Fall* tell us more about the audience's needs than anything the play depicts. Many Americans feel a need to make Marilyn Monroe into a perfect icon—the ideal, desirable women, who can reflect the possibility of an ideal world—and they become angry when Miller undermines this image with his portrait of a flawed and damaged human being.

However, Miller's Maggie is nearer the true Monroe, and actually allows her far more human complexity than the stylized icon which has been built up by the media. The world is not perfect, and to try to pretend that it is by creating a perfect, female icon, is a potentially dangerous form of denial—far worse than anything Quentin does. He learns to recognize the existence of flaws in himself and others, through Holga's assistance, and embraces his own "idiot child." By accepting some responsibility for the evil that goes on around him, and acknowledging that perfection is largely an illusion, Quentin no longer hides in paralyzing denial and is able to get on with his life. To dismiss *After the Fall* as confessional autobiography is shortsighted, as it prevents us from acknowledging the wisdom which lies within the play. Although not seen as autobiographical, reactions to *Broken Glass* betray similar prejudices on the part of the audience.

Many early reviews of *Broken Glass* relate how dissatisfied critics felt on leaving the theater, but rather than a failing of the play, this could be taken as an indication of its true effectiveness. As a playwright, Miller intends to discomfort his audience: the repetition of the eerie cello music before each scene is an indication of this. There is a sense of menace from the start, as the strident cello begins its pulsing rhythms. In *Timebends*, Miller points out how audiences, in America particularly, have a tendency to resist plays which challenge and ask them to judge themselves. Maybe the final dissatisfaction with *Broken Glass* stems from learning that this menace is not so much the expected Nazism, as it is the common failings within each and every one of us, all too often preventing us from fully connecting with our fellow human beings. After all, the lesson of Kristallnacht, which should have warned people about what was happening to Jews in Germany, was not heeded until *after* the elimination of six million Jews—there is a guilt attached to that neglect which we all must continue to share, and from which we can learn. The Gellburgs may begin to uncover the roots of their problems, but they are still a long way toward solving them. Sylvia regains her feet by the close of the play and seems to have regained her sense of balance; however, although she stands, it remains unclear as to what she stands for, and to where her first steps might lead. Miller is suggesting that it is partly the audience's responsibility to help create a world in which Sylvia can safely walk.

Sylvia's paralysis is a reflection of the moral paralysis many of us experience in the face of continuing human atrocities. Miller warns us against a paralysis of spirit which seems to have become as much national policy as personal inclination, and indirectly asks us to do something about it before it is too late. *After the Fall* and *Broken Glass* are plays which insist on involving their audiences: Quentin's whole delivery to the supposed "Listener" is nothing more than a direct address to the audience seated before him. Each play asks its audience to reconsider its own sense of responsibility, and though audiences often do not want to accept the responsibility Miller asks them to take on, such resistance only offers proof of Miller's accusations that our current society dangerously relies too much on denial to survive.

7

House Un-American Activities Committee: *The Crucible* (1953)

The Crucible is Miller's most resilient play, in that its sheer craft makes it nearly impossible to turn out a bad production, and that its subject and theme continually fascinate audiences throughout the world. Being one of the easiest to perform, it has consequently been the most performed of his plays. It tells the story behind the Salem witch trials of 1692, centering our attention on the effect these trials had on the Proctor family, as well as making an analogous critical commentary on the actions of the House Un-American Activities Committee (HUAC) in the 1950s. Despite its later success, the play's initial reception was poor, but this may have been partly a fear of the repercussions of liking a play which was critical of current politics. Audiences cheered "Bravo!" at the end of its premier performances, but many critics were quick to condemn both play and playwright. *The Crucible* first appeared in January 1953, but it was not until the 1960s that it became widely popular, needing some separation of time from the "communist hunts" of HUAC, against which it so bravely spoke.

The printed play contains extensive notes detailing the historical background of Salem society in the 1690s, and detailed facts regarding the actual lives of the main characters involved. Miller wanted his critics to know that he had not made up these events, but that people really allowed such things to occur. These notes illustrate the extensive research which Miller undertook to write *The Crucible*. The following plot and setting outline concentrates on the performed text, although Miller's notes are referenced in other sections of the chapter.

SETTING AND PLOT DEVELOPMENT

The Crucible is set in the spring of 1692, in Salem, Massachusetts, which is described as a newly founded, small, religiously devout township. A communal society has formed, which has allowed the church to have political control to help it attain the discipline necessary for survival. Salemites are naturally suspicious of individuality, seeing it as a threat to their imposed sense of order. They have worked hard to survive, constantly threatened by the surrounding wilderness. Concentrating on survival has left them little opportunity to misbehave, but ironically, although their recent ancestors came to this land to avoid persecution, they have become an intolerant society, and are constantly judging each other's behavior. Their way of life is strict and somber, and the witch trials will offer them a release of pent-up frustration and emotion. Under the guise of morality, they will be given the opportunity to express envy of and hostility toward their neighbors, and take vengeance.

The play begins in the bedroom of Reverend Samuel Parris's daughter, Betty. It is a sparse Puritan room, purely functional with no extraneous decoration. Parris kneels in prayer, weeping at the bedside of his ten-year-old daughter, who is in some sort of coma. The family slave, Tituba, fearfully joins them, but despite her evident concern, is immediately sent away. Parris allows entry to his teenage niece, Abigail Williams, and young Susanna Walcott, a servant who has been sent by the doctor for information on Betty's condition. Susanna tells Parris that the doctor suspects witchcraft, a suggestion which, as the community's leading religious figure, worries Parris, and he sends her away. Although he insists that "unnatural causes" cannot be at fault, he has already sent for an outsider, the Reverend Hale, to look into such possibilities.

Prior to Betty's coma, Parris caught her and Abigail dancing "like heathens" in the forest. The shock of discovery caused Betty to faint, and she has not regained consciousness. Parris is more worried about how his enemies may use this against him than he is about his daughter's health. He presses Abigail for more details about their exploits, but she insists they were only dancing. Abigail was dismissed from the Proctors' service seven months prior, and although she insists it was maliciousness on Elizabeth Proctor's part, Parris is suspicious of Abigail's behavior. Ann and Thomas Putnam, a village couple respected more for their wealth than sensibility, arrive with stories of Betty flying like a witch, clearly determined to believe the worst. Their daughter, Ruth, is also behaving strangely, neither eating nor talking, as if she were a sleepwalker. Both are highly superstitious and want this to be witchcraft, ignoring Parris's requests for them not to jump to wild conclusions. Ann Putnam lost seven babies prior to Ruth, an occurrence not uncommon in the seventeenth century, but is determined to blame someone. She had sent Ruth to Tituba, whom she believes to have supernatural powers (mostly because she is a black foreigner), to discover who "murdered" her babies.

The Putnams press Parris to publicly declare that witchcraft is involved, but he is reluctant because he sees this as reflecting badly upon himself; however, he agrees to lead the gathering villagers in a prayer. These three leave, and Abigail remains to talk with the Putnams' servant, Mercy Lewis, who had entered just before the others left. Mercy came to tell them Ruth had shown signs of life by sneezing, but it is an excuse to check on Betty. They are joined by another teenager, Mary Warren, who replaced Abigail as the Proctors' servant. The girls discuss what really went on in the forest, which was more than innocent dancing—Mercy had been naked, and Abigail had drunk blood to make a revengeful spell against Elizabeth Proctor. Mary Warren had only watched the others, but she is the most fearful of what will happen once the truth comes out. Abigail shakes Betty and threatens her with violence to wake her out of her stupor, and Betty momentarily revives. She tries to fly out of the window, but is held back by Abigail who threatens them all not to give anything away. Betty reverts to her coma as John Proctor enters. He has come to fetch Mary, who had been ordered not to leave the house.

Proctor sends Mary home, and Mercy follows her out, leaving he and Abigail together. Abigail is attracted to Proctor, and as she flirts with him, we see him initially flirt back, but her desire for him becomes overwhelming, and he tries to behave in a more austere manner. Abigail tells him that no witchcraft is involved in the girls' behavior, but is angered by his insistence that he will have nothing more to do with her. They have had relations in the past, and Abigail refuses to believe that Proctor does not prefer her to his wife, even though he insists that she give up such hopes. By insulting his wife, Abigail pushes Proctor too far, and he physically shakes her in warning.

A hymn about Jesus drifts in from outside, and Betty begins to scream. Parris, the Putnams, and Mercy Lewis rush in to see what is happening, shortly joined by two respected elders of the village, Rebecca Nurse and Giles Corey. Rebecca calms Betty down with her presence, and suggests that the children's odd behavior is childish mischief which they would do best to ignore. Proctor is angered by the belief of Parris and the Putnams that devils are present, and accuses Parris of being a poor preacher. They begin to squabble viciously, with Parris accusing Proctor of being one in a faction against him, while Rebecca tries to calm them down. As soon as she resolves one argument, they find another to pursue, and they are all arguments involving property rather than religion. As Putnam threatens to serve a writ on Proctor and Giles for stealing his lumber, Reverend John Hale arrives.

Hale's serious attitude calms tempers, and Proctor leaves as Hale begins to examine Betty. Hale insists they forget their superstitions and accept his authority in matters of the Devil; they agree and proceed to inform him of their suspicions. Rebecca disapproves of the malicious tone of these proceedings and leaves, while Giles questions Hale about his wife Martha's tendency to read books. Parris and Hale question Abigail about the children's exploits in the forest, and she accuses Tituba, saying that the slave called the Devil and made her drink blood. Tituba is brought in. She declares that she has nothing to do with the Devil, but was making a charm for Abigail. Defensively, Abigail accuses Tituba of lying and all kinds of evil, and the adults take Abigail's side. Hale insists that Tituba wake up Betty, and threatens her with death. Tituba tries to escape by suggesting that someone else is "witchin' these children," and in her fear, allows them to lead her into confessing complicity with the Devil to save her own life, and to name others who are supposedly witches, such as Sarah Good and Goody Osburn. Abigail joins in and names others, and Betty rouses to add more names as the adults scurry to arrest the accused.

Act 2 begins eight days later in the Proctors' house. The initial stage business tells us much about the Proctors. In contrast to Parris, the self-absorbed parent, we hear the caring Elizabeth singing her children to sleep. As John Proctor enters, he furtively adds salt to the stew on the fire, showing he has a different taste to that of his wife, and yet he will compliment her on her seasoning upon eating the stew, which implies that he wants to make her happy, but also is capable of a mild deception. Elizabeth joins her husband, and serves his meal while they discuss the crops.

There is some tension between the two; both speak and behave overcautiously with each other. Proctor wishes Elizabeth to be warmer toward him, while she is suspicious that he has been seeing more of Abigail. Their servant, Mary, now an official of the court which has been set up in town to try the accused, has found the confidence to openly defy her employers and leave the house whenever she wants. Matters have escalated, and there are now fourteen people in jail faced with hanging unless they confess to witchcraft. The town supports the trials, as Abigail leads the other girls to accuse more people. Elizabeth, knowing Abigail's deviousness, asks Proctor to try to stop this dangerous nonsense, but he is uncertain that anyone will believe him if he denounces Abigail. Elizabeth responds with suspicion and jealousy, believing it to be Proctor's feelings for Abigail which prevent him from going, but Proctor responds angrily since he feels her suspicions are unfounded and becoming tiresome. Mary appears to deflate their argument with her arrival.

Mary gives Elizabeth a small rag doll, called a poppet, which she made in court. If the accused confess their allegiance with the Devil, they go to jail, but if they refuse to confess, they are hanged as unrepentant witches; a declaration of innocence carries little weight. Mary and the other girls have accused twenty-five more people, and the court has declared that Goody Osburn must hang. Hysteria seems to be sweeping the town, with the girls allowing their imaginations to run riot, inventing offenses, and seeing evil in innocent gestures. Sarah Good was condemned a witch for not being able to name the Ten Commandments. Even Elizabeth has come under suspicion (both the Proctors suspect this is from accusations by Abigail), but the court dismissed the idea when Mary defended her. Mary is realizing the power she now wields, and it gives her new confidence.

After Mary has gone to bed, the Proctors seriously worry about what might happen. Elizabeth asks Proctor to go to Abigail, knowing that Abigail is plotting to get rid of her to take her place, and that she is in danger. Elizabeth wants Proctor to make sure Abigail knows he will not allow this, hoping this will stop her. Proctor agrees to go, just as Hale arrives, looking guilty. Hale is unsure of the girls' accusations, and is investigating further, having just come from Rebecca whom, on examination, he cannot believe is involved in witchcraft. However, he is convinced that witchcraft is about, and he questions the Proctors involved their religious adherence. Proctor's church attendance has been poor, and his third son was never baptized. This is because of his dislike of Parris, but Hale sees it in a more sinister light. Hale asks Proctor to name the Ten Commandments, but Proctor significantly forgets "adultery," until delicately reminded by his wife, which gives Hale further misgivings. Elizabeth presses Proctor to tell Hale about Abigail's admission that there was no witchcraft going on. Hale is shocked and asks Proctor to testify to this in open court, but Proctor is sensibly reluctant, for it will be his word against Abigail's. Hale is suspicious of the Proctors' refusal to believe that witchcraft is present in Salem, seeing such a belief as ungodly.

They are interrupted by Giles and Francis Nurse, arriving to announce that their wives have been arrested on ridiculous charges of witchcraft. This news shakes Hale, but he insists they accept the justice of the court, and allow no one to be above suspicion. Marshal Herrick arrives with his men to arrest Elizabeth, asking to search for a poppet which he has been told is Elizabeth's, and proves her witchery. Abigail has stuck herself with a needle and declared that Elizabeth sent a spirit to do this; they find a needle sticking in the poppet. When fetched, Mary explains that the poppet and needle are hers, but they still aim to take Elizabeth. Proctor rips their warrant and sends them away, but Elizabeth offers to go rather than cause trouble. Proctor promises to free her shortly, and they take her off in chains. Giles and Proctor urge Hale to see the girls' accusations as the vengeful frauds they are, but Hale stands firm that such confusion would not have fallen on the town if all were innocent. In the guilt of his recent adultery, Proctor falls quiet. As the rest leave, Proctor remains with Mary, whom he insists must speak to the court to clear Elizabeth, but Mary refuses because she is scared of what Abigail can do to her. Proctor says he is prepared to confess his own adultery if it will help to destroy the court's faith in Abigail and free his wife.

At this point, there is an additional scene between acts 2 and 3 which is not always included. It was added by Miller toward the end of the initial Broadway run to try to better explain Abigail. Taking place five weeks after Elizabeth has been arrested, the day before she goes to trial, Proctor has arranged to secretly meet Abigail to warn her to tell the truth or he will expose her. But Abigail refuses, believing she has a hold over Proctor, and that he wants his wife to die so he can have her. He threatens to confess their adultery, but she does not believe him, and leaves. Abigail is close to madness in this scene; she has a deep passion for Proctor, and has convinced herself that the others are witches out to hurt her. Her body is covered in scars that she says have been caused by spirits, but which Miller leads us to realize are self-inflicted.

In act 3, we move to an anteroom outside the courtroom, but not into the court itself. Miller is not interested in the proceedings as much as the motivations behind them, and the fears of those involved. We hear Judge Hathorne questioning Martha Corey in the adjacent courtroom, but our attention is focused on her husband, Giles, who tries to speak the truth to save his wife and is brought into the anteroom by the judges for questioning. Governor Danforth, leading the panel of judges, demands Giles be less disruptive and offer his evidence in a proper affidavit. Meanwhile, Francis Nurse, whose wife, Rebecca, has been condemned, insists to the shocked judges that the girls are deceiving frauds. They threaten him with contempt, but he stands firm. Proctor enters with Mary, who has taken sick absence from court for the last week. After being constantly encouraged by Proctor, she has agreed to tell the truth about the girls' deceit.

Although Hathorne and Parris are against even considering that the girls are lying, Danforth, although suspicious, does listen. He questions Proctor regarding his motivation for presenting Mary, fearing Proctor is trying to undermine the court, rather than just save his wife. Danforth has jailed and condemned many on the word of the girls, and he is loathe to accept that he has been deceived, as it would badly affect his authority. We learn that Elizabeth has declared herself pregnant, although the judges are unsure whether or not to believe her. Proctor insists that this must be so because his wife would never lie. To test him, they offer to let Elizabeth live to have their child if Proctor will drop his protest, but in all conscience he finds he cannot, as too many other innocents are condemned. Danforth is angry at this threat to his court, but agrees to hear Proctor's deposition.

Proctor begins by offering a list which Francis has compiled of locals who have signed to declare their good opinion of Elizabeth, Rebecca, and Martha. At Parris's insistence, and to Francis's dismay, the judges agree that all these people will be arrested for examination. Next, Proctor offers Giles's deposition accusing Thomas Putnam of prompting his daughter to cry witchery on people to get their property. Danforth insists that Giles name the witness who heard Putnam betray this. Knowing that to name the man would send him to jail, Giles refuses, despite Danforth's threats. Hale reasons with Danforth, explaining that the people's fear of court is understandable, but Danforth strongly objects to such reasoning and arrests Giles for contempt.

Proctor turns to Mary, reminding her to tell the truth. Hale asks Danforth to pay close attention to this charge and allow proper lawyers to present it. He is having doubts about some of the people he has helped condemn to die. Danforth refuses to allow any lawyers, and he, Hathorne, Parris, and Hale all read Mary's deposition while the others nervously wait. Danforth harshly questions Mary, and points out that she has condemned herself to jail for lying either then or now, but Mary stands firm. Susanna Walcott, Mercy Lewis, Betty Parris, and Abigail are brought in to face their accuser, and Danforth asks them for their response. Abigail insists that Mary is lying, and is questioned further. Her answers divert the men to argue over Elizabeth's poppet, but Proctor redirects their attention to Abigail, insisting she is trying to murder his wife. His accusations of Abigail laughing during services and leading the girls to dance naked begin to have some affect on Danforth. Hathorne steps in and asks Mary to show how she pretends to faint in court, but Mary cannot do this without the proper atmosphere, which restores the judges' belief that she is the one lying.

Danforth asks Abigail if the spirits were real, but her vehement insistence on her own innocence weakens his resolve. Abigail acts out that Mary has sent a spirit against her, and the other girls join in, shivering and accusing Mary. Mary becomes hysterical, beginning to lose control, so Proctor attacks Abigail directly, calling her a whore and confessing his adultery. Abigail denies the charge, so Danforth calls for Elizabeth (whom Proctor has told us never lies) to support Proctor's accusation. Not knowing that her husband has confessed, Elizabeth cannot publicly betray him, so she lies and declares no adultery took place. Hale suggests that this is "a natural lie to tell," but Danforth is firm, and decides it must be Proctor who has lied. To seal his decision, Abigail and her followers once more pretend that Mary's spirit is attacking them, drawing the judges into their performance. Mary is reduced to a whimpering heap, and under threats from Danforth and continued pressure from the girls, cries out against Proctor to save herself. All the judges except Hale (who now denounces the proceedings) are convinced by this performance, and have Proctor arrested.

Act 4 takes place three months later inside the jail where a drunken Marshal Herrick moves Sarah Good and Tituba (both confessed witches who escaped hanging, but now languish in jail) to make space for the judges to meet. Ironically, Sarah and Tituba call to the Devil to take them from jail, which they see as hell. Many are to hang this morning, and Herrick's drunkenness indicates a dissatisfaction with his involvement. Parris and Hale are praying with the condemned, and Danforth and Hathorne are concerned. They are unsure of Hale's support, and suspect that Parris is losing his grip. Hale is trying to persuade the condemned to confess, in order to save their lives. Parris joins Danforth and Hathorne, and tells them Abigail and Mercy have absconded after stealing his savings. A nearby town, Andover, has been rebelling against the witch courts, and the girls have fled for fear Salem may follow suit and turn on them as instigators. So far, Salem has only hanged disreputable characters, but today they are hanging a formerly respectable group, and are unsure of public reaction. There is the fear of riot, and Parris has had his life threatened; he suggests they postpone the hangings. Danforth refuses any delay.

Twelve people have been executed, and to pardon the next seven accused would cast doubt on the guilt of those already hanged. If one of the seven would confess, it would make the others look guilty, so Danforth suggests using Elizabeth to lead Proctor to confession. Hale pleads with Elizabeth to get Proctor to lie to save his life. She is suspicious of his motives, thinking they are trying to trick her, but offers to speak with her husband. He is brought in, and, as with Elizabeth, we see a change in appearance. Both Proctors are chained, dirty, and gaunt from the bad treatment they have received in jail. They are happy to see each other still alive, and at Hale's request they are left alone to talk.

Elizabeth tells how Giles died under torture, refusing to answer questions so that he could not be found guilty and have his lands forfeited. Proctor suggests to Elizabeth that he may as well confess and continue living, as he feels too dishonest to hang with such morally pure people as Rebecca and Martha. Elizabeth insists that he decide this for himself, but assures him she does not see him as dishonest. She confesses her own feelings of blame in his adultery, because she has been cold to him in the past, and says she trusts him to make the right decision. As Hathorne reenters, Proctor declares he will confess, even though he knows this is wrong, because it is untrue. The judges are elated, and proceed to record his confession.

As they lead Proctor to admit he has bound himself to the Devil, Rebecca is brought in to witness this in the hope she will follow suit. She adamantly refuses, and is shocked that Proctor has agreed. The judges try to get Proctor to damn the others by saying he saw them with the Devil, but to Danforth's displeasure, Proctor refuses to name anyone but himself. They ask him to sign his confession, which he reluctantly does, but then refuses to hand over the document. He has confessed to them before God, and will not allow them to put his confession on public display since he knows it will badly reflect on the others who are condemned. Overwrought, he admits that his confession is a lie. Proctor sees by his own reaction that he is not as morally bad as he believed, and so rips the confession apart, deciding to die beside the others rather than become a hypocrite. Danforth orders all seven to be hanged at once, and Herrick escorts Proctor and Rebecca outside. Parris and Hale beg Elizabeth to get Proctor to change his mind, but despite the pain she feels at losing him, she honors his decision to die for his beliefs, and refuses. The curtain falls to the sound of the drums heralding the executions. In an afterword, Miller relates subsequent events, in which Parris is forced from office, Abigail becomes a Boston prostitute, and Elizabeth eventually remarries. Twenty years after these proceedings, the government awarded compensation to the victims still living, and to the families of the dead.

CHARACTER DEVELOPMENT

Although the original John Proctor was not a major figure in the Salem trials, Miller's Proctor is the central protagonist of *The Crucible*. Proctor represents the voice of common sense in the play, being rightly skeptical of the whole procedure. A freer thinker than many of his neighbors, he consistently insists that the whole idea of witchery is a sham. However, this is a period of time when common sense has flown out of the window, and his skepticism only works against him, making him appear more suspicious to the biased judges.

Proctor dislikes Reverend Parris, seeing him as materialistic and insufficiently godly, and refuses to attend his church or have his third son baptized. These honest reactions to Parris, and the evident conviction Proctor shows in his beliefs, also work against him. Proctor is very human and not without fault; not only is he impatient and quick to anger, but he has committed adultery in the past with Abigail. However, he is fully repentant, and Miller expects us to forgive him his lapse, even if he cannot do so himself. He definitely loves his wife, Elizabeth; he is keen to please her, and does everything he can to save her once she has been arrested, even to the point of endangering himself.

Proctor faces the dilemma of the innocent person who must falsely confess to a crime in order to save his own life. He considers telling this lie because he feels guilty over an adultery for which he has not been punished. In sleeping with Abigail, he committed a sin against his own standards of decent conduct, and when Hale suggests that the town is being punished for some secret "abomination," Proctor takes this to heart. He realizes, too, that were it not for his former relationship with Abigail, his wife would not be in danger. When Elizabeth effectively absolves him of his guilt in their final meeting, declaring her faith in his judgment, Proctor can reject the temptation to lie and die with honor.

Proctor's refusal to go along with the confession indicates his awareness that he has a responsibility to himself and his community, and he would rather hang than participate in the false judgment of either. Through Proctor, and the others who die with him, Miller wishes to show the heroism of these victims, leading us to recognize and celebrate the existence in the world of such personal integrity. It will not come as a surprise that when faced by HUAC three years later, just like his hero John Proctor, Miller himself refuses to name names, and accepts the consequences of his refusal.

Elizabeth Proctor, like her husband, is a sensible person, which is why she also finds it hard to believe in witchcraft, a notion which shocks Hale. Although we see her returning her husband's regard, she begins the play angry and suspicious of him, having recently discovered his adultery. She bravely allows herself to be taken to jail, secure in her own feelings of innocence, and because she is later found to be pregnant (evidence that she and Proctor have continued relations since Abigail left their employ), manages to survive a death sentence.

Elizabeth's love for her husband is emphasized by her lying for him about the adultery (her only lie ever) in an effort to save him embarrassment; it is ironic that it is this lie which condemns him in the eyes of the judges. Her suffering in jail has caused her to reflect on her former treatment of Proctor, and in their final meeting she confesses she has been cold toward him in the past, and takes on partial responsibility for driving him into the arms of Abigail. This helps to sufficiently release Proctor from his own guilt in the affair to allow himself to accept death as an honorable man.

Reverend Parris was previously in business in Barbados, and he runs his ministry like a business. He has estranged honest men like John Proctor from his church because of his evident materialism and concentration on negative aspects of their religion. He translates any dissension from his views within his community into personal persecution. As a minister of God he strikes an ungodly figure; He is petulant, selfish, conceited, unmerciful, and awkward in his relationships with others, especially children. Parris's first thought on his daughter's bewitching is how it affects him and his standing in the community. It is he who brings in the witch finders and gets the trials happening, and he is a staunch advocate of condemning anyone the girls name without allowing them any proper defense. Too wrapped up in himself and his image, he learns nothing from these events, and it seems that just shortly afterward, he gets voted out of office and sent away.

The Reverend John Hale begins the play a conceited figure, seeing himself as a superior intellect to these villagers, happily determined to uncover their evil spirits; but, events conspire to make him reassess all of this. The strength of his belief in the world of spirits is tested, and we watch as his convictions are eroded by doubt. Initially, he lets his fascination with devils and witchcraft overwhelm the evidence of his sense, and he allows this to continue past the point when he can stop what he has begun. His questioning comes too late, but it helps to expose the closed logical system of the judges when one of their number turns so strongly against them. In contrast to the other judges, by honestly considering the evidence before him, Hale shows himself to be more rational and conscientious. On having his eyes opened to the deception of the girls, Hale has the courage to denounce the proceedings and redeem himself by trying to save the victims, but he has become too cynical in response. He urges people he knows are innocent to confess in order to save their lives, casting aside any possibility of honor or nobility in such people. He is, in the end, a lost figure, no longer knowing in what he should believe, and unable to understand the nobility in the Proctors' behavior.

Judge Hathorne is described as a "bitter, remorseless" man, and he is certainly more concerned with his own power than he is with uncovering the truth. His refusal to even listen to others makes him contemptible, but Danforth is actually worse. Deputy Governor Danforth is a grave figure, equally determined, but more sophisticated than his fellow judges, which makes him more dangerous. Although he listens to counterarguments, it is not with an open mind, and when he finally hangs the condemned even with full knowledge of their innocence, trying to justify that this is for a higher good, we should recognize in him an evil force. Miller sees him as the "rule-bearer" who fixes boundaries for these proceedings which, in fear and ignorance, he refuses to allow to be crossed. The security he seeks comes at a high price, and he does more evil than he intends merely by refusing to go beyond the narrow boundaries he has set for himself and others.

Thomas Putnam is an example of a sour man filled with grievances against others, most of which have been created by his own imagination, sense of self-importance, or greed. He delights in how having witches present could damage Parris's reputation, for he had wanted the minister's position to go to his wife's brother-on-law, but had been outvoted. It is to satisfy men like him, who have power in Salem because of their wealth, that Parris calls in the witch finders, rather than allow the town to deal with their rebellious children more rationally. Greedy and argumentative, Putnam is not above manipulating truth and law to his own vindictive ends, and it is entirely credible that he has persuaded his daughter, Ruth, to cry out against men whose land he wants to take. His wife, Ann Putnam, is no less self-absorbed and vindictive, and for a religious woman, ascribes far too much value to silly superstition. The Putnams are typical of the worst kind of Puritan, whose religion has become mere show and who live narrow, mercenary, and selfish lives, which ultimately damage themselves as much as their community.

Giles and Martha Corey, along with Rebecca and Francis Nurse, offer the kinder face of Puritanism. Even though Giles may be argumentative, it is without malice, and he has a courage which reminds us of the strength of the pioneer stock from which he sprang. At heart he is a good man, and he dies for his beliefs no less bravely than John Proctor. Martha Corey and Rebecca Nurse are ideal Puritans who live their faith, showing kindness and compassion to others, and displaying a gentleness in their lives which is rightly respected. The fact that such women can be accused of witchcraft and condemned to die helps underline the ludicrousness of the proceedings. Francis Nurse is the opposite of Thomas Putnam, being a man who puts others before himself and lives a genuinely moral life. In the past, Francis has acted as the unofficial judge of town disputes and has been a voice of calm reason, but it is a voice which becomes lost in the hysteria of the moment. The fact that, despite his evident goodness, he is unable to save his wife, displays Miller's concern that goodness and reason are no protection against the forces of evil.

Tituba and Sarah Good confess to witchery rather than hang, and they are readily believed because neither has a good reputation in the town. The first group hanged were of a similar low standing, which is why Salem so easily went along with the judges' decisions. Sarah Good is a vagrant, and as a black foreigner, Tituba has already been judged by this racist township as having an allegiance to dark forces (hence Ann Putnam's assumption that Tituba will be able to summon up her dead children's spirits). The children incorporate Tituba into their nighttime romps, as she holds an even lower status in the community than they, and can offer no threat. These two women survive, but there is no triumph in their survival, for they have lost everything by confessing to something they have not done.

Abigail Williams is the most complex of the girls who cry out against their elders. She has been awakened to her sexuality a few months previously after a brief affair with her former employer, John Proctor, and is no longer content to play the role of meek serving girl. She seems to honestly believe that Elizabeth is her only impediment to a happy future with Proctor. An orphan who has been dependent on her churlish uncle, Parris, Abigail sees in Proctor the first person who treated her as a woman rather than as a childish nuisance. Her desire for him seems to transcend the physical, and she has magnified the importance he holds in her life beyond reasonable expectation.

Evidently still in love with Proctor despite her dismissal (for which she blames his wife), Abigail cleverly uses the town's superstitious leanings to her own advantage, to claim greater respect in the community and revenge herself upon Elizabeth, whom she sees as having "blackened" her name with her dismissal. A master manipulator and actress, Abigail solicits the complicity of many of the town's young girls in accusing numerous townspeople of witchcraft. The way she sacrifices former friends like Tituba to the court, without care, suggests an amorality in her nature. The scene Miller added in which she and Proctor meet even suggests a mental imbalance, as she seems to sincerely believe in her own inventions of witchcraft. She eventually turns on her beloved Proctor in an act of self-preservation, and when the possibility arises of the town turning against the court, she quickly flees, stealing the Reverend Parris's savings on the way, as if to prove what a truly disreputable character she is.

Mercy Lewis, Susanna Walcott, Betty Parris, Ruth Putnam, and Mary Warren are among the young girls who follow Abigail's lead. All have led limited lives up until this point, bullied by employers, forced to be quiet and subservient. Abigail offers them a chance to be at the center of attention, and treated as special. They are attracted to the power they see themselves holding over the townspeople as they offer the judges any names they like. Their deceit in these matters seems clear, partly by Mary's initial confession, and finally by their running away to avoid any repercussions when the villagers start to object.

THEMATIC ISSUES

Miller insists that while McCarthyism, by which HUAC, led by Senator McCarthy, strove to discredit and destroy what it saw as a subversive element in the country, may have been the historical occasion of *The Crucible*, it is not its theme. We need to look beyond specific history for the thematic issues of the play, toward its universal aspects. One issue which concerns Miller is the tension people experience between conscience and their predilection toward selfishness, and the inevitable moral consequences of allowing the latter an upper hand. *The Crucible* exposes the extent to which many people use troubled times, such as the trials, to pursue selfish ends. In contrast to these types, Miller elevates and celebrates people of individual conscience, such as the Nurses and the Proctors, who refuse to do this.

The Crucible depicts how unscrupulous people, from the Putnams to the trial judges, declare the presence of evil and the Devil to cripple whoever disagrees with them, not just religiously, but politically and socially. Such people assume a moral high ground, and anyone who disagrees with them is deemed immoral and damned. Tituba and the children were certainly trying to commune with dark forces, but if left alone, their exploits would have bothered no one—their actions are an indication of the way people react against repression rather than anything truly evil. But Miller does view evil as being at large in the world, and he believes that anyone, even the apparently virtuous, has the potential to be evil given the right circumstances, even though most people would not admit this. Miller offers Proctor as proof: a good man, but one who carries with him the guilt of adultery. But men like Danforth also fit this category, because they do evil deeds under the pretense of being right.

In *The Crucible*, Miller wanted to go beyond the discovery of guilt, which has motivated his plots in many earlier plays, into a study of the results of such guilt. He centers this study on John Proctor, a man with an initially split personality, caught between the way in which others see him and the way he sees himself. His private sense of guilt leads him into an ironically false confession of having committed a public crime, although he later recants. What allows him to recant is the release of guilt given to him by his wife's confession of her coldness and inability to blame him for his adultery. Elizabeth insists that he is a good man, and this finally convinces him that he is.

Miller sees *The Crucible* as being a companion piece to *Death of a Salesman*, in the way both explore the realm of conscience. Through Willy Loman and John Proctor, Miller examines the conflict between a person's deeds and that person's conception of himself. While Loman never resolves this conflict and consequently never discovers who he is, Proctor finally comes to some understanding, evidenced in the way he claims his identity in the form of his "name." In *The Crucible*, Miller explores what happens when people allow others to be the judge of their conscience; in *Death of a Salesman*, the central character does not get this far because Loman refuses to allow his guilt any reality. Both plays explore the social forces which operate on people, to show the falsity of our belief in individual human autonomy. Both Proctor's and Loman's actions are largely dictated by forces outside of themselves, which seem to demand of them reactions and sacrifices they have little choice but to give. Total freedom, Miller suggests, is largely a myth in any working society.

Some critics like to view *The Crucible* as a debate on the theme of marriage, and what a marriage requires to make it work. Issues of trust, love, and what a marriage partner owes the other are all discussed in the play. It is Giles Corey's idle tongue and lack of trust in his wife which gets her hanged. But it is the marriage of John and Elizabeth Proctor which lies at the center of the play, and the love triangle Miller creates between Abigail and the Proctors. When we consider that at the time of writing this play, Miller himself was pursuing an adulterous affair with Marilyn Monroe while still married to Mary Slattery, it is unsurprising that such issues would have been on his mind. Although John and Elizabeth love each other, seven months before the play began, he had an affair with their serving girl, Abigail. Abigail has been sent away, but trust between the married couple is gone. Miller depicts the toll this places on the Proctors' marriage. Insecure of her own attractiveness, Elizabeth constantly looks for signs that her husband is beginning again to stray. Tortured by guilt at what he sees as a moment of weakness, Proctor vacillates between apologetic attempts to make his wife happy and anger at her continued distrust. It is not until both suffer at the hands of the court that they come to a purer understanding of each other, and rediscover their mutual love.

HISTORICAL CONTEXT

Miller's interest in the Salem witch trials was partly prompted by reading Marion Starkey's *The Devil in Massachusetts*. While researching witch trials at the Historical Society in Salem, Massachusetts, Miller found the core of his plot in Charles W. Upton's nineteenth-century book, *Salem Witchcraft*. Here, he found references to most of the main characters who appear in his play. In terms of the play's historical accuracy in portraying the Salem witch trials of 1692, in a note at the start of the play's script, Miller declares that his play is predominantly accurate with regard to facts, but he has made some changes for "dramatic purposes."

There are many details in the play which are firmly backed up by trial transcripts and other records of the time, such as Tituba's confession, Sarah Good's condemnation on being unable to cite the Ten Commandments, Rebecca's steadfastly claimed innocence, Giles Corey's complaints against his wife preventing him from saying his prayers, and Mary Warren's poppet being given to Elizabeth. The notable details which appear to have arisen more from Miller's imagination are the presentation of Abigail and her lust for Proctor; the development of both the Proctors, with John especially depicted as a liberated thinker for those times; and Proctor's subsequent confession and recantation. Miller also makes Governor Danforth a lot more accommodating than the original, who would never have listened to any counterarguments. But the original prosecution was really as blind to facts and as relentless as they appear in the play, and there were many, like the Putnams, who took full mercenary advantage of the situation.

Miller initially resisted the idea of depicting the HUAC hearings in the form of an old-fashioned witch trial as too obvious. However, as the HUAC hearings grew more ritualistic, and more cruelly pointless, he could no longer resist, despite the obvious risks, for the parallels were far too apt to ignore. He saw how both sets of hearings had a definite structure behind them, designed to make people publically confess. In both cases, the "judges" knew in advance all of the information for which they asked. The main difference was that Salem's hearings had a greater legality because it was against the law in America to be a witch, but not a communist. Miller does not attempt a one-to-one analogy between his characters and those involved in HUAC, because this would have made the play too temporal. The reason the play has remained so popular is that it offers more than a simple history lesson of either the original witch trials or of HUAC—what Miller explores are the prevailing conditions which cause such events.

The 1950s communist scare which gave HUAC its power had disgusted Miller. It was a period in which he saw the civilities of public life stripped away as everyone became unsure of what innocent comment or gesture could ruin them. Many "great and noble citizens," Miller tells us, were "branded traitors, without a sign of real disgust from any quarter" (*Timebends* 1987, 312), and with as little real truth, evidence, or reason for it. Miller feels that HUAC taught him about the fluidity of reality, and the patent fictionalizations with which many of us live. Miller had attended some meetings of communist writers in his past, but had not given his support to them, any more than he now gave his support to their oppressors. What worried him most about these years was that American democracy seemed under threat of dissolution. Although many stayed cautiously silent about what was happening, Miller felt he had to publically respond in some way to the committee's behavior, "For if the current degeneration of discourse continued, as I had every reason to believe it would, we could no longer be a democracy, a system that requires a certain basic trust in order to survive" (330). Miller's response was to write *The Crucible*.

LITERARY DEVICES AND CRAFT

Miller created his own poetic language for this play, based on the archaic language he had read in the Salem documents. Wanting to make his audience feel they were witnessing events from an earlier time, yet not wanting to make his dialogue incomprehensible, he devised a form of speech for his characters which blended into everyday speech, an earlier vocabulary and syntax. Incorporating more familiar archaic words like "yea," "nay," or "goodly," Miller creates the impression of a past era without overly perplexing his audience. Words like "poppet" instead of "doll," are easily understood, just as the way he has the women addressed as "Goody" instead of "Mrs." The alterations of syntax are as subtle, such as the use of double negatives, as when Mary declares she "never saw no spirits," or using "let you" to act as the imperative. Miller alters various verb conjugations and tenses to conform more readily with those of the period, substituting "he have" for "he has," or "be" for "are" and "am," to give his audience just the flavor of seventeenth-century English.

While Miller's mastery of language in *The Crucible* seems most evident in the way he manages to create everyday speech, which appears to be of the period, it rises to the level of poetry with its sophisticated metaphors. The "cruci-ble" of the title is a place where something is subjected to great heat to purify its nature—as are the central characters of Proctor, Elizabeth, and Hale. All en-dure intense suffering to emerge as better, more self-aware individuals. Com-plex imagery is built up through the concerns and language of the play—ideas of heat and light against cold and dark are played off against our common con-cepts of heaven and hell, good and evil. Numerous images of cold and winter, along with the hardness of stone are used to indicate the harshness of the Puri-tan life: trapped in a cycle of toil, unrelieved by leisure (singing, dancing, or any frivolous behaviors are not allowed), by both the hard landscape they strive to tame, and their own restrictive religion. Abigail tells John that he is "no wintry man," which is true in that he refuses to abide by many of the strictures of his community, and determines to have a mind of his own.

For the people of Salem, Satan is alive and nearby in the dark forest. The for-est acts as a representation of hell to be avoided at the cost of sin, and godly folk stay home at night. The main sin is sex, which has been notoriously equated with the Devil by way of original sin. The girls dance illicitly in the dark woods around a fire (another hellish symbol), some naked, while Abigail drinks blood to cast a spell on Elizabeth, in order to try to break up a marriage. This is no in-nocent fun, but an evocation of all that these townspeople fear. Abigail's devil-ment is continually reinforced by the symbols which surround all she says and does: she has been initiated into the joys of sex by her former employer through her "sense for heat," and still feels Proctor "burning" for her. He is described in his adulterous lust as a "stallion," in other words, less than human. But is the sexual affair of this couple sufficiently evil to bring judgment down on the whole town, as Hale seems to suggest at the close of act 2?

The imagery becomes more complex as Miller plays with our expectations. It becomes difficult to decide with which body of imagery we most sympa-thize. Miller associates the idea of good with mixed images of cold and light, and evil is associated with images of heat and darkness. While light seems un-deniably positive against the darkness of evil, the idea of heat would seem to be better than coldness—heat denoting life and coldness its restriction. Given the town's restrictions, is the dark forest the entrance to hell, or a place of liberation and freedom? Is the heated sexual crime of Proctor and Abigail worse than the cold, mercenary greed and malice of the Putnams? More than this, just as good and evil are so often mixed, we begin to see the imagery overlap between sup-posedly good and bad characters alike, most noticeably in the way Miller uses images of blood.

Blood is a dominant image of the play, in the idea of it being heated and equated with sexual passion, and in its association with murder. Bad deeds are often kept hidden until "blood" betrays their presence. The images are initially associated with Abigail, who comes from a history of blood, having lain beside her parents as their heads were caved in by native assailants. Her heated blood leads her into a sexual liaison with Proctor, and she drinks blood to cast a spell on his wife. But the blood is transferred to the hands of the supposedly righteous judges who begin to hang innocent people. By fixating so much on sin and the religious right, men like Parris and Danforth become sinful and turned from God. Early in the play, Proctor accuses Parris of preaching too much "hellfire and bloody damnation" (28) and saying too little about God; this becomes a kind of prophesy as Parris and the judges become more devilish in their treatment of others. It is significant that where they send the supposedly "saved" Sarah Good and Tituba who have falsely confessed becomes for the women a hell from which they pray to be saved by the Devil. The fires of Hell seem to consume the supposedly righteous rather than the "guilty" witches.

ALTERNATE PERSPECTIVE: A DECONSTRUCTIONIST READING

Deconstruction is a term which defines the philosophical position of the inevitability of error and misreading whenever we approach a text. Deconstructing a text is, in large part, an ironic task, since at its heart deconstruction implies that clear meaning is impossible, because there are contradictions in everything, and all writing is ultimately unstable because of this. There is a tendency toward playfulness when critics deconstruct a text; rather than hide from the irony, they enjoy it and allow imagination full play. To deconstruct is to try to expose a text's self-contradictions, rather than provide answers. Many critics find this approach interesting because it allows them to open texts up to new and imaginative interpretations by insisting they be viewed from new positions. Instead of attempting to fix a single meaning, they try to expand a text's possibilities to discover many new meanings.

A deconstructionist critic looks for ideas contained within a text which seem to contradict each other, but can also both be true. Then they decide which of these opposing ideas appears to be the one that the writer believes. Then, they look for evidence in the text which contradicts this favoring, and allows us to suspect that although the writer supports one view, their text can be viewed as supporting the opposite. It is possible, through deconstruction, to show how texts often work against their own supposed purpose; for example, the conventional reading of *The Crucible* is to view John Proctor as the hero, but what if we read the play in an entirely different way which makes Abigail the hero?

Consider Abigail's position: a young, orphaned girl who has been seduced by her boss (an older, family man and respected member of his society) and deflowered in an age when virginity was a prerequisite for marriage. She then gets thrown out of the house on orders from his wife, and utterly rejected. She, perhaps naively, tries to win back his affection, resorting to casting spells on his wife to remove her from competition. When she does meet him again, she declares her love, but is ignored and again rejected, and the man even threatens the girl whom he has ruined that he will make her a disgrace in the town. It is not until he publically confesses their relationship that she finally attacks him, and this is to protect herself rather than a malicious act of revenge. Surely we should be sympathizing with such a character, rather than condemning her as a wanton whore.

Although many critics prefer to view John Proctor as the innocent Christian martyr who has been seduced by the devilish whore, Abigail, there is enough evidence in the play to allow for a very different reading. Why would a simple whore try to get rid of a lover's wife? Abigail, far from being irredeemably wicked, is sincerely in love with Proctor, which her actions prove. Having been awakened by her affair with Proctor from a slumbering servitude to see her potential as a human being, Abigail struggles to uncover a sense of self in a highly restrictive society. She creates for herself a position of respect, outside of the more usual marriage, by becoming the voice of accusation which all fear. She bravely refuses to accept a patriarchal society which strives to silence and denounce independent female spirits. Her gulling of the judges and eventual escape with the mercenary reverend's savings before the town turns against her depict her as victorious—a woman who refuses to be controlled and who wins herself freedom through her own quick thinking.

The concept of Puritan restriction is in clear opposition to individual freedom, and the play depicts this division with the Salem authorities being against the young girls of the town. The authorities claim themselves to be righteous (even while doing much harm), therefore, anyone going against them must be evil. But wanting freedom should not be considered evil, but natural, for any free-spirited individual. The Salem authorities represent order and security, but such come at a heavy price, and it is a price not all girls are prepared to pay. Note how often adults (including John Proctor) suggest whipping one of the young girls of whose actions they disapprove—it must have been a common treatment at the time for any infringement of their harsh rules. The young, unmarried girls of this town are considered more as chattels than viable members of the community, and are allowed to make no independent decisions for themselves, not even to decide when they should go to bed. What avenues are they offered to earn respect, outside of marriage (which merely transfers them from one "owner" to another)?

In the forest, the girls dance and their spirits and desires can run free; it is no wonder they find such escapades exciting. They carry this freedom forward into the courtroom as Abigail leads them to cry out against many of the town's elders. But such actions are also a dangerous threat to their community. They are introducing a form of chaos into a tightly ordered society, as their actions go against everything this society holds sacred. Parris's fear that Abigail and her friends are going into the woods at night to dance naked and invoke the Devil is justified, for this is precisely what the girls are doing. Their actions attack the foundations of their society: its religious beliefs, its social conventions, and the sanctity of marriage (by Abigail plotting to take Elizabeth's life so that she might replace her). But when a society consistently restricts an individual and will not allow a person to show independence, it is effectively killing off that individual's spirit. In any land that calls itself a democracy, that person should be encouraged to attack such a society any way he or she can in order to be free of it. Therefore, given this interpretation, we should applaud rather than condemn the heroic behavior of Abigail Williams.

8

Continuing Concerns:
The Ride Down Mt. Morgan
(1991)

Even in his eighties, Arthur Miller has not slowed down, and although he continues to experiment with form and theme, there remain perennial concerns to which he finds himself drawn as society itself continues to change. Foremost are the needs, desires, and responsibilities of the American family, and even more specifically, the American male. These considerations were dealt with in *Death of a Salesman* in 1949, and reconsidered fifty years later through the social climate of the 1990s in the evolving story of Lyman Felt in *The Ride Down Mt. Morgan*.

There are many similarities between Willy Loman and Lyman Felt, beyond the echo in their names. Both are salesman, selling the materialistic American dream of wealth and success by denying certain aspects of reality. But there is an intrinsic difference: Lyman Felt is what Willy Loman wanted to be—handsome, well liked, and successful. Lyman possesses a self-confidence that Loman cannot attain, partly because he has never faced the disgrace of impending failure. He has been better suited to play the capitalistic game by his more resistant personality and his ability to find scapegoats to deflect his own responsibilities. While Loman was a man striving against the inherent difficulties of living during the forties and fifties, Lyman is a man for the eighties, and unlike Loman, a successful businessman. Where Loman is powerless, Lyman is fully empowered. But we can also see, even more clearly than *Death of a Salesman* displays, just how misguided Willy's desires were, as we witness the dangerous and unsatisfactory life Lyman has created with all those skills and advantages for which Willy longed.

Miller premiered *The Ride Down Mt. Morgan* in 1991 in London, England. Tired of the harsh realities of getting a serious play produced on the Broadway stage, he allowed it to run where he felt it would meet with a warmer and kinder reception. Although a hit in London, the play was not produced in America until the summer of 1996 at the Williamstown Theater Festival, where it appeared in a rewritten form, and then later for a limited run on Broadway in 1998. Although the plot remains essentially the same in both versions, the 1999 published version tries to make the transitions between scenes smoother and easier for the audience to follow, and reduces the role of the father.

SETTING AND PLOT DEVELOPMENT

The opening scene reveals Lyman in a hospital bed, his body wrapped in incapacitating casts, and the silent, ghostly presence of his father standing over him. Lyman talks in his sleep, imagining he is addressing a business conference, while Nurse Logan listens in amusement. Dreaming of his father wakes Lyman up, and he chats with the nurse, who fills him in on his injuries, which were caused by him skidding his car down a mountain. She then worries him by announcing that his wife, Theo, and daughter, Bessie, are waiting to see him. Lyman has been doing something wrong. He tries to imagine what they must be saying as they sit in the waiting room, and we witness the possible scene in which they show a brave face, complain about Lyman's mother being too possessive, and meet Leah, who has also been notified of the accident. Lyman is a bigamist, and Leah is his second wife. The prospect of his two wives meeting both horrifies and fascinates him, as he imagines the slowly dawning realization between the two that they are both currently married to the same man.

The differences between Lyman's two wives is clear from their reactions to life in general. Theo is accepting and complacent, though capable of anger when she sees her security threatened. Leah is tougher and more worldly; a consummate businesswoman who copes more efficiently with stress. Theo faints from the shock of discovering her husband is a bigamist, and the scene switches to a subsequent discussion between Leah and Lyman's friend and lawyer, Tom Wilson, as Leah decides what to do about this situation. She is mostly concerned regarding money, wanting to ensure that their son, Benjamin, is not disinherited. We also learn that the life Lyman has been leading with Leah is entirely different to his life with Theo. With Theo he played the cautious family man, but with Leah he liked to take risks.

Lyman convinced Leah he had divorced Theo, but never actually went through with it. Tom is fascinated by what Lyman has been up to, and now recalls to Leah a past discussion he had with Lyman about the feasibility of bigamy, in which Lyman had told him that he was in love with another woman. From Lyman's discussion with Tom (re-created for us onstage), we realize his marriage to Leah was partly a desire to change the life he was leading, in which he was suffering a midlife crisis filled with affairs and fears of impending death, still being accosted by people criticizing him for betraying his business partner to the authorities. Leah re-creates the scene for Tom how when she got pregnant with Benjamin she had refused to continue being the mistress, and Lyman had promised to marry her. Leah was highly attracted to Lyman's great appetite for life, but is now thoroughly disappointed with him.

The scene returns to Lyman's bedside and we realize everything so far may have been purely in his imagination, but then Tom enters and tells Lyman that his two wives have indeed met, and Lyman's imagination has followed reality fairly closely. Theo and Bessie come to talk with him; both are very angry, and Lyman tries to hide by pretending to be asleep, as he decides what to do. To Theo's annoyance, Leah joins them. In his imagination, Lyman creates a scene in which after some initial wrangling, he is able to control all three women, getting Theo and Leah to lie beside him on the bed. He re-creates his first liaison with Leah, and they seem close as he confides in her many details about his past and upbringing. In a phone call he made at this time to Theo, we see their relationship was far more conventional and less open. But this scene fragments as it switches back to when Theo and Leah first came in, and we see Lyman's imagination has not created a realistic outcome, as the two women prepare to fight and Lyman loses control.

Act 2 begins with Theo and Tom in the waiting room discussing what Theo should do; she is very confused. Leah joins them and tells them how Lyman's car accident is looking suspiciously like a purposeful act, and they wonder if he might be suicidal. The hostility between Theo and Leah is revealed in numerous petty comments they make to each other, but both are primarily concerned about how their respective children will cope with this whole mess. Theo is astonished at the different type of person Lyman has been with Leah, and is unsure how much to believe. Considering this other side of his nature, she tells Tom about a time she imagines Lyman tried to kill her by letting her go into shark-infested waters. She re-creates the scene in a number of ways until it becomes unclear as to what really happened—it is even possible that he saved her life. Their marriage has had its ups and downs in the past, and Theo has no idea of what she should do next.

Meanwhile, Lyman is sleeping, and having a strange fantasy about his wives which gets played out onstage. In his dream, Theo and Leah seductively compare their culinary skills and seem to be deciding how best to share their husband. At first, their advances seem provocative, but turn threatening as they begin to eat him. His father enters to add a further threat to this nightmare as he antagonizes his son over money. The nurse wakes Lyman and calms him down, sympathizing with him and telling him about her family. Tom enters to talk to his friend, telling him he thinks Theo may take him back. Lyman tries to rationalize his behavior, admitting he has been selfish and betrayed people, but justifying it by saying that is how the world works, and he has been truthful on one level. Lyman wants to find a way to keep both women, and at this point, Bessie and Theo reenter.

By Lyman's responses, we realize Theo is acting strangely as she berates her husband for past annoyances. She recalls when they went skinny-dipping at the start of their relationship, wanting to ascertain his sincerity at that time to discover when he began to stray. It is evident she has loved him. Their daughter, Bessie, gets incensed by this talk and tries to break it up, but Theo refuses to leave and asks Bessie to wait outside. Lyman tries to convince Theo that their marriage was stronger after he took up with Leah because he was more tolerant with both of them, knowing he had the other to turn to. Instead of placating Theo, this idea turns her against him, deciding he is incapable of love. At this point, Lyman re-creates a series of memories to explain his behavior, beginning with a safari on which he had gone with Theo and Bessie shortly after marrying Leah, when he confronted a lion.

Lyman sees his moment with the lion as a turning point in his life, for it was then he made the decision to never feel guilt. The lion backs off, and Lyman is exhilarated by his own sense of power, feeling an affinity with this "king of beasts." His high spirits infect both Theo and Bessie, whose evident love and respect for Lyman at this point severely contrasts with their current feelings in the hospital. Lyman next recalls how he felt blackmailed into marriage by Leah who had threatened to abort their child. He explains that his need to marry Leah and keep Benjamin is partly fueled by guilt from an earlier illegitimate boy he had had for whom he had refused to divorce Theo and marry the mother. He then explains how he tried to ask Theo for a divorce, but had not had the courage to go through with it. Leah has the baby even though she knows he is not yet divorced, but then threatens to marry someone else, which provokes Lyman to try again.

We briefly return to the present, as Leah comes to visit Lyman in the hospital to discuss their son, about whom she is worried. While she tries to get Lyman to confess some guilt, he responds by trying to get her to accept some responsibility. Like Theo, his response turns her against him, and she also sees him as someone incapable of love. She recalls a time when he stayed with her in a hotel near his home with Theo, so he could walk by the house with Leah, as if to mock his first wife. Our sense of his audacity increases as he relates how he had sent Leah back to their hotel while he went to see Theo and make love to her. He was glorying in his own power over two separate women, and feeling like a god. Leah had not known about this, and is disgusted. She insists that he give her their house and business, and will not allow him to see Benjamin until he signs a quitclaim. They argue over what he should tell Benjamin about this whole thing, but are interrupted by Bessie, who comes with the news that Theo is acting very strangely.

Theo has taken off her skirt to indicate her decision to go against convention, and admit her own sexuality. Deciding she wants Lyman back, she is even willing to share him. To her daughter's horror, Theo accepts responsibility for her husband's adultery, seeing herself as having provoked and deserved it. This acquiescence excites Lyman, who sees her return to him as possible. Leah tries to make Theo see Lyman as untrustworthy, but he works on her too, to convince her he has really done her a favor. Bessie continues to stand firm against him, as everyone bursts into tears. Tom tries to take control, telling the women to stop loving Lyman before he destroys them all, and attempting to get Lyman to confess to having a conscience. He has better luck with the former than the latter; Lyman refuses to accept any guilt, but Theo and Leah decide to leave.

Once again, Lyman sees his father's ghost, which drives him to confess to Leah what he was doing on the mountain—trying to surprise her by arriving unexpectedly, because he was suspicious she had a lover. Bessie tries one last time to get her father to think of others, but he seems incapable of looking beyond his own selfish needs. Leah is not impressed and leaves on the heels of the others, and Lyman is left alone with the nurse. They talk again about her family, and she kisses his forehead before she leaves. Suddenly touched by the sheer contentment and simplicity of the nurse's life, Lyman seems to reach some kind of epiphany at the close, but in his isolation is unsure what next to do. The play ends with his anguished cry, belying what he has insisted on all along, that he feels no guilt, fear, or pain, and allowing the audience to join with the nurse in sympathizing with this lost soul.

CHARACTER DEVELOPMENT

The father appears at the start of the play to signify his importance to Lyman Felt. The father is a figure of hope and fear, inspiration and intimidation; his memory both encourages and restricts the son. Lyman's father died at fifty three, and Lyman worries about his life when he reaches the same age; this is when he makes all these strange and daring changes in his life. The father's first speech is fraught with images of restriction placed on his son: he will not buy Lyman skates, restricting his movement (literally and symbolically); he warns him strongly about having anything to do with women, thereby restricting Lyman's future relationships and ability to connect with women; and he criticizes Lyman's looks and abilities, telling him he is "stupid" and a "great disappointment" (2), which must restrict Lyman's intrinsic self-esteem. However, Lyman has seemingly overcome these restrictions, and it is this which makes us aware of Lyman's great spirit. In the world he inhabits, he is a great success—a wealthy man with not one, but two attractive women to show off; he has come a long way from his father's humble origins. But, he is to learn in the course of the play that he has really remained firmly within his father's restrictions, for his success is false—he has not progressed spiritually, he has little connection with either of his women, and he still desperately seeks his father's approval.

The father's advice to Lyman regarding business and passion fully illustrates his son's inner conflict. Lyman is torn between the practical—the male world his father invokes of cold cash and WASP principles—and the emotional—a female world of sex, recklessness, and the Jewish lust for life. The two seem at odds; while his father demands that the first take precedence, Lyman, rightly, needs a balance between them. Caught between his primal love for the Jewish Leah and the sexuality she offers, and the admiration he feels for the more reserved, WASPish Theo, he wants a combination of both, but that is hard to achieve.

Despite the wrong he commits, it is hard not to like Lyman, and our attraction to him is an integral aspect of his characterization, without which we are in danger of missing the point. Lyman is a truly American figure, multiethnic in background and sympathies. He has employed African Americans for years, and James Baldwin views him with brotherly affection. Also, he has had an Hispanic business partner, his sexual preferences are not race restricted, and he is half Jewish and half Albanian—the son of an immigrant. As a second generation American, he epitomizes both the strengths and weaknesses of the American vision. He has pursued and caught the traditional twentieth-century American dream of success, having enough cash to keep two beautiful women in beautiful homes—though we are also shown the essential hollowness of that dream. Underneath it all, Lyman is not happy but constantly suffering, and it is this suffering with which he is finally left once the rest gets stripped away.

Despite our sympathy, however, we should not believe Lyman when he tells us that you can be true to yourself or to others, but not to both. The first law of life is betrayal, Miller insists, largely because we are human and therefore fallible—but we can fight this. We need to recognize that the root of Lyman's problem is that he has not been honest to himself. Lyman does what he wants, but in the end he is wracked with guilt and suffers for this selfishness. Lyman is a victim not only of social restrictions, but also his own excesses. So it would be best not to follow his example, but listen to the quiet voice of reason that Bessie offers—you have to be more socially responsible in life, whatever your desires, for your own good. Bessie may be a small voice in the throng, but that should not make what she says any less important. "There are other people" (138) she tells her father, and the balance Lyman needs will involve those other people. By refusing to emphasize Bessie, Miller allows us to risk missing the truth she states, as Lyman does.

Theo and Leah seem to offer Lyman two very different alternatives, yet on a closer look their characters become more complex. There are similarities between them—symbolized by their identical fur coats—as well as a profound contrast. Theo's inflexible nature seems assured from the start, as she is described as "stiff and ungainly." Theo is very practical and offers Lyman a sense of order, a sense that "everything ultimately fits together . . . and for the good" (8). Lyman feeds off her naive optimism. She comes from a sheltered family background which has given her a limited outlook on life. She has idealized the American concept of the small town, refusing to acknowledge its darker side, and looks back nostalgically to her past. Theo seems to stand for a certain honesty, and Lyman is drawn to her strong sense of reality, yet with the shark episode this becomes questionable. Theo may be as capable of lying and manipulation as her husband. Apparently a homebody, she is conventional and accommodating, but she is controlling as well as controlled. She exhibits a need to control Lyman in the way she likes to identify his quotes—it is for her a way of identifying and fixing him. Her association with truth, we learn, is based more on pretense than reality.

While Theo lives largely in the past, Leah is a figure of the future. At the start, Leah seems the more wily of the two, the one more capable of being a liar, and yet ironically she becomes the one more capable of accepting lies as much as truth. She is, throughout, fully aware that life is dangerous. With her greater verve, she is willing to make a scene. She has been attracted to a similar hunger for life in Lyman. A strong businesswoman, Leah is the modern woman of ambition, a role which seems beyond Theo. Like Theo, she enjoys control, and can be manipulative, despite her claims to the opposite. A clear example of this is the way she manipulates Lyman over the baby and getting married, where she forces him into matrimony by playing on his jealousies, morality, and sense of guilt.

Importantly, Lyman is different with each of them—the ultimate split personality—seeing himself as two warring identities: the Jew, which he associates with lawyers and judges, against the Albanian, which he associates with bandits and anarchy. His two wives reflect this split: Theo the conservative, judgmental type who lives strictly according to rules, and Leah the anarchist who will break those rules. He loves both in his way, for each offers him something he needs. With Theo he can be the strong provider and play it safe—a secure existence. With Leah he can be the playboy with fast cars, planes, hunting—the apparent free spirit who can face fear with a casualness that belies his inner turmoil. As the play progresses, we see Theo and Leah gradually swap roles, with Theo becoming the rebel and Leah the conservative. Theo changes, as she sheds her skirt, along with many of her former inhibitions, and becomes more comfortable with herself and her position—even offering to share Lyman. She recognizes the inadequacy of her earlier conformist views regarding socialism and Christianity, and seems ready for compromise, though this horrifies the others.

Lyman's lawyer, Tom Wilson, advises Lyman to lie and be dishonest because the truth is often hurtful. Such moments allow us to question Tom's complicity, even though he finally takes a stand against his friend. Self-effacing Tom has lived vicariously through Lyman, allowing him to take the risks. Tom is a kind of everyman figure in the play, because we are all prone to letting others live the sensational lives as we stand by and watch—becoming virtual "Uncle Tom" figures in our "yes man" complacency; through the ineffectual figure of Tom, Miller warns us against such complacency.

SOCIAL AND HISTORICAL CONTEXT

The action of *The Ride Down Mt. Morgan* takes place in troublesome times, and addresses the difficulties of living in an amoral, chaotic postmodern society. The play is an evocation of life in America in the eighties and nineties, and the importance of Reaganism to this play, with its emphasis on materialistic consumption and consumerism ahead of all other concerns, has been recognized. Lyman's marriage to Leah occurs in the same year Ronald Reagan became President, and Lyman's bigamous behavior becomes a reflection of the values and type of leadership America subsequently experienced. The play portrays a harsh, hostile world filled with conflict and betrayal. The constant threat that their lives could fall apart at any moment is a fact that all the characters must face: it is something with which they must learn to live. The sense of control toward which Miller has many of the characters strive is shown to be necessary, to a degree, and exhibits a healthy desire for self-determination—but too much control can be as dangerous as too little control. Characters like Leah, who insist on complete control, become limited and limiting, while a man like Tom, who has too little control, has his potential partly wasted. A balance must be sought between these two extremes to allow for both individuals and society to function within an encouraging network of possibilities, and to avoid the pitfalls of living in a postmodern age.

Clearly, postmodern concerns impact our contemporary lives. A play such as *The Ride Down Mt. Morgan* depicts a mean-spirited world, but also offers strategies by which we may create a viable alternative for the future. Miller suggests means by which people can rebuild their threatened sense of stability and order, and this is partly achieved through the existence of the play itself; the organized form of the play creates an antidote to counter the chaos of real life.

Miller sees the theater as a place of connection, as he explains in one of his many essays on the theater: "By whatever means it is accomplished, the prime business of a play is to arouse the passions of its audience so that by the route of passion may be opened up new relationships between a man and men, and between men and Man. Drama is akin to the other inventions of man in that it ought to help us know more, and not merely to spend our feelings" (*Theater Essays* 1995, 168). Another major way in which a play provides unity is not just through the action or message of the play itself, but through its audience, because attending a theater is a communal activity. In his autobiography, Miller recalls during a French production of Jean Giraudoux's *Ondine*, "I was bored by the streams of talk and the inaction onstage, but I could understand that it was the language that was saving their souls, hearing it together and being healed by it, the one unity left to them and thus their one hope" (*Timebends* 1987, 159).

Arthur Miller realizes that we must acknowledge the chaotic state of the postmodern world in which we live before we can discover the means to be content in such a world. *The Ride Down Mt. Morgan* presents a picture of such a chaotic world. This play satisfies Miller's directive that drama should heighten people's awareness of what living in contemporary times involves. It conveys the uncertainty of everyday life where a person must battle objectification and the pitfalls of an overcommercialized culture, and the effect all of this has on the people who must live those lives. Both individualism and any sense of a supportive society are under threat. We witness the characters in this play trying to live lives which contain dignity and a certain amount of nobility. Even though Miller leaves the struggle unresolved, through the calm voices of Bessie and Nurse Logan, he offers some powerful directives for our contemporary consideration: think of others and be satisfied with less.

THEMATIC ISSUES

A central issue of *The Ride Down Mt. Morgan* is Miller's perennial concern with discovering the right balance between social and individual responsibilities in order to live a useful and contented life. In the play, Miller does not try to show us a single ideal American, but asks us to uncover a compromise between the various characters we meet. While Lyman fluctuates between deception and sincerity, so do the rest of the cast. Each character is a complex mix of lies and truth—consider Theo's recollections about the shark, Leah's explanation of why she marries Lyman and her manipulations to achieve this, and the way Tom leads a vicarious life through Lyman while on the surface condemning him.

Lyman is the play's central figure, and most duplicitous with his two wives and two lives, struggling between his relationship to both Jewish and WASP lifestyles. He is a man simultaneously trapped by his casts (and responsibilities), yet free in his imagination—but he is not alone. The act of finding a balance among these conflicting desires, needs, and beliefs is complicated because it inevitably involves others. Lyman dreams of an ideal situation in which his two women unite and give him everything he wants, but we are shown the unreality of such an expectation. Lyman's dream swiftly turns into a nightmare as the women begin to devour him (sucking his fingers). However, Leah and Theo are as conflicted as Lyman. Both latch onto Lyman and insist that he provide a bedrock of stability in their lives. The wives fool themselves into thinking they have control. They too need to learn that nothing can be that certain and secure; they too need to face the uncertainties of real life.

Another theme Miller seems to suggest is that vision is integral to leading a satisfactory life, for it is needed in order to create the better fictions toward which we aim. Lyman's greatest strength is that he has vision. He has great potential, and at times we inevitably get sucked in to his energy for life, even accepting some of his rationalizations, but in the end we should realize that it all comes down to the fact that he has lived selfishly and only listened to half-truths (his own, ignoring those of others). He suffers for this, as he had all along needed a balance to be whole and content. He has lived his life, for all its apparent variety, too one-sidedly. When you live for yourself alone, that is with whom you are finally left.

Miller reveals a total disconnection between the characters in *The Ride Down Mt. Morgan*, but he replaces this sense of disconnection with a desire for connections that is made evident through notions of responsibility, mostly voiced through Bessie. Miller has characters in the play embody the various traps people face during their development into useful, satisfied human beings. By so doing, he warns his audiences against some of the pitfalls they too must face. Theo and Tom tend to restrict themselves by relying on conventions and allowing others to dominate their lives. Being overly conservative turns out to be as restricting as being overly selfish like Lyman, who is ultimately restricted by false feelings of superiority. This is similar to the self-defeating trap of anarchy into which Leah falls, which damages herself and others, because it continuously insists on isolating rebellion rather than socializing compromise.

We should recognize the subtle contrast to Lyman provided by Nurse Logan. She talks more of her family than of herself, listening rather than telling. She is satisfied and content with no sign of angst. She does not need everything explained or understood, but accepts mystery and is satisfied. In this light, it may be Lyman's ambition which ultimately reduces him. His desire for continued excitement escalates, as does his need to take greater and greater risks; a fall was inevitable. But we see him go full circle. By the end, the commonplace events and concerns described by Nurse Logan have become unusual and exciting to Lyman, for he has gone so far from that kind of life it now seems strange and alien to him. The Logans have the simpler response to life that was perhaps his father's, and they have that contentment Lyman has sought.

The play suggests that modern society forces us all to live increasingly complicated lives—but humanly we cannot keep up and should not try. Lyman's final confession is given more to the audience than to Leah, as he describes the similarity between facing that mountain and the lion. "All obligations spent. Is this freedom?" Lyman asks. He is beginning to realize that freedom is not what he wanted after all. Complete freedom means no connections at all, which is awful. He ends the play alone, shaken and sobbing—with only the nurse's compassion to mitigate his isolation. We can find hope for his future in that he does seem closer in touch with the simple reality of the nurse and her family.

LITERARY DEVICES AND CRAFT

Discussing *The Ride Down Mt. Morgan* with theater scholar Jan Balakian, Miller explains: "Formally speaking it's very free flowing, a little bit like *Salesman* was. But this one spills in all directions; time is rather plastic. While the story is moving forward, it's also moving sideways and out" ("Conversation" 1990, 162). We cannot trust our eyes when watching *The Ride Down Mt. Morgan* for the line between reality and illusion is so carefully blurred, and the scenes flow together with no clear-cut beginnings or endings. The work is an example of the way in which Miller likes to play with notions of both reality and time in his writing, both structurally and thematically.

In classic dreamplay tradition, it becomes impossible to say for sure if any of *The Ride Down Mt. Morgan*'s events exist outside Lyman's imagination as he lies prone in his hospital bed. Indeed, is Lyman's crash and hospitalization even real, or just the product of a guilty conscience? Opening the play with a man asleep is Miller's way of warning us that this whole play could turn out to be nothing more than one man's dream (or nightmare) with the patient waking, perhaps, only at the close with a strangled cry, or perhaps never waking at all. We are kept deliberately unsure as to what exactly is real, and we must pass judgment without the nicety of certainty. In his dreams, at least, we see Lyman able to escape the human limitations of his casts and also, perhaps, the human limitations of his guilt, conscience, and sense of responsibility—all of which trouble him. This is no slice-of-life realism, but symbolic representation of a man trying to come to terms with who he is, much like *After the Fall.*

As in so many of Miller's plays, the names of central characters and the play's title have symbolic meaning. While in *Death of a Salesman*, Willy Loman's name tends to evoke discussion of him as a "low man" in terms of his abilities, character, or prospects, Lyman's name with its possibilities of outrageous deceit (lies), passion (to lie with), and, as critic June Schlueter suggests, the concept of one who is "lionized" ("Scripting" 1995, 143), clearly evokes a different sense of being. Meanwhile, Lyman's actual "ride" down, what one critic refers to as "Mount More-Gain," is emphasized by the title, which can be taken as a metaphor for the dizzying experience of life toward the end of the millennium—comparable to hurtling down an ice-covered mountain. The last nine years for Lyman, since his encounter with the lion, have been a metaphorical ride down a steep slope, dangerous and out of control, hurtling toward an inevitable crash. Completing such a run without spinning off is a skill we must learn in order to survive. Lyman gets somewhat broken in the process of his ride, but he survives, which should draw our attention to the qualities he possesses which allow for this.

ALTERNATE PERSPECTIVE: A MYTHIC READING

A mythological approach to literature looks for elements in a work which provoke in the reader some kind of instinctual human response. Such responses are innate, and if we look hard enough, we find that they continually recur because they are part of what psychoanalyst Carl Jung calls our "collective unconscious." This is a body of responses, beliefs, and images with which Jung believes every human being is born. A collection of archetypes, which are models of behavior which tend to repeat themselves, has evolved from this concept, and they are used to explain those natural processes and common human experiences to which we respond with a sense of familiarity. When we witness a recurrent pattern of action, images, or character types, we describe them as archetypal. For example, when someone nobly sacrifices himself or herself for others, we describe their behavior as "Christ-like" because it fits the pattern of the life of Christ. The templates for many of our archetypes come down to us through folklore, myth, and religious tracts. In the case of *The Ride Down Mt. Morgan*, there are striking allusions to aspects of the Bible, and a mythic reading of these helps delineate the varying importance and impact of the characters and situations involved, and how they might be interpreted. The central characters in *The Ride Down Mt. Morgan* portray certain archetypal relationships which are signposted by their names, and other symbols with which they are associated.

A religious/Jewish connection between the characters is evidenced in a network of predominantly biblical naming and symbolism in the play. Situationally, Lyman can be seen as related to Jacob, famous for his two wives (though perfectly legal in his society). Also, Lyman's mother was Esther, invoking the Esther whom Jews recall every Purim. Esther thwarted the plots of Haman to kill the Jews by using her feminine wiles on the king, and through her actions she keeps the Jews alive. We should note that Lyman's mother was very disappointed that Theo was not Jewish, because Jewishness is passed on matrilineally and so Bessie is not technically Jewish. Lyman eventually marries a Jewish woman in order to preserve his Jewish heritage (passed on to him by his mother) and he names his son Benjamin after his mother's grandfather—Ben also being Hebrew for his son—and so finally preserves the Jewish line. In this way, Esther is once more victorious.

Lyman's Jewish wife is Leah. In the Bible, Leah was one of Jacob's two wives, her sister, Rachel, being the other. Between them, Leah and Rachel are the matriarchs of Israel, bearing to Jacob the children who will eventually be the founders of the tribes of Israel. Jacob also had children by another woman, a servant he never married, which could relate to Lyman's illegitimate child—but he was married to both Rachel and Leah, though Rachel was his preferred wife and given primary status. Jacob fathered a Ben too, though with Rachel rather than Leah. But Lyman calls his son Benjamin Alexander, the Alexander being his father's name, a man for whom religion had no import. Alexander is not a Jewish name; historically it recalls Alexander the Great, the Macedonian warrior, and also Alexander Hamilton, one of America's founders. It seems that in the naming of his son, Lyman illustrates the ambivalent nature of the child's heritage—he becomes an archetypal Jewish American and therefore the true offspring of Lyman, caught between dueling cultural heritages.

Lyman's daughter, Bessie, by his Christian wife, Theo, may bring to mind the New Testament figure of Elizabeth, Mary's cousin who gave birth to John the Baptist. Bessie too is a prophetlike figure who offers words of wisdom which are largely ignored, words which are also strongly suggestive of New Testament philosophy in their insistence that you consider others before yourself. Even Theo's name has a religious connotation with its root connection to theology, the study of religion—perhaps emphasizing her extremely rational nature. She is the hub around which religious concepts spin in America, and her father was a preacher. Tom Wilson, the Quaker, another representative of the New Testament may bring to mind the famed "doubting Thomas." At a point near the close of the play, when Theo seems to be won over to Lyman's outlook, we find Tom seeming to distance himself entirely from the group. Like the doubting-Thomas figure he may represent—he wants to believe, but has trouble committing himself to a more audacious set of beliefs. Furthermore, in Aramaic the name Thomas means "twin," and in many ways Tom is a twin to Lyman, being a would-be Lyman, only without the necessary spirit.

From a mythic standpoint, the scene between Lyman and the lion is also an important piece—we see in it an archetypal act of identification and test of the self. Getting close to death makes Lyman feel more alive, but it is fraught with danger. Lyman lives life dangerously and tempts the fates by wild acts which are motivated by over-blown pride. It is as if he wants to be a god—not for the power that would entail, but because a god does not have to feel guilt, and it is this which continually threatens his peace. The laws of tragedy insist the hero must suffer for his pride when at the peak of his existence, which is at the point Lyman faces the lion. Lyman declares that this was when he lost his guilt and felt most godlike; but, this is a lie, and it is the lie of which he is most guilty. We know his guilt exists—after all, why marry Leah and give his son a legal father but for the social mores which insist on such actions as right, and also, as he tells us, to assuage the guilt he feels from an earlier illegitimate child?

It is with the lion that Lyman decides to keep two wives, and be "lion-like" with his "pride." A further comparison of Lyman to that Lion of Judah, King David, seems applicable. David was a great uniter of warring factions who tried to build a golden ideal, but was eventually torn apart by the conflict between public appearance and private indiscretions—a similar dynamic to Lyman's life. When we finally learn the truth as to why Lyman was on the mountain, we discover not a god but a very human being—he is jealous (in a way he is not allowing his wives to be). In the end, he will not be able to avoid guilt because he is human, and not a god. As Lyman gets caught between the issues of desire and need, he overreaches himself, in the end losing everything for which he has striven.

Bibliography

PLAYS BY ARTHUR MILLER

After the Fall. New York: Viking, 1964.

The American Clock *and* The Archbishop's Ceiling: *Two Plays*. New York: Grove, 1989.

Arthur Miller's Collected Plays, Vol.1. New York: Viking, 1957.

The Creation of the World and Other Business. New York: Viking, 1973.

The Crucible. New York: Viking, 1953.

Danger: Memory! New York: Grove, 1986.

Death of a Salesman. New York: Viking, 1949.

An Enemy of the People. New York: Viking, 1951.

The Golden Years *and* The Man Who Had All the Luck. London: Methuen, 1989.

Incident at Vichy. New York: Viking, 1965.

The Last Yankee *and* Broken Glass. Harmondsworth, UK: Penguin, 1994.

A Memory of Two Mondays. In A View from the Bridge: *Two One Act Plays by Arthur Miller*. New York: Viking, 1955.

Mr. Peter's Connections. New York: Penguin, 1999.

Playing for Time. Woodstock, IL: Dramatic Publishing, 1985.

The Price. New York: Viking, 1968.

The Ride Down Mt. Morgan. New York: Penguin, 1992.

Two-Way Mirror. London: Methuen, 1984.

A View from the Bridge *and* All My Sons. Harmondsworth, UK: Penguin, 1961.

SCREENPLAYS AND OTHER FICTION BY ARTHUR MILLER

Everybody Wins. New York: Grove Weidenfield, 1990.
Focus. New York: Reynal and Hitchcock, 1945.
Homely Girl, A Life. New York: Viking, 1995.
I Don't Need You Anymore. New York: Viking, 1967.
Jane's Blanket. New York: Collier-Macmillan, 1963.
The Misfits. New York: Viking, 1961.

ARTICLES, ESSAYS, AND OTHER NONFICTION BY ARTHUR MILLER

"American Theatre: The Responsible Man." *Economist* 316 (14 Jul. 1990): 91.
"Arthur Miller on McCarthy's Legacy: Address, April 30, 1984." *Harper's* 269 (Jul. 1984): 11–12.
"How the Nazi Trials Search the Hearts of All Germans." *New York Herald Tribune*, 15 Mar. 1964: 24.
"My Wife Marilyn." *Life* 45 (22 Dec. 1958): 146–47.
"Our Guilt for the World's Evil." *New York Times Magazine*, 3 Jan. 1965: 10–11, 48.
"Red and Anti-Red Curbs on Art Denounced by U.S. Playwright." *New York Times*, 13 Feb. 1956: 9.
Salesman in Beijing. New York: Viking, 1984.
Situation Normal. New York: Reynal and Hitchcock, 1944.
The Theatre Essays of Arthur Miller. Ed. Robert A. Martin and Steven R. Centola. Rev. ed. New York: Viking, 1995.
Timebends: A Life. New York: Grove, 1987.
"With Respect for Her Agony—But with Love." *Life* 56 (7 Feb. 1964): 66.
"The Writer as Independent Spirit: The Role of P.E.N." *Saturday Review* 49 (4 Jun. 1966): 16–17.
Miller, Arthur, and Inge Morath. *Chinese Encounters.* New York: Farrar, Straus and Giroux, 1970.
———. *In Russia.* New York: Viking, 1969.
———. *In the Country.* New York: Viking, 1977.

WORKS ABOUT ARTHUR MILLER

Miller's autobiography, *Timebends*, contains the most detailed description of his life, and he has given numerous interviews in which he has discussed his plays, opinions, and life. However, no book-length biography of Miller exists to-date, though some critical works include chronologies and other biographical elements—the best of which are the following.

Allen, Jennifer. "Miller's Tale." *New York* 16 (24 Jan. 1983): 33–37.

Balakian, Jan. "A Conversation with Arthur Miller." *Michigan Quarterly Review* 29 (Spring 1990): 158–70.

Bigsby, C.W.E. *A Critical Introduction to Twentieth-Century American Drama, Vol. 2.* Cambridge: Cambridge University Press, 1982–1985.

———, ed. *Arthur Miller and Company.* London: Methuen, 1990.

Carson, Neil. *Arthur Miller.* New York: St. Martin's, 1982.

Centola, Steve R., ed. *Arthur Miller in Conversation.* Dallas: Contemporary Research Associates, 1993.

Cheever, Susan. "The One Thing That Keeps Us from Chaos." *New Choices for Retirement Living* 34.8 (1994): 22–25.

Clurman, Harold. "Arthur Miller's Later Plays." In *Arthur Miller: A Collection of Critical Essays.* Ed. Robert Corrigan. Englewood Cliffs, NJ: Prentice-Hall, 1969: 143–68.

Dunham, Mike. "Society, Art and Obligations: Conversation with Arthur Miller." *Anchorage Daily News,* 1 Sep. 1996: 3H.

Kaplan, James. "Miller's Crossing." *Vanity Fair* (Nov. 1991): 218–21, 241–48.

Kunitz, Stanley J., and Vineta Colby, eds. *Twentieth Century Authors; First Supplement.* New York: Wilson, 1955.

Miller, Arthur. "A Boy Grew in Brooklyn." *Holiday* 17 (Mar. 1955): 54–55, 117, 119–20, 122–24.

Moss, Leonard. "Biographies and Literary Allusion in *After the Fall.*" *Educational Theatre Journal* 18 (1966): 34–40.

Nelson, Benjamin. *Arthur Miller: Portrait of a Playwright.* New York: McKay, 1970.

Roudané, Matthew C., ed. *Conversations with Arthur Miller.* Jackson: University Press of Mississippi, 1987.

Rowe, Kenneth T. "Shadows Cast Before." In *Arthur Miller: New Perspectives.* Ed. Robert A. Martin. Englewood Cliffs, NJ: Prentice-Hall, 1982.

Schlueter, June, and James K. Flanagan, eds. *Arthur Miller.* New York: Ungar, 1987.

Strickland, Carol. "Arthur Miller's Latest Message to Humanity." *Christian Science Monitor,* 26 Apr. 1994: 12.

CRITICAL STUDIES

Bhatia, Santosh K. *Arthur Miller: Social Drama as Tragedy.* New York: Humanities, 1985.

Bigsby, Christopher, ed. *The Cambridge Companion to Arthur Miller.* New York: Cambridge University Press, 1997.

———. *Modern American Drama 1945–1990.* Cambridge: Cambridge University Press, 1992.

Bloom, Harold, ed. *Arthur Miller.* New York: Chelsea House, 1987.

———, ed. *Modern Critical Views: Arthur Miller.* New York: Chelsea House, 1987.

Brater, Enoch. "Ethnics and Ethnicity in the Plays of Arthur Miller." In *From Hester Street to Hollywood.* Ed. Sarah Blacher Cohen. Bloomington: Indiana University Press, 1983: 123–36.

Centola, Steven R., ed. *The Achievement of Arthur Miller: New Essays*. Dallas: Contemporary Research, 1995.

Corrigan, Robert W., ed. *Arthur Miller: A Collection of Critical Essays*. Englewood Cliffs, NJ: Prentice-Hall, 1969.

Evans, Richard I. *Psychology and Arthur Miller*. New York: Dutton, 1969.

Gordon, Lois. "Arthur Miller." In *Contemporary American Dramatists*. Ed. K. A. Berney. London: St. James, 1994: 407–14.

Griffin, Alice. *Understanding Arthur Miller*. Columbia: University of South Carolina Press, 1996.

Hayman, Ronald. *Arthur Miller*. New York: Ungar, 1972.

Hogan, Robert. *Arthur Miller*. Minneapolis: University of Minnesota Press, 1964.

Huftel, Sheila. *Arthur Miller: The Burning Glass*. New York: Citadel, 1965.

Isser, Edward. "Arthur Miller and the Holocaust." *Essays in Theatre* 10.2 (1992): 155–64.

Martin, Robert A., ed. *Arthur Miller: New Perspectives*. Englewood Cliffs, NJ: Prentice-Hall, 1982.

———. "Arthur Miller: Public Issues, Private Tensions." *Studies in the Literary Imagination* 21.2 (1988): 97–106.

Martine, James J., ed. *Critical Essays on Arthur Miller*. Boston: Hall, 1979.

Moss, Leonard. *Arthur Miller*. 2nd. ed. New York: Twayne, 1980.

Murphy, Brenda. "Arthur Miller: Revisioning Realism." In *Realism and the American Dramatic Tradition*. Ed. William W. Demastes. Tuscaloosa: University of Alabama Press, 1996: 189–202.

Murray, Edward. *Arthur Miller: Dramatist*. New York: Ungar, 1967.

Panikkar, N. Bhaskara. *Individual Morality and Social Happiness in Arthur Miller*. Atlantic Highlands, NJ: Humanities, 1982.

Parker, Dorothy, ed. *Essays on Modern American Drama: Williams, Miller, Albee, and Shepard*. Toronto: University of Toronto Press, 1987.

Partridge, C. J. *Arthur Miller*. 1970. New York: Ungar, 1972.

Savran, David. *Communists, Cowboys, and Queers: The Politics of Masculinity in the Work of Arthur Miller and Tennessee Williams*. Minneapolis: University of Minnesota Press, 1992.

Welland, Dennis. *Miller: The Playwright*. 2nd. ed. New York: Methuen, 1983.

White, Sidney H. *Guide to Arthur Miller*. Columbus: Merrill, 1970.

Zeineddine, Nada. *Because It Is My Name*. Devon, UK: Merlin, 1991.

REVIEWS AND SELECTED CRITICISM

DEATH OF A SALESMAN

Reviews

Atkinson, Brooks. "At the Theatre." *New York Times*, 11 Feb. 1949: 27.

Barnes, Howard. "A Great Play Is Born." *New York Herald Tribune*, 11 Feb. 1949: 14.

Beaufort, John. "Arthur Miller's New Play an Absorbing Experience." *Christian Science Monitor*, 19 Feb. 1949: 12.

Clurman, Harold. "Theatre: Attention!" *New Republic* 120 (28 Feb. 1949): 26–28.

Coleman, Robert. "*Death of a Salesman* Is Emotional Dynamite." *Daily Mirror*, 11 Feb. 1949. In *New York Theatre Critics' Reviews* 10 (1949): 360.

Dash, Thomas. "'Life' of a Salesman." *Women's Wear Daily*, 24 Feb. 1949: 51.

Gibbs, Wolcott. "The Theatre: Well Worth Waiting For." *New Yorker* 24 (19 Feb. 1949): 58, 60.

Krutch, Joseph Wood. "Drama." *Nation* 168 (5 Mar. 1949): 283–84.

Criticism

Altena, I., and A. M. Aylwin. *Notes on Arthur Miller's* Death of a Salesman. London: Methuen, 1976.

Bloom, Harold, ed. *Arthur Miller's* Death of a Salesman. New York: Chelsea House, 1988.

———, ed. *Willy Loman*. New York: Chelsea House, 1991.

Brater, Enoch. "Miller's Realism and *Death of a Salesman*." In *Arthur Miller: New Perspectives*. Ed. Robert A. Martin. Englewood Cliffs, NJ: Prentice-Hall, 1982: 115–26.

Centola, Steven R. "Family Values in *Death of a Salesman*." *College Language Association Journal* 37.1 (1993): 29–41.

Dukore, Bernard F. Death of a Salesman *and* The Crucible: *Text and Performance*. Atlantic Highlands, NJ: Humanities, 1989.

Gelb, Philip. "*Death of a Salesman*: A Symposium." *Tulane Drama Review* 2 (1958): 63–69.

Harshburger, Karl. *The Burning Jungle: An Analysis of Arthur Miller's* Death of a Salesman. Washington, DC: University Press of America, 1979.

Hurrell, John D., ed. *Two Modern American Tragedies: Reviews and Criticism of* Death of a Salesman *and* Streetcar Named Desire. New York: Scribner's, 1961.

Koon, Helen Wickam, ed. *Twentieth Century Interpretations of* Death of a Salesman: *A Collection of Critical Essays*. Englewood Cliffs, NJ: Prentice-Hall, 1983.

Meserve, Walter J., ed. *The Merrill Studies in* Death of a Salesman: *A Collection of Critical Essays*. Columbus, OH: Merrill, 1972.

Murphy, Brenda. *Miller:* Death of a Salesman. Cambridge: Cambridge University Press, 1995.

Murphy, Brenda, and Susan C. W. Abbotson. *Understanding* Death of a Salesman. Westport, CT: Greenwood Press, 1999.

Roudané, Matthew, ed. *Approaches to Teaching Miller's* Death of a Salesman. New York: Modern Language Association, 1995.

————. "*Death of a Salesman* and the Poetics of Arthur Miller." In *The Cambridge Companion to Arthur Miller*. Ed. Christopher Bigsby. New York: Cambridge University Press, 1997: 60–85.

Shockley, John S. "*Death of a Salesman* and American Leadership: Life Imitates Art." *Journal of American Culture* 17 (Sum. 1994): 49–56.

Weales, Gerald, ed. *Arthur Miller:* Death of a Salesman: *Text and Criticism.* New York: Viking, 1967.

ALL MY SONS

Reviews

Atkinson, Brooks. "Arthur Miller's *All My Sons* Brings Genuine New Talent into the Coronet Theatre with Expert Cast of Actors." *New York Times*, 30 Jan. 1947: 21.

Barnes, Howard. "Too Many Duds." *New York Herald Tribune*, 30 Jan. 1947: 15.

Chapman, John. "A Lot Goes On but Little Happens in Backyard Drama, *All My Sons*." *New York Daily News*, 30 Jan. 1947. In *New York Theatre Critics' Reviews* 8 (1947): 478.

Hawkins, William. "*All My Sons* a Tense Drama." *New York World-Telegram*, 30 Jan. 1947. In *New York Theatre Critics' Reviews* 8 (1947): 475.

Morehouse, Ward. "*All My Sons*, Intelligent and Thoughtful Drama, Superbly Played at Coronet." *New York Sun*, 30 Jan. 1947. In *New York Theatre Critics' Reviews* 8 (1947): 477.

Watts, Richard, Jr. "A Striking but Uneven Drama about the Soldier's Return." *New York Post*, 30 Jan. 1947. In *New York Theatre Critics' Reviews* 8 (1947): 476.

Criticism

Bloom, Harold, ed. *Arthur Miller's* All My Sons. New York: Chelsea House, 1988.

Centola, Steven R. "*All My Sons*." In *The Cambridge Companion to Arthur Miller*. Ed. Christopher Bigsby. New York: Cambridge University Press, 1997: 48–59.

Loughlin, Richard L. "Tradition and Tragedy in *All My Sons*." *English Record* 14 (Feb. 1964): 23–27.

Marino, Stephen. "Religious Language in Arthur Miller's *All My Sons*." *Journal of Imagism* 3 (Fall 1998): 9–28.

Robinson, James A. "*All My Sons* and Paternal Authority." *Journal of American Drama and Theatre* 2.1 (Winter 1990): 38–54.

Wells, Arvin R. "The Living and the Dead in *All My Sons*." *Modern Drama* 7 (1964): 46–51.

Yorks, Samuel A. "Joe Keller and His Sons." *Western Humanities Review* 13 (Autumn 1959): 401–7.

A VIEW FROM THE BRIDGE

Reviews

Findlatter, Richard. "No Time for Tragedy?" *Twentieth Century* (Jan. 1957): 56–62.
Hartley, Anthony. "Waterfront." *Spectator*, 19 Oct. 1956: 538–40.
Hope-Wallace, Philip. "Theatre: *A View from the Bridge*." *Time and Tide* 37 (1956): 1267.
Trewin, J. C. "Quick Change." *Illustrated London News*, 27 Oct. 1956: 720.
Webster, Margaret. "A Look at the London Season." *Theatre Arts* 41 (May 1957): 28–29.
Worsley, T. C. "Realistic Melodrama." *New Statesman and Nation*, 20 Oct. 1956: 482.

Criticism

Alter, Iska. "Betrayal and Blessedness: Explorations of Feminine Power in *The Crucible, A View from the Bridge*, and *After the Fall*." In *Feminist Rereadings of Modern American Drama*. Ed. June Schlueter. Rutherford, NJ: Fairleigh Dickinson University Press, 1989:
Carson, Neil. "*A View from the Bridge* and the Expansion of Vision." In *Modern Critical Views: Arthur Miller*. Ed. Harold Bloom. New York: Chelsea House, 1987: 93–102.
Centola, Steven R. "Compromise as Bad Faith: Arthur Miller's *A View from the Bridge* and William Inge's *Come Back, Little Sheba*." *Midwest Quarterly* 28.1 (Autumn 1986): 100–103.
Costello, Donald P. "Arthur Miller's Circles of Responsibility: *A View from the Bridge* and Beyond." *Modern Drama* 36.3 (1993): 443–53.
Epstein, Arthur D. "A Look at *A View from the Bridge*." *Texas Studies in Literature and Language* 7 (Spring 1965): 109–22.
Hurd, Myles R. "Angels and Anxieties in Miller's *A View from the Bridge*." *Notes on Contemporary Literature* 13 (Sep. 1983): 4–6.
Popkin, Henry. "Arthur Miller: The Strange Encounter." *Sewanee Review* 68 (1960): 34–60.
Styan, J. L. "Why *A View from the Bridge* Went Down Well in London: The Story of a Revision." In *Arthur Miller: New Perspectives*. Ed. Robert A. Martin. Englewood Cliffs, NJ: Prentice-Hall, 1982: 139–48.
Wertheim, Albert. "*A View from the Bridge*." In *The Cambridge Companion to Arthur Miller*. Ed. Christopher Bigsby. New York: Cambridge University Press, 1997: 101–14.

THE AMERICAN CLOCK

Reviews

Barnes, Clive. "This *Clock* is a Bit Off." *New York Post*, 21 Nov. 1980. In *New York Theatre Critics' Reviews* 41 (1980): 81–82.

Beaufort, John. "*American Clock.*" *Christian Science Monitor*, 24 Nov. 1980. In *New York Theatre Critics' Reviews* 41 (1980): 83.

Kalem, T. E. "Broke and Blue." *Time* 115 (9 Jun. 1980): 65.

Manifold, Gay. Review of *American Clock*. By Arthur Miller. *Theatre Journal* (Mar. 1985): 106–7.

Nathan, David. Review of *American Clock*. By Arthur Miller. *Plays and Players* 397 (Oct. 1986): 22.

Rich, Frank. "Miller's *Clock* at Spoleto USA: The Hoover Years." *New York Times*, 27 May 1980: C7.

Wilson, Edwin. "New Drama By Miller." *Wall St. Journal*, 21 Nov. 1980. In *New York Theatre Critics' Reviews* 41 (1980): 82–83.

Criticism

Bennetts, Leslie. "Miller Revives *American Clock* Amid Resonances of 30s." *New York Times*, 14 Jul. 1988: C23.

Schlueter, June. "Miller in the Eighties." In *The Cambridge Companion to Arthur Miller*. Ed. Christopher Bigsby. New York: Cambridge University Press, 1997: 152–67.

Schonberg, Harold C. "Joan Copeland Remembers Mama—And So Does Her Brother Arthur." *New York Times*, 16 Nov. 1980, sec. 2: 1, 5.

Weales, Gerald. "Watching the *Clock*." In *The Achievement of Arthur Miller*. Ed. Steven R. Centola. Dallas: Contemporary Research, 1995: 127–34.

THE CRUCIBLE

Reviews

Atkinson, Brooks. "*The Crucible.*" *New York Times*, 1 Feb. 1953, sec. 2 : 1.

Beyer, William H. "The State of the Theatre: The Devil at Large." *School and Society* 77 (21 Mar. 1953): 183–87.

Brown, John Mason. "Witch-Hunting." *Saturday Review* 36 (14 Feb. 1953): 41–42.

Gibbs, Wolcott. "The Devil to Pay." *New Yorker* 28 (31 Jan. 1953): 47–48.

Kerr, Walter F. "*The Crucible* Retells Salem's Violent Story." *New York Herald Tribune*, 1 Feb. 1953, sec. 4: 1.

Kirchway, Freda. "*The Crucible.*" *The Nation* 176 (7 Feb. 1953): 131–32.

Raymond, Henry. "*The Crucible*, Arthur Miller's Best Play, Dramatizes Salem Witchcraft." *Daily Worker*, 28 Jan. 1953: 7.

Wyat, Euphemia Van Rensselaer. "Theatre." *Catholic World* 176 (Mar. 1953): 465–66.

Criticism

Adler, Thomas P. "Conscience and Community in *An Enemy of the People* and *The Crucible*." In *The Cambridge Companion to Arthur Miller*. Ed. Christopher Bigsby. New York: Cambridge University Press, 1997: 86–100.

Alter, Iska. "Betrayal and Blessedness: Explorations of Feminine Power in *The Crucible, A View from the Bridge*, and *After the Fall*." In *Feminist Rereadings of Modern American Drama*. Ed. June Schlueter. Rutherford, NJ: Fairleigh Dickinson University Press, 1989.

Bergeron, David. "Arthur Miller's *The Crucible* and Nathaniel Hawthorne: Some Parallels." *English Journal* 58 (1969): 47–55.

Blau, Herbert. "The Whole Man and the Real Witch." In *Arthur Miller: A Collection of Critical Essays*. Ed. Robert W. Corrigan. Englewood Cliffs, NJ: Prentice-Hall, 1969: 123–30.

Bloom, Harold, ed. The Crucible: *Modern Critical Interpretations*. New York: Chelsea House, 1999.

Dukore, Bernard F. Death of a Salesman *and* The Crucible: *Text and Performance*. Atlantic Highlands, NJ: Humanities, 1989.

Ferres, John H. *Twentieth Century Interpretations of* The Crucible. Englewood Cliffs, NJ: Prentice-Hall, 1972.

Hendrickson, Gary P. "The Last Analogy: Arthur Miller's Witches and America's Domestic Communists." *Midwest Quarterly* 33.4 (1992): 447–56.

Marino, Stephen. "Arthur Miller's 'Weight of Truth.'" *Modern Drama* 38.4 (Winter 1995): 488–95.

Martin, Robert A. "Arthur Miller's *The Crucible*: Background and Sources." *Modern Drama* 20 (1977): 279–92.

Martine, James J. The Crucible: *Politics, Property, and Pretense*. New York: Twayne, 1993.

Schissel, Wendy. "Re(dis)covering the Witches in Arthur Miller's *The Crucible*: A Feminist Reading." *Modern Drama* 37.3 (1994): 461–73.

Warshow, Robert. "The Liberal Conscience in *The Crucible*." In *Arthur Miller: A Collection of Critical Essays*. Ed. Robert W. Corrigan. Englewood Cliffs, NJ: Prentice-Hall, 1969: 111–21.

Weales, Gerald, ed. The Crucible: *Text and Criticism*. New York: Viking, 1971.

AFTER THE FALL

Reviews

Chapman, John. "*After the Fall* Overpowering." *New York Daily News*, 24 Jan. 1964. In *New York Theatre Critics' Reviews* 25 (1964): 374.

Hanscom, Leslie. "*After the Fall*: Arthur Miller's Return." *Newsweek*, 8 Feb. 1964: 50–51.

Hewes, Henry. "Quentin's Quest." *Saturday Review*, 15 Feb. 1964: 35.

Kerr, Walter. "Miller's *After the Fall*—As Walter Kerr Sees It." *New York Herald Tribune*, 24 Jan. 1964: 1, 11.

McClain, John. "Arthur Miller's *After the Fall* Tour de Force by Robards." *New York Journal American*, 24 Jan. 1964. In *New York Theatre Critics' Reviews* 25 (1964): 376.

Nadal, Norman. "Miller Play One of Inward Vision." *New York World-Telegram*, 24 Jan. 1964. In *New York Theatre Critics' Reviews* 25 (1964): 375.

Taubman, Howard. "Theater: *After the Fall*." *New York Times*, 24 Jan. 1964: 18.

Watts, Richard, Jr. "The New Drama by Arthur Miller." *New York Post*, 24 Jan. 1964: 38.

Criticism

Alter, Iska. "Betrayal and Blessedness: Explorations of Feminine Power in *The Crucible, A View from the Bridge*, and *After the Fall*." In *Feminist Rereadings of Modern American Drama*. Ed. June Schlueter. Rutherford, NJ: Fairleigh Dickinson University Press, 1989.

Balakian, Janet N. "The Holocaust, the Depression, and McCarthyism: Miller in the Sixties." In *The Cambridge Companion to Arthur Miller*. Ed. Christopher Bigsby. New York: Cambridge University Press, 1997: 115–38.

Bigsby, Christopher. "The Fall and After—Arthur Miller's Confession." In *Essays on Modern American Drama: Williams, Miller, Albee and Shepard*. Ed. Dorothy Parker. Toronto: University of Toronto Press, 1987: 68–105.

Centola, Steven R. "The Monomyth and Arthur Miller's *After the Fall*." *Studies in American Drama 1945–Present* (1986): 49–60.

Engle, John D. "The Metaphor of Law in *After the Fall*." *Notes on Contemporary Literature* 9.3 (1979): 11–12.

Moss, Leonard. "Biographies and Literary Allusion in *After the Fall*." *Educational Theatre Journal* 18 (1966): 34–40.

Stanton, Stephen S. "Pessimism in *After the Fall*." In *Arthur Miller: New Perspectives*. Ed. Robert A. Martin. Englewood Cliffs, NJ: Prentice-Hall, 1982: 159–72.

Unger, Arthur. "Arthur Miller Talks of His Holocaust Drama." *Christian Science Monitor*, 19 Sep. 1980: 19.

Weales, Gerald. "Arthur Miller in the 1960s." In *Arthur Miller: New Perspectives*. Ed. Robert A. Martin. Englewood Cliffs, NJ: Prentice-Hall, 1982: 97–105.

BROKEN GLASS

Reviews

Canby, Vincent. "Arthur Miller Still Holds to His Moral Vision." *New York Times*, 1 May 1994: 5.

Gerard, Jeremy. Review of *Broken Glass*. By Arthur Miller. *Variety*, 25 Apr. 1994. In *New York Theatre Critics' Reviews* 55 (1994): 128.

Lahr, John. "Dead Souls." *New Yorker*, 9 May 1994. In *New York Theatre Critics' Reviews* 55 (1994): 124–25.

Nightingale, Benedict. "Smashed Certainties." *Times*, 6 Aug. 1994: E5.

Peter, John. "A Raw Slice of Humanity." *Sunday Times*, 14 Aug. 1994, sec. 10: 20–21.

Richards, David. "A Paralysis Points to Spiritual and Social Ills." *New York Times*, 25 Apr. 1994. In *New York Theatre Critics' Reviews* 55 (1994): 129–30.

Simon, John. "Whose Paralysis Is It, Anyway?" *New York*, 9 May, 1994. In *New York Theatre Critics' Reviews* 55 (1994): 127–28.

Wolf, Matt. "Splintered Factions." *Times Literary Supplement*, 19 Aug. 1994: 18.

Criticism

Abbotson, Susan C. W. "Issues of Identity in *Broken Glass*: A Humanist Response to a Postmodern World." *Journal of American Drama and Theatre* 11.1 (Winter 1999): 67–80.

Bigsby, Christopher. "The Chill Factor." *Independent Magazine*, 5 Mar. 1994: 16, 18, 21.

————. Miller in the Nineties." In *The Cambridge Companion to Arthur Miller*. Ed. Christopher Bigsby. New York: Cambridge University Press, 1997: 168–83.

Hopkinson, Amanda. "A View from the Bridge." *New Statesman and Society*, 5 Aug. 1994: 31–32.

Neill, Heather. "Leading Role." *Times Educational Supplement*, 9 Sep. 1994: A15.

THE RIDE DOWN MT. MORGAN

Reviews

Borak, Jeffrey. "Miller At 80 Fine-Tuning Play's American Performance." *Berkshire Eagle*, 4 Jul. 1996: B1, B4.

Brantlcy, Ben. "Arthur Miller, Still Feeling the Pain After the Fall." *New York Times*, 25 Jul. 1996: C13, C16.

Christiansen, Richard. "Arthur Miller Opens New Play in London for Good Reason." *Chicago Tribune*, 13 Nov. 1991, sec. 1: 24.

Eck, Michael. "Williamstown Theater Festival's *Mount Morgan* Is Pure Arthur Miller." *Times Union*, 24 Jul. 1996: D6.

Greer, Herb. "*Mount Morgan* A Bumpy Ride: Miller Plays Solemn Premise for the Laughs." *Washington Times*, 24 Nov. 1991: D6.

Henry, William A. III. "Arthur Miller, Old Hat at Home, Is a London Hit." *Time* 138 (11 Nov. 1991): 100–101.

Lewis, Peter. "Change of Scene for a Mellow Miller." *Sunday Times*, 3 Nov. 1991, sec. 6: 6.

Peter, John. "Review of *Ride*." *Sunday Times*, 3 Nov. 1991, sec. 6: 7.

Watts, Janet. "*The Ride Down Mount Morgan*." *The Observer*, 3 Nov. 1991: 59.

Criticism

Bigsby, Christopher. "Miller in the Nineties." In *The Cambridge Companion to Arthur Miller*. Ed. Christopher Bigsby. New York: Cambridge University Press, 1997: 168–83.

Schlueter, June. "Scripting the Closing Scene: Arthur Miller's *Ride Down Mount Morgan*." In *The Achievement of Arthur Miller*. Ed. Steven R. Centola. Dallas: Contemporary Research, 1995: 143–50.

RELATED SECONDARY SOURCES

Adler, Thomas. *American Drama, 1940–1960: A Critical History*. New York: Twayne, 1994.

Berkowitz, Gerald M. *American Drama of the Twentieth Century*. London: Longman, 1992.

Cohn, Ruby. *New American Dramatists 1960–1990*. New York: St. Martins, 1991.

Demastes, William. *Beyond Naturalism: A New Realism in American Theatre*. Westport, CT: Greenwood Press, 1988.

Foulkes, Peter A. *Literature and Propaganda*. New York: Methuen, 1983.

Freedman, Morris. *American Drama in Social Context*. Carbondale: Southern Illinois University Press, 1971.

Halberstam, David. *The Fifties*. New York: Fawcett Columbine, 1993.

Herman, William. *Understanding Contemporary American Drama*. Columbia: University of South Carolina Press, 1987.

Kazan, Elia. *A Life*. New York: Knopf, 1988.

Mielziner, Jo. *Designing for the Theatre: A Memoir and a Portfolio*. New York: Bramhall, 1965.

Porter, Thomas E. *Myth and Modern Drama*. Detroit: Wayne State University Press, 1969.

Scanlan, Tom. *Family, Drama, and American Dreams*. Westport, CT: Greenwood Press, 1978.

Schneider, Daniel E. *The Psychoanalyst and the Artist*. New York: Farrar, Strauss, 1950.

Schroeder, Patricia R. *The Presence of the Past in Modern American Drama*. Cranbury, NJ: Associated University Press, 1989.

Sievers, W. David. *Freud on Broadway: A History of Psychoanalysis and American Drama*. New York: Hermitage, 1955.

Spindler, Michael. *American Literature and Social Change: William Dean Howells to Arthur Miller*. Bloomington: Indiana University Press, 1983.

Index

About the Author

SUSAN C. W. ABBOTSON has taught English for over fifteen years, both at the high school and university levels. She currently teaches at the English Department of Rhode Island College. She is coauthor of *Understanding Death of a Salesman* (Greenwood 1999). She is also author of the Drama section in *Resources for Teaching: Literature and Its Writers* (1997) as well as numerous articles on Literature and Drama.